It Usually Begins With Ayn Rand

It Usually Begins With Ayn Rand

Revised and Updated

Jerome Tuccille

Author of **The Gospel According to Ayn Rand, Trump**, *the best-selling biography of Donald Trump, and other books*

ASJA Press

New York Lincoln Shanghai

It Usually Begins With Ayn Rand

ASJA Press
an imprint of iUniverse, Inc.

iUniverse books may be ordered through booksellers or by contacting:

iUniverse
2021 Pine Lake Road, Suite 100
Lincoln, NE 68512
www.iuniverse.com
1-800-Authors (1-800-288-4677)

Because of the dynamic nature of the Internet, any Web addresses or links contained in this book may have changed since publication and may no longer be valid.

The views expressed in this work are solely those of the author and do not necessarily reflect the views of the publisher, and the publisher hereby disclaims any responsibility for them.

ISBN: 978-0-595-47757-9

Printed in the United States of America

This book is dedicated to the new generations of readers who discovered *It Usually Begins With Ayn Rand* and have kept the book in print since it was first published in 1971

Contents

Introduction by the Author

This edition of *It Usually Begins With Ayn Rand* contains much of the text that appeared in the original edition—revised and edited to conform to modern style—plus new chapters dealing with events that took place after the book was first published. Some of the new material deals with my campaign for Governor of New York as the Free Libertarian Party candidate, a discussion of events that transpired on the American political scene after that benighted campaign, plus thoughts on my current political and spiritual leanings. The perennial success of *It Usually Begins With Ayn Rand* has startled no one more than me. Sales started slowly, then began to pick up over the years, until the book became an underground classic that has gained readership over the decades. *It Usually Begins With Ayn Rand* should be read as political memoir, a first-hand account of a political movement, mostly fact, but with fictional elements and hyperbole added for effect. A reviewer once said that most memoirs are neither fact nor fiction; they are the truth as the author remembers it. So it is with *It Usually Begins With Ayn Rand*.

PART I
The Overview

1

The Whim Worshipers

It usually begins with Ayn Rand.

The young crusader in search of a cause enters the world of *The Fountainhead* or *Atlas Shrugged* as though he were about to engage in unheard-of sexual delights for the first time. He has been warned beforehand. There is no need to search any further. The quest is over. Here is all the truth you've been looking for contained in the tightly packed pages of two gargantuan novels.

He steps inside, cautiously at first, perhaps even skeptically, but before long he is swept away by the rampaging prose of the author and the heroic activities of her characters. Here are Dominique Francon, newspaperwoman determined to destroy her man before the altruists can get to him; Howard Roark, architect, designing skyscrapers and dynamiting public housing projects; John Galt, hero par excellence, creating his anarchist utopia in the middle of the Rocky Mountains; Dagny Taggart, beautiful and courageous, running off in a billowing evening gown to save her railroads from extinction; Ragnar Danneskjold, anarchist, blowing up foreign-aid ships on the open seas.

The titles of Rand's nonfiction works give a good indication of the basic tenets of her philosophy: *The Virtue of Selfishness*; *Capitalism: The Unknown Ideal*; later still, *The Romantic Manifesto*. Ayn Rand was not the first to advocate individualism and economic *laissez faire*, but she was certainly the first to elevate selfishness to the level of a philosophical absolute. To Rand it was simply not enough to believe in individual liberty and the efficacy of the marketplace; you had to have a proper understanding of the fact that altruism is the root cause of all the evil that has ever existed on the face of the earth, and that selfishness

3

(less arrogantly translated into "rational self-interest") is the only proper motivation for all human conduct. All forms of altruism—including voluntary communes and even private charity—are viewed as inherently evil, since they will eventually lead to an altruistic political order: communism, a welfare state, any government designed to protect collective egalitarianism.

For this reason unregulated capitalism is much more than just an efficient economic system to Rand and her followers. It is a moral absolute and the cornerstone of the Randian code of ethics, which has its base not in mere voluntarism, but in selfishness in all areas of human activity. Understanding this, it becomes easier to see why the dollar sign is revered by the Randian with the same fervor Christians reserve for the cross, Jews for the star of David, Moslems for the crescent, middle Americans for Old Glory.

It is all quite heady, this stuff, when fed in massive doses to the impressionable young mind all at once. It is especially appealing to those in the process of escaping a regimented religious background—particularly young Jews and renegade Roman Catholics, ripe for conversion to some form of religion-substitute to fill the vacuum. The crumbling walls of doctrinaire Catholicism, or heavy-fisted Judaism, leave you with a feeling of vulnerability. Your protective shell is cracking. You're gradually becoming more and more exposed to the great agnostic world out there that the priests and brothers and rabbis have been warning you about since you were five years old. You realize you can't go home again, but where *do* you go?

And then you discover Galt's Gulch at the end of *Atlas Shrugged* and you know everything is going to be all right forevermore. The world is still intact and so are you.

You've become a devout Objectivist.

After eight years of grade-school nuns, four years of prep-school Jesuits, and four more of Christian brothers in college, I emerged at the end of my formal education with a pronounced distaste for all things papal and divine. Pugnacious, iconoclastic, more libertine than libertarian, I charged into the workaday world in search of icons to smash. Show me anything boasting of security, happiness, or certitude in any area, and—wham—I would swing out with my anti-icon stick in an effort to bring it down with a crash. If there was anyone in the Western Hemisphere with a lower resistance to the heady wine of Objectivism, I can't imagine that he or she existed at the time. I later discovered there were legions more like myself back in the early '60s, eager to make that Great Leap—and who actually did, with reckless abandon. For the moment I considered myself unique, a lone and courageous individual who had found the Holy Grail after years of floundering.

Objectivism can be a wonderfully appealing religion-substitute for disaffiliated Jews and Catholics from the middle class who turn to it with a mania formerly reserved for their ancestral religion—and also to the sons and daughters of old American WASPS, brought up on the Protestant ethic of hard work and self-sufficiency. It is a closed system of ideas, even more so than the conservative Catholicism in vogue until the middle '60s. Under the most doctrinaire of Catholic upbringings there is a certain margin for flexibility. The boundaries are clearly defined, but you are permitted an area of deviation from the straight and narrow before stepping onto the wild shores of heresy. To a lesser extent the same holds true for Judaism.

Not so under the tutelage of the Rand.

Objectivism is an inflexible package deal. Ayn Rand, having established herself as a radical individualist, an uncompromising muckraker and free thinker by the 1950s, then proceeded to erect a tight system of logic embracing every conceivable area of human endeavor. Economics, politics, psychology, child-rearing, sex, literature, even cigarette-smoking—Rand had written about them all, issuing her pronouncements on each subject in turn. Curiously enough, for a woman who started out as a champion of the independent mind, she began to consider her own ideas as natural corollaries of truth and objectivity.

"Objective reality" was what Rand said it was.

"Morality" was conformity to the ethic of Ayn Rand.

"Rationality" was synonymous with the thinking of Ayn Rand.

To be in disagreement with the ideas of Ayn Rand was to be, by defi-nition, irrational and immoral. There was no allowable deviation under the tenets of Objectivism—which, following the publication of Rand's major philosophical novel, *Atlas Shrugged*, in 1957, quickly became a kind of New Marxism of the Right. A generation earlier, the same con-verts now flocking to her would just as enthusiastically have joined the Marxist bandwagon tearing down the rocky road of the '30s. If Marx-ism, with its promise of a proletarian utopia, was tailor-made to the aspirations of the working-class crusader, Objectivism and its ethic of self-sufficiency and achievement was intoxicating to the sons and daughters of the middle class, graduating from college at the end of the Eisenhower era. The watertight, compartmentalized structure of Ran-dian logic was every bit as self-delineated as that of Karl Marx, con-demned by Rand as the paragon of human immorality and depravity. The purges occurring behind the scenes at the Nathaniel Branden Insti-tute, the headquarters of Objectivism, throughout the 1960s were a right-wing replay of Communist Party purges in the 1930s. And devia-tionism, even today the dirtiest word in the Marxist dictionary, became the cardinal sin for followers of Objectivism.

The dogmatic nature of Objectivism does not become apparent on first contact. Looking back, we can see that a good many people grow-ing up in the 1950s developed a profound disgust for the American *sta-tus quo*. The demoralizing atmosphere of the Corporate State, so effectively analyzed by Charles Reich in *The Greening of America*, was already perceived on a subconscious level by many people in the years following the Truman administration. It did not take long to recognize that Eisenhower, rather than charting a new and exciting course that would give people a greater measure of control over the institutions that dominated their lives, was doing little more than slowing down tempo-rarily our mad rush toward a dictatorship by bureaucracy.

Something was radically wrong with America. There was a feeling in the air, an intimation that we were no longer in control of forces that propelled us faster and faster toward a goal no one had yet been able to

define. The American state itself was out of control. This giant apparatus we had come to know as government seemed to be building an inevitable momentum, while operating with a bizarre technocratic
intelligence of its own. People with strong opinions on political and
social issues ten years earlier shrugged their shoulders as if to say,
"What's the use?" "The government" seemed to be running the country
with a disembodied intelligence, and even the politicians could do little
more than attempt to apply the brakes from time to time.

The world had grown too complicated.

There were forces at work in the world that the average citizen
couldn't be expected to understand.

"They"—those hazy and mysterious people in command—had more
information than "we the people" did. "They" would see us through all
right.

It was comforting to have a benevolent father figure—Dwight D.
Eisenhower—at the helm. He was a good man, a just and honest man: a
real American. We could trust him to guide us through these confusing
times in one piece. We could—we had to—place our future in his
hands. He was the father of the American people. He *was* the American
people, for Christ's sake! The world was suddenly too big and too complex; the individual's confidence in his ability to conduct the affairs of
his own life had shrunk to zero.

The individual *was* a zero, a pygmy, a cipher in the vast machinery of
the Corporate State. This was the age of giant bombs, giant nations, corporations, unions; giant and unfathomable political issues. Individualism was obsolete in this era of the Organization Man, the Man in the
Gray Flannel Suit, the Suburban Sprawl, and the Super Highway. In an
era of sameness and conformity, the sacrifice of the individual and his
idiosyncrasies to the rigid pattern of the giant American Shopping Center seemed logical. No one was going to rock the boat, to interfere with
Father Eisenhower in his divinely ordained task of steering the American nation to safety. Anyone who did was a "Commie," a "Red." He
was a goddamned "un-American."

And then along came Ayn Rand.

There was no one more radical than she in championing the autonomy and supremacy of the individual through the rhetoric of her novels. Philosophically, she was a wild and freaky anarchist, an iconoclast, a radical individualist. She created fictional heroes who challenged the authority of Corporate America, who fought the conformity of the American nation-state, who plotted against it and bombed its institutions and brought it down with a resounding crash.

This was the allure of Ayn Rand at the outset—her anarchism, her individualism, her revolutionary radicalism. Ayn Rand said to hell with conformity, to hell with sameness, to hell with Corporate America.

Ayn Rand said "Fuck you!" to Dwight David Eisenhower.

And then, sadly, the seeds of rigidity implanted in her novels bore fruit. This champion of the individual, of the beauty and variety of the unfettered mind, proceeded to erect her own house of cards. She developed her own system of compartmentalized logic, her own form of religion-substitute, which negated every principle she had established in the abstract such a short time before. Those who flocked to Objectivism for the breath of fresh air it promised in the midst of a choking miasma of political and cultural stagnation soon found themselves trapped in a different kind of intellectual straitjacket—all the more mystifying since it was unexpected.

The ray of hope offered the individual in the basic principles of Ayn Rand's Objectivism was quickly dimmed by its originator. The fact that her followers could later look back and analyze the "tragic flaw" in her philosophy provided little comfort. It was all the more frustrating because she had given them their first awareness of what they were looking for—and then destroyed her own ideal with narrow vision and ego-crippling rigidity.

Her protégé Nathaniel Branden had been Rand's chief disciple since he had written her a fan letter in the early 1950s after deciding that *The Fountainhead* was the "most rational book" he had ever read. Rand was quick to recognize the incisive clarity of Branden's mind.

In view of his obvious brilliance, it was only logical that Rand selected him for private instruction in the rudiments of objectivism. By the time *Atlas Shrugged* came out in 1957, Rand had transformed Branden into the second-most rational person in the world—after herself, of course. Rand created the Nathaniel Branden Institute to market her philosophy via a series of twenty-five lectures, given as a course each spring and fall. Every week the initiate would be treated to a discourse, usually delivered by Branden in his curious, singsong, Canadian Northumbrian burr, about a different aspect of objectivism: objectivist epistemology, the nature of reason and knowledge; objectivist morality, the objectivist theory of politics and economics; objectivism and art; objectivism and literature; objectivist psychology; even the objectivist view of sex.

Here one was introduced to the heady world of second-handers (those who lived off the accomplishments of others); whim-worshipers (those who had faith in the supernatural); muscle mystics (those who led others by exercising spiritual or physical power over them); America's persecuted minority (successful businessmen); A is A (a thing is what it is); altruism (collectivism); collectivism (altruism); the Cult of Moral Grayness (the notion that there are degrees of good and evil); heroes and heroines (individualists in *The Fountainhead* and *Atlas Shrugged*); thugs and hoodlums (collectivists in *The Fountainhead* and *Atlas Shrugged*); rationalists (those who did not question the teachings of Ayn Rand and Nathaniel Branden); and degenerates (those who did).

Until the institute moved into larger offices in the Empire State Building, the lecture series was presented in the old Sheraton-Atlantic Hotel on 34th Street and Broadway in Manhattan. Students were warned at the outset that it was immoral to call themselves objectivists until they had taken the basic course at least twice, the advanced course at least once, and had read the entire body of Randian literature and pronounced themselves in total agreement with it. They were then formally admitted to the Senior Collective, the inner circle of a hard-core group of undeviating "individualists." Everyone else was a mere *student* of objectivism, and those outside the collective who referred to themselves as objectivists were quickly denounced as second-handers—or worse, whim-worshipers.

Once agreeing to this basic ground rule, the new student entered the Spartan rigidity of the lecture hall determined above all else to prove himself a worthy candidate for the Senior Collective. Each course attracted over a hundred youthful aspirants, all of them convinced that the Law of Natural Selection would propel himself or herself to the top of the heap. There was little smiling or joking as the latest batch of novices, neatly groomed and manicured right down to the last individual, filed past the photographs of Rand and Branden in the anteroom (where student employees carefully checked admittance tickets, ever on the lookout for "frauds and thugs"), past the prominently displayed lineup of Rand's books and officially approved pro-capitalist, anti-collectivist literature, into the main hall with its soldierly rows of straight-back metal chairs.

Smiling, when it happened at all, was indulged in surreptitiously, since humor in the Objectivist handbook was considered immoral and anti-life, a device contrived to destroy man's capacity for greatness; besides, there was little amity among the students to begin with, since they all considered themselves competitors in the race for recognition as full-fledged Objectivists. Admission to the Senior Collective was in fact a kind of Atheists' Armageddon, a sweepstakes competition for capitalistic Jehovah's Witnesses, with the major prizes awarded for syllogistic rather than spiritualistic perfection. With room at the top for only a chosen few, each student became in effect the enemy of his neighbor; there was very little to smile about.

My first reaction to all of this was awe, the stunned awe of a true-believing convert as devout now in my atheistic capitalism as I had ever been in the baroque Catholicism of the 1950s. Here one was surrounded by a veritable battalion of superior human beings, Galt-like in the no-nonsense jut of their jaws and the drilling determination issuing forth from eyes that never blinked. And heroines galore, many with capes swirling behind them as they swept toward their seats, dollar-sign brooches glinting conspicuously over their hearts, smoking cigarettes through long holders the way Dagny did in *Atlas Shrugged*.

Sweet Jesus! It was so easy to imagine a world populated by such as these, rational and self-sufficient individuals, all conducting their lives in accordance with the Objectivist code: "I swear—by my life and my love of it—that I will never live for the sake of another man, nor ask another man to live for mine." When Branden stepped out—tall, striking, his hair cascading in blond waves over his forehead and his eyes sparkling like blue ice—the setting was complete. There wasn't a student in the hall who didn't believe, deep down in the far recesses of his being, that the days of the collectivists—the thugs and hoodlums and irrational muscle mystics—were coming to an end.

Lecture by lecture I found my New Credo beginning to crack. As much as I wanted to believe that the Objectivist package deal held all the answers, the doubts arose one by one until I had no choice but to face them as I had with Catholicism several years before.

Try as I might I could not swallow whole the idea that altruism was responsible for all the ills afflicting the world of the early 1960s. I saw the issue as a question of individual freedom versus the authority of the state; and the notion that state-corporate monopolies, economic and military imperialism, racism, violence, crime, alienation, etc., all had their roots in an altruistic ethic was too much of a strain even on the most impressionable of mentalities.

My second crisis of conscience revolved around the Randian theory of literature. For someone whose tastes in literature ran the gamut from Hemingway to Maugham to Fitzgerald to Steinbeck to Duerrenmatt to Cheever to Mailer to Salinger to Evelyn Waugh to Perelman to Vonnegut, naturalists and satirists to the last, it was a bit difficult to accept the theory that naturalism and comedy were immoral and anti-life, or that Mickey Spillane and Ian Fleming were the greatest living practitioners of the romanticism of Victor Hugo.

The final straw was the Objectivist theory of sex, a form of atheistic Puritanism as severe as that of the most dogmatic Marxist. According to

Rand, it was the height of immorality for a man and woman to hop in bed simply because they liked the shape of each other's buttocks. Disciples were permitted carnal bliss only if they were intellectually compatible and shared the same values, the same sense of life, the same moral code.

Rand's analysis of how people were supposed to know when and if they were intellectually compatible had some curious twists. Obviously, lengthy philosophical discussions were extremely time-consuming and distracting, particularly if one had an itch to satisfy his sexual needs. No fear. Rand provided students of Objectivism with a short cut. It was not necessary for would-be bedmates to probe each other's psyches at length to determine whether they could make it together or not. Truly rational people had the capacity of recognizing each other *on sight*. Intellectual compatibility, it seemed, could be discerned in the set of someone's jaw or the direct, confident glare of his or her eyes. Rational men and women were invariably tall, beauteous, and lean, with thick, wavy hair, drilling eyes, and strong jutting jaws. This posed a problem for short, dumpy individualists who could practice eye exercises forever, but could never alter their stature and bone structure no matter how hard they tried. From all this one might have assumed the crowning height of ecstasy to be raped on the steps of the New York Stock Exchange by a philosophical heir of William Graham Sumner.

By the time the five-month course was over I had already begun to drift away from the straight and narrow Randian road. The feeling I had experienced back in 1959 when the Dean of Manhattan College warned me of "incipient heresy," skillfully employing the imagery of sizzling flesh and the Pit of Darkness, began to simmer once again.

No matter.

It was always too late to turn back. The time had come to move on to other fields.

2

The Rational Dancer

Behind it all was a search for the libertarian ideal.

While various people had translated the basic principles of libertarianism into differing schools of political philosophy—ranging from radical libertarianism or anarchism to the more conservative variety of classical liberalism, in which a government would be created for the sole purpose of providing defense services and a judicial system for its citizens—there were certain fundamental areas in which the most radical and conservative of libertarians could find common ground.

Libertarians started with a distrust of government in all its forms, believing that all governments tend to accumulate power the longer they go on and will inevitably abuse that power. Thomas Jefferson warned right from the start of the American experiment in government that it would require a revolution every generation or so to keep the freedoms he and our other forefathers had fought for. He might have been talking about a nonviolent revolution, but that's not clear. Libertarians who believed in *any government at all* wanted one that would limit itself to keeping the peace by protecting its citizens from internal and external threats to their wellbeing. The functions of government would essentially be limited to running the military and maintaining a judicial system to enforce contract law, protect private property, and protect people against fraud. Libertarian anarchists wanted even those institutions run by private enterprises.

Ideally, a libertarian society would be one in which everyone would be free to choose his or her own lifestyle, own property or not own property, trade freely in an open marketplace without interference from anyone else as long as no one else's rights were violated in the process.

They wanted a society in which all citizens would be free from coercion as long as they did not damage someone else's person or property, did not injure another's reputation by libel, did not defraud others, did not spew pollutants into the environment where they were likely to infringe on everyone else's rights to clean air and water, and didn't violate the terms of any contracts they entered into voluntarily.

Libertarians believed in the absolute right of self-defense, including the right to bear arms peacefully to protect themselves and their property. They believed people had a right to structure their social institutions as they saw fit—their education, housing and cohabitation arrangements, police protection, fire prevention, sanitation, judicial, economic relief and welfare programs, and other systems necessary for a civilized existence. Ideally, user fees would be charged to finance these services when government provided them, and the most radical libertarians were opposed to any type of taxes at all. Libertarians who called themselves classical liberals and were willing to tolerate a strictly limited government preferred a simplified tax system such as a flat income or sales tax.

Libertarians were also opposed to a military draft, regarding it as the severest form of slavery when people were forced to risk their lives fighting for a cause they wanted no part of. In short, they were against aggression in all its forms, whether initiated by individuals or by government against its people.

This was the libertarian society in its most ideal form. These were the values we subscribed to, if only in a vague and hazy way at the time, as we left Manhattan College and points west and continued our search.

Of course, the United States had moved so far away from that ideal during the past couple of centuries and had continued in the direction of more government controls, not less, that any reversal in momentum away from the modern mega-state and latter-day empire would have been seen as a breath of fresh air blowing across a miasmic swamp.

From the early 1950s, Murray N. Rothbard, an economist and writer living in New York City who went on to become one of the foremost proponents of the Austrian School, had been the most radical right-wing anarchist in the United States. He had been an anarchist from his earliest years, subscribing to that school of libertarianism that maintains that all essential services, including military defense and a judicial system, could be provided by an unregulated free enterprise system without the agency of government.

Rothbard and his close friend Leonard Liggio, later to head several libertarian think tanks, including the Cato Institute, had been active in the Youth for Taft movement in 1952. Both were strong supporters of what came to be referred to as the Old Isolationist Right, the right wing of H.L. Mencken, Garet Garrett, Albert Jay Nock, Frank Chodorov, Leonard Read; the Old Right that used to condemn the liberals for involving the United States in overseas adventures such as Korea and even World War II; the Old Right that the New Left started to sound so much like at the beginning of the anti-war movement in 1965.

Rothbard and Liggio also found common ground in the economic theories of Ludwig von Mises, the leading Austrian economist in the United States. They attended the Mises lectures at New York University and then sat around talking afterward in various Greenwich Village cafes, a touch of European intellectual life favored by the Viennese economist. Rothbard's reputation as Mises' chief disciple began to grow in right-wing circles, and he and Liggio (whose field was historical revisionism, another common bond between the Old Right and the New Left of William Appleman Williams and Gabriel Kolko) started to attract a satellite group of their own personal followers. George Riesman, later to become a member of Rand's Senior Collective, was converted to Austrian *laissez faire* primarily through the efforts of Rothbard; Robert Hessen, another budding Objectivist, was a protégé of Liggio. Others who joined the circle in the middle and late 1950s were Ronald Hamowy and Ralph Raico, who founded the *New Individualist Review* to challenge William F. Buckley-style conservatism in the early 1960s. Another convert was Ed Nash, later the head of his own publishing firm in Los Angeles, whose main interest at the time was establishing a kind of Radio Free Bronx at his home in the University Heights section of that borough. He operated a radio transmitter with a broadcasting radius of about ten city blocks, and eagerly piped right-wing messages to anyone he could reach.

Murray Rothbard had met Ayn Rand around 1950, but they lost contact when Rand moved out to the West Coast for a while shortly afterward. When *Atlas Shrugged* was published in 1957, Rothbard's letter congratulating her on its success got him an invitation to attend the weekly *salons* she was conducting in her apartment in midtown Manhattan.

It was there that Rothbard met Nathaniel Branden and his wife, Barbara, for the first time. Each week the size of the assemblage grew: Ralph Raico, George Riesman, Robert Hessen, and Leonard Liggio were followed by Leonard Peikoff (who would become Rand's primary heir after her death in 1982), Alan Greenspan (Chairman of the Federal Reserve from 1987 to 2006), Edith Efron (who would write a best-seller attacking the liberal media in the 1970s), and a gaggle of professors, economists, students, and right-wing hangers-on who were disenchanted by William F. Buckley's brand of right-wing religious zeal. A bit later, Branden conceived the idea of an institute and a series of public lectures for a fee.

Through it all, Liggio was the least infatuated with the mounting Randian groundswell. From the beginning he detected a kernel of evangelical anti-communism in her thinking that would give her politics a conservative coloration in the 1960s. He also regarded her historical analysis of the individual roles of the United States and the Soviet Union in world affairs as shallow and unsophisticated. When he discovered that Rand refused to even *listen* to ideas that contradicted her own, whatever interest he had in Rand evaporated altogether.

On Rand's part, she was not sorry to see Liggio's attendance at her weekly *salons* begin to fall off. For one thing, he was still a practicing Catholic, which could only mean that his basic premises were in a state of degeneration, if not total disrepair. And if that were not enough, he had developed the antilife habit of falling asleep on her sofa whenever she was speaking at any length.

She had no place for hoodlums of that sort in her living room.

Murray Rothbard's enthusiasm began to flag when Rand decided to hold her salons twice a week. Since it was only logical that rational men and women required the frequent companionship of other rational people to maintain their peace of mine, Rand decided to hold her meetings semiweekly. To miss a session for any reason other than death or debilitating illness was considered an irrational and immoral act; it meant you were sacrificing a higher value—conversation with Rand—to a less productive activity.

"Where were you last night, Murray?" Branden inquired by phone the morning after Rothbard missed his first salon. Branden had added a slight Russian accent to his Highland burr, possibly an unconscious assimilation of Rand's vocal pattern.

"I was tired, Nathan. I decided to stay home and get some sleep."

"You were tired! You were too tired to discuss the philozophical development of muzzle mysticism in the thirteenth and fourteenth zenturies?"

"I didn't get any sleep the night before, Nathan. I just couldn't make it."

"I zee. I zuppose I will just have to tell Ayn that Murray Rossbott was too tired to attend her Tuesday salon. Is *that* what you want me to do?"

"Well, I suppose so. I mean, it's the truth."

"You will be along tomorrow night, of course?"

"Sure, I'll be down.'

"We look forward to zeeing you."

Shortly afterward, Ayn discovered that Rothbard's wife, Joey, was a devout Protestant, a practicing Episcopalian who actually believed that faith and altruism had a positive moral value. When the last tremors of this revelation faded away, a pall of silence fell over the living room. There was a Christian in the house. Not a renegade Christian who acknowledged the sins of her past and was ready to make amends for them. Not an apostate Christian who had forsaken the principles to which she formerly adhered. But a real, live, breathing, dedicated Protestant who admitted belief in the existence of a supreme being! A heretic such as this was occupying a chair in Ayn Rand's living room. And was married to one of Rand's most gifted apostles, no less!

Well, if Murray Rothbard's wife was a Christian, there could only be one logical explanation for it: she had obviously never read Ayn's proof that a supreme being does not, did not, will not, and could not exist. Ever.

Branden hustled her into an adjoining room and sat her down with a handful of Rand's anti-God essays. Joey, relieved to be out of earshot of all this talk about second-handers, floating concepts, and whim-worshipers, pored through the pamphlets while the meeting continued in the other room. When she completed her assignment and returned to the group, all conversation suddenly stopped, and she was skewered by twenty sets of drilling eyes.

Branden took the initiative. "Well?"

"I found it all very interesting, Nathan."

"She found it very interezting," Branden repeated the information at no extra charge. "Anything elze?"

"The arguments are very good, but I'm still not an atheist, if that's what you're getting at."

Rand was clearly irked and decided to take over. This was clearly a matter that required her personal intervention. "You haf read ze proofs?"

"They're all very good and thought-provoking, Ayn, but you don't shake a lifetime of religious faith with a few articles. I'll have to think about it for a while."

"You haf read ze proofs, and you still inzist on wallowing in your mindless myztizism? Faith is irrational, which means ..."

"Which means zat faith is immoral," said Branden.

"Which means it is antilife," said Greenspan.

"Which means it is antiman," said Robert Hessen.

"Which means—"

"Enoff," said Rand, cutting off Barbara Branden. "Zere has been enoff zmall talk for vun night. Do you haf any more questions to ask me?"

This was the signal that the meeting was adjourned for the evening. No. No one had any questions. Rand was getting a headache. It was time for everyone to go home.

This episode marked the beginning of the end of Murray Rothbard's eminent position in the Objectivist hierarchy. He, like Liggio, had begun to question the wisdom of many Randian attitudes on political and, particularly, historical affairs. He compounded his crime of being happily married to a practicing altruist at the following meeting when he refused, at the insistence of Rand and Branden, to leave his wife and take a more rational mate. There were any number of Dagny Taggart types, complete with capes, cigarette holders, and dollar-sign brooches, whom he might have considered.

Shortly afterward there was a meeting at which he found himself denounced for not smoking cigarettes. Cigarettes were pro-life and pro-man since they were manufactured by productive capitalists for human enjoyment; to be against tobacco on the grounds that it was destroying your lungs was to be against the creative efforts of industrialists who had gone through all their trouble for consumers who didn't appreciate what was being done for them. It was a paradigmatic case of ingratitude at the least; an argument could even be made that it was immoral.

Then there was the *salon* at which everyone rose individually, Alcoholics Anonymous-style, and gave a brief testimonial on the one person in their lives who had made the greatest impact.

"Ayn Rand has influenced me most because …"

"The one person who has affected me most was Ayn Rand. This woman more than anyone else …"

"The writings of Ayn Rand have opened new horizons …"

And so it went around the circle until one young fellow stood up and said, "The person who had the greatest influence on my life was Rocco Fantozi. Rocco helped—"

Branden leaped to his feet. "Who in bloody hell is Rocco Fantozi?"

"Why, he was a friend of mine in high school. When I was sixteen I had a rough period after my parents got a divorce, and Rocco pulled me through. I don't think—"

Needless to say, he was purged on the spot.

By this time Rothbard just about had his fill. In addition to everything else that was taking place, he was tired of hearing his named pronounced *Rossbott* all the time. There was some excuse for the Russian-born Rand, but none at all for Branden, born and raised in a predominantly English-speaking country, notwithstanding his eclectic and variegated accent.

Around this time a slick dance instructor from Brooklyn, who gave dancing lessons at Don Pallini's or Fred Astaire's or some similar emporium, discovered Rand and declared himself in total agreement with her ideas. Rand was instantly taken by the sheen of his hair and the rapier-like sharpness of his mind. Having already decided that it was immoral for Objectivists to socialize voluntarily with nonbelievers, she now decided that the cha-cha, tango, mambo, and samba were the highest social skills yet developed by man. When she entreated him to teach his terpsichorean skills to members of the Senior Collective, Rothbard decided to bid farewell. The addition of a rational dancer to the Senior Collective was more than he could stomach.

The climax to this crucial episode in American history came in the summer of 1958. Since it was unthinkable for anyone to leave the Randian nest of his own accord, Rand called an emergency meeting of the Senior Collective to hear the various charges of deviationism that had been compiled against Rothbard over the past six months. Leonard Liggio was offered the chance to sit in and register his own vote, but he missed his opportunity for moral redemption by dismissing the affair as "silly and unimportant."

The vote to purge Rothbard from the World of Reason was not unanimous but, alas, Riesman and Hessen, former colleagues of Rothbard and Liggio from an earlier time, cast their votes with the majority—as they did ten years later when Branden's turn finally came and he, too, was ejected from the world he had worked so hard to create.

3

With a Jaw Like That He Can't Lose

Those libertarians disillusioned with Ayn Rand and her Objectivism were left, for the time being, without a home of their own. There were others in the country who felt the way they did, of course. You knew about them because you exchanged letters with them once in a while, and you came across their articles now and then in some obscure journal no one else had ever heard of. Their ideas were usually buried in an avalanche of ponderous tracts on economic theory—the ones that were sprinkled throughout with mathematical formulae and technical language that gave you a headache if you read them too carefully. Or else they were mimeographed on those defective little machines with pale blue ink and broken letters that made you squint for hours afterward.

It was a time of disillusionment and uncertainty. And frustration, because you knew things were getting worse instead of better. Somehow you had been caught between generations. Having gone to school in the age of Pat Boone, Johnnie Ray, and Dwight D. Eisenhower, you'd come along too late to be fully a part of the Beatnik world of Jack Kerouac, Lawrence Ferlinghetti, and Alan Ginsberg. By the late 1950s the Beatnik subculture was already on the wane, and cool, progressive jazz—the one medium you could really understand and call your own—was rapidly leaving the American continent for Paris and London. The age of flower children and rock music was a few years away, and by the time it got going you would be a little too old to identify with the under-twenty-five youth subculture anyway.

Adrift as you were—culturally, generationally, politically—you entered the decade of the 1960s convinced that the world would never last another five years. Sooner or later the Bomb would go off. It didn't matter, really, who dropped the first one, the Russians or ourselves. The general effect would be the same. Death, destruction, radioactive clouds all over the whole planet. *On the Beach* was real. It was only a question of how much longer. The Bomb was so big and out of control, so far beyond the reach of you, the individual. There was nothing you could do about it. Shrug your shoulders and dismiss it all with a hopeless gesture. Invest your life savings in a fallout shelter for the backyard, next to the barbecue pit. There was little reason for optimism.

If, miraculously, the powers that be managed to control their paranoia and restrain themselves from totally destroying the earth, there was still no doubt that American society was in an imminent state of collapse. The death throes had already begun; the final hours were now at hand. The presidential election of 1960 was proof enough of that. To the libertarian, John F. Kennedy typified everything that had been wrong with the corporate, liberal, technocratic elite for nearly thirty years. If elected, he would move into Washington with an army of think-tank intellectuals and pragmatic social engineers to dictate a scientistic policy that would touch every conceivable area of human activity. No stone would be left unturned, no corner of the country would be left free of regulation by the social planners in Washington. 1961 would be 1984 before its time.

On the other hand, Richard M. Nixon was a thoroughly inadequate opponent from a libertarian viewpoint. He had been a sorry figure under Eisenhower, representing the worst aspect of conservatism—obsessive anti-communist hysteria—without any noticeable traces of real economic and civil libertarianism. He seemed capable only of me-tooing the state-corporate programs of the Kennedy liberals, instead of challenging the basic concepts themselves. By parroting the Kennedy nostrums about what must be done to save American society, stipulating only that somehow *he* could implement them more effectively, he offered no philosophical opposition to the liberal elitism of JFK.

Oh, if somebody pressed you to it, you admitted reluctantly that you did prefer Nixon to John F. Kennedy. But it was certainly not a strong enough preference to prod you into the polling booth.

You didn't even bother to vote that year.

In the midst of your disillusionment and frustration, in the midst of this cultural and political and philosophical vacuum in which you found yourself adrift, a storyland politician—the likes of whom you had never seen before—suddenly and unexpectedly stepped into the spotlight. Who was he? What was he saying? Could it be that an American politician was actually saying things like that at this time and in this place? It was overwhelming. It was too much to be believed.

It was time for Barry Goldwater.

Barry Goldwater was a Randian character with a jaw Rand might have created. One look at him and you knew he belonged in Galt's Gulch, surrounded by striking heroes with blazing eyes and lean, dynamic women with swirling capes.

In building the characters for her books, Rand invariably described the altruists as flabby men with shifty eyes, poor muscle tone, and names like Ellsworth Toohey or Wesley Mouch; the egoists, of course, were beauteous and tall, and their names when spoken rang with the hardness of steel and granite. This was a built-in absurdity in Rand's fictional characterizations that exposed her to a great deal of criticism from both the Left and Right. Her either-or philosophy and Goldwater's no-compromise political attitudes were ready-made to dovetail with each other in an era when "pragmatism" was the order of the day, absolutism and consistency were out, compromise and relativistic problem-solving were in; when anyone who believed in a firm and consistent set of principles was regarded as single-minded or shallow.

But by reducing consistency of principle to the level of a Hegelian dialectic, Rand committed an error in reverse logic. Rereading *The Fountainhead* and *Atlas Shrugged* with the benefit of hindsight, one can see that this either-or distinction Rand creates—most obviously through her characterizations—laid the groundwork for a similar Hegelian dialectic when she developed her political philosophy. Man is *either* hero *or* villain; he is *either* good *or* bad; he is *either* tall, lean, and heroic *or* short, squat, and villainous.

By the time Goldwater appeared on the scene, Rand had already embraced the Cold War dialectic, which translated into: it's *either* the United States *or* the Soviet Union; if we are the apotheosis of virtue, they become by definition the embodiment of evil. While it was true that the United States was infinitely preferable to the Soviet Union in that Americans enjoyed basic freedoms while Soviet citizens had none, Rand made no allowances for unfathomable stupidity in U.S. foreign policy. Rand's error in challenging the pragmatism and anti-absolutism of her era is the old one of tossing out the baby with the bathwater; if compromise and day-to-day problem-solving is wrong, then a black-and-white, either-or value structure must be right. Consequently there can be no such thing as shades of gray, no such thing as degrees of good and evil. It was therefore all but inevitable that her Hegelian code would translate into political conservatism in the Cold War era. Since she had selected the United States over the Soviet Union, this choice necessarily shaped her politics with the view that the United States and the Soviet Union were locked in irreconcilable conflict. The notion that each side might be partly right and partly wrong in its dealings with the rest of the world was unthinkable.

At the same time there was no question that this dichotomy appealed to many libertarians, especially those who tended to view the world in Darwinian terms. Social Darwinism—particularly the survival-of-the-fittest approach to life—has always had a strong influence on the individualist Right.

When Goldwater's *The Conscience of a Conservative* came out in 1960, it naturally made its mark on many of the same people who had already been turned on by *The Fountainhead* and *Atlas Shrugged*. There was a strong libertarian undercurrent running through the book, with the same disgust for the expanding Corporate State and its totalitarian tendencies that was dramatized in Ayn Rand's novels. And the either-or anti-communism of Goldwater meshed almost perfectly with the Objectivist logic. But more important than his message was Goldwater's visual impact: he managed to *look the part* as though he had been made for it.

He was from the Southwest, still a frontier area in many respects. He was tall, well set up, and ruggedly youthful in his middle age. He looked better in jeans and rawhide than he did in suits and ties. And that jaw! Jumping Jesus on roller skates, his jaw could have been chiseled by Rand herself. It was perfect. So strong and hard and it stuck out just the right amount. No one else in the country had one quite like it—well, Kirk Douglas maybe, but he was way over on the Left, which didn't fit the Randian stereotype at all. Things would never have been the same had *The Conscience of a Conservative* been written by a fat, balding man with cigar ashes dribbling down his shirtfront.

Nor would the book have had the same impact had it been written by an author named Wesley Mouch. Wesley Mouch, individualist, somehow wouldn't have made it. But Barry Goldwater! Barry, by itself, was a bit swishy perhaps; but when coupled with Goldwater? The last name was perfection. *Gold*, with all its connotations of hard currency and the free market. And Gold*water*! It rippled, it shone, it glittered. The combination was dynamite. Students all over the country who hated the Corporate State and wanted to see it replaced by an individualistic way of life were freaked out by Goldwater. There was no one else like him.

Rand and then Goldwater, in fact, seemed to offer the only real alternatives to the American Leviathan. There was no one else. *Atlas Shrugged* had hit a certain segment of American political and cultural consciousness with the impact of a lightning bolt. For all its flawed imagery and comic-strip characterizations, it was the first revolutionary outcry against the unbearable *status quo* of Organization Man America, the first truly radical critique and denunciation of the gargantuan U.S. power structure. A few years later, along came Barry Goldwater, a hero straight from the pages of *Atlas Shrugged*. The combination and timing couldn't have been more effective had the whole thing been staged by a Hollywood press agent.

It is probably safe to say that without the one-two punch of the Rand-Goldwater assault on the American psyche, the New Left radicalism of the middle 1960s would have taken a different form entirely. The initial anarchism of the New Left in its earliest days owed much of its basic formulation to the Rand-Goldwater inheritance. Their anti-establish-mentarianism was admired by many of the original leaders of the New Left such as Tom Hayden and Carl Oglesby, even as they rejected the anti-communism and free-market economics of Rand and Goldwater. Without this burst of anarchistic individualism in the early 1960s, the radical Left uprisings against the political structure would have been more closely bound up in the state socialist and Marxist concepts of the Old Left. The gradual dissipation of libertarian forces in the New Left movement may have been partly due to the element of conservatism inherent in Rand and Goldwater's thinking. Put another way, the basic flaws in the Rand-Goldwater brand of libertarianism may have planted the seeds for the dissolution of libertarian elements in the New Left movement that came later.

When Goldwater ran for president in 1964, the enthusiasm surrounding his candidacy matched or exceeded that of the McCarthy youth movement that followed in 1968. A mania had gripped those of us who supported Goldwater. He was more than just a candidate; he would be more than just a president. His followers hero-worshiped him, embodying as he did everything we held sacred. His philosophy seemed quasi-Randian, but he was a *politician*—potentially the most powerful one in the world. And unlike other politicians, he would never compromise with the pragmatists and knee-jerk problem-solvers in Washington. He epitomized the free market, self-sufficiency, and a style of life that was being eroded a bit more each day.

He had to win, there were no two ways about it. Everything was at stake. If he lost, it would mean a return to the same old crap for another four years. Four more years of LBJ, of the Great Society. Barry would change all that. We never considered for one moment that his will would be stymied by a recalcitrant Congress. All he had to do was drill those flabby, compromising Congressmen with his ice-blues and the opposition would dissolve before him.

The first trepidations began to set in during the early stages of the campaign. Who was advising the man? Who was conducting his battle for the presidency?

"Did you hear what Goldwater said last night?"

"No. What?"

"No more farm subsidies. To an audience in the middle of Kansas, no less."

The day before, he had told a Golden Age Club gathering that Social Security would have to go. A week earlier he called for an end to import quotas—before a group of textile magnates. If that wasn't enough, he was telling white Mississippians that black people had the same rights they did. Or pacifists that we had to defoliate the jungles of Southeast Asia.

"What's the matter with him?"

"He's dumb."

"He's crazy."

"He's not dumb, he's just honest. He's got principles, for Christ's sake!"

"Principles don't win elections."

If only he would keep his mouth shut. If only he would just walk around and let people look at his jaw! With a jaw like that he didn't have to say anything.

Now LBJ was beginning to cut into his physiognomy vote. Some people were beginning to suggest that LBJ looked a little like John Wayne. Oh my God, not John Wayne! John Wayne was one of ours. Why the hell couldn't Goldwater be running against somebody like Adlai Stevenson? Stevenson didn't look like John Wayne. Stevenson looked like an altruist. Adlai Stevenson looked like Wesley Mouch.

Barry Goldwater would have been a shoo-in against Adlai Stevenson.

When it was over the whole world had fallen in. John Galt had been buried in a landslide. It was overwhelming. It was incredible. The

American voter was incorrigibly irrational. The fabric of American society was corrupt and rotten all the way through. Ragnar Danneskjold had the right idea. You had to blow the whole system sky-high. That was the only way to get rid of it. No more of this crapping around with elections and reform. No more bullshit. Reform within the system was impossible.

Goldwater was dead. Howard Roark, John Galt, and Hank Reardon had been rejected by an overwhelming majority of the American people. Sixty-five percent of the population was degenerate and anti-life. Galt's Gulch receded farther away into the clouds. There would never be an opportunity like this again.

Overnight, a reaction against Goldwater began to set in among his supporters. He let us down. He had all the right ingredients—a jaw, a name, a book—and he blew it. He was a phony hero, a fake. He didn't belong in the same league as John Galt. He was an imposter, a whim-worshiping second-hander, a muscle mystic. He was a tin hero with mixed premises. And he was also a religionist. His inconsistencies stuck out like warts all over his face. If you took a closer look you could detect a certain shiftiness about the eyes. There was a weakness there that belied the strength and hardness of his jaw.

If only Nathaniel Branden had run for president instead of Goldwater. There was a man whose consistency on every basic issue was incontestable. Or Ayn Rand, for that matter. The first woman President of the United States.

But both of them were born outside the country. Only a native American could run for the highest office. There was no one else. After Goldwater, there was simply no one else to turn to.

Reform within the system was impossible. That left only one alternative. Dare one say the word? It ran against the grain of the whole conservative frame of mind. And yet …

Ragnar Danneskjold! Where were you now that we needed you more than ever?

4

The Impact of Ivy League Hegelianism

William F. Buckley, Jr. had never really turned us on that much. His appeal to the right-wing mentality had never been primarily libertarian in nature, despite his joking reference to himself as an "anarchist" in his earliest days.

In 1965 he emerged as an active political candidate for the first time, raising high the banner of the Conservative Party in his race for Mayor of New York City. You campaigned openly for him, mainly because you lived in the city and wanted life there to be as agreeable as possible while you did, and you saw no hope in either of the two major candidates. John Lindsay, the Republican nominee, was an unimaginative corporate-liberal on the order of Senator Jacob Javits, representing a point of view that was not all that different from European democratic socialism, and Abraham Beame was a dim-witted populist Democrat who was in bed with the city's monopolistic, racist, mostly white trade unions. The war in Vietnam was not yet the crucial issue it was to become a year or two later, so you found yourself supporting Buckley even though his brand of right-wing elitism was markedly different from your own.

Back in the early 1950s, when Buckley had hit the country with *God and Man at Yale*, his conservative philosophy was peppered throughout with a generous dash of libertarianism. In the beginning, the terms libertarian and anarchist held no shock value for him personally, and he delighted in using both of them to describe that part of his philosophy which advocated economic *laissez faire* and personal freedom from government intervention. He found common ground in the thinking of such Old Right libertarians as Albert Jay Nock and Frank Chodorov, whose philosophies ranged from total anarchism to a radical form of severely limited government. "The amount of government I believe in would fit inside my kitchen," was a favorite slogan of Chodorov's.

Buckley, in the beginning, was able to incorporate this type of anarchistic individualism into his own philosophy and to espouse it with an apparent degree of sincerity. Within a short time, however, it became obvious that there was another side to the Buckley mentality, a side that contradicted and was at total variance with his libertarianism, a side that was later to grow and dominate the other until the remaining elements of libertarianism in his thinking were reduced to little more than weak rhetoric. The dominant anti-libertarian side of Buckley's conservatism can best be described as crusading, even evangelical anti-communism.

The Hegelian dichotomy in Buckley's mentality presented itself in the following manner: simultaneously, he held two irreconcilable premises to be absolute truths. The first stated that the individual had the right to remain free from all outside intervention in his life so long as he conducted his affairs in a non-aggressive manner. This was libertarian philosophy, pure and simple. The second premise stated that the existence of atheistic communism was the single greatest evil mankind faced on earth, and that a powerful American nation-state was the only effective means of protecting our Western heritage from destruction by this insidious Red menace. This, of course, was the conservative anti-communist side to the Buckley mentality, which was to become increasingly dominant throughout the balance of the 1950s and the decade to follow.

He attempted to maintain this precarious balancing act between a call for unobtrusive government, and a strong nation state with a large, powerful, and aggressive government that existed only to combat the "Red disease" in the international arena, while maintaining at the same time a hands-off policy in domestic affairs. When he later realized that this concept was an impossible dream—primarily because a large military establishment depends heavily on a military draft and high taxation, profoundly anti-libertarian measures—he was forced to readjust his political formulation and speak of the "temporary suspension of individual liberties" until international communism could be defeated. By the middle 1950s the escalation of Buckley's conservative anti-communist philosophy and the de-escalation of his individualist libertarianism were well under way.

Having solved this Hegelian dilemma to his own satisfaction, he was able to concentrate more thoroughly on the development of a sophisticated intellectual foundation for his anti-communist conservatism. Since he had now reconciled the libertarian-conservative dialectic by "temporarily" suspending most libertarian goals, it became possible for him to live with such measures as a "temporary" military draft, "temporary" confiscatory taxation, and "temporary" abridgment of civil liberties at home to support a large "temporary" anticommunist, militaristic nation-state. He would have preferred to have Americans *voluntarily* give themselves bodily, spiritually, and monetarily to the creation of an anticommunist juggernaut. This would have enabled him to eat his cake and have it at the same time, to have a *voluntary* slave state without having to violate what remained of his libertarian sensibilities. But, if Americans were too unsophisticated to realize that a condition of "temporary servitude" was actually in their own best interests, then it became necessary to save them from their wrong-headedness despite themselves.

It was their own fault, goddamnit!

If the people were too stupid to realize what was good for them, it wasn't Buckley's fault, was it? He was willing to give them a chance to flock to the banner of the Crusades. If the foolish creatures couldn't understand that the "moral climate" of Western society was being eroded a little bit more every day by insidious heresies, somebody had to see that the proper measures were taken to safeguard their traditions.

Of course, all this was interwoven with religious considerations. Buckley was reflecting an attitude that has long been prevalent, not only in Western society but throughout the world. Over the centuries the institutions of religion and government have somehow become inseparable. There has never been a true "separation of church and state" on a practical level. Men have merely transferred their devotion to God and religion to the institution of government. The "Divine Right to Rule" is still very much a part of the psychological makeup of many human beings. There have been few patriots who did not believe in—and who were not willing to risk their lives to defend—the concept that God was on the side of their particular nation-state. "God" is simultaneously "on the side of" the Germans, the Italians, the French, the Japanese, the Irish, the Arabs and Israelis, and the Americans even as they have butchered one another over the centures. No man has ever died for his "country" alone, and very few men have ever died to defend their "freedom." Most men who go willingly to war have believed, very strongly, that they were fighting "God's cause."

Understanding this, we begin to see a little more clearly why so many Americans have waxed violent over the so-called issue of flag desecration. What is being spat or shat upon is not merely a piece of cloth with red and white stripes and white stars on a blue background; it is "God's face" that is being bombarded; it is Jesus on the cross who is being trampled underfoot. And so the overlay of the peace symbol on the flag during Vietnam was considered "desecration," while the super-imposition of a B-52 on the same flag was regarded as "patriotic." Bigger and Better Bombs for Jesus might well be the rallying cry of American super-patriots, who see the American nation-state as the sacred repository of Western religious traditions. Nuke the Reds and Bomb Hanoi! Rape the earth in the name of Christ!

Consciously or not, the highly sophisticated Buckley began to appeal to these unsophisticated attitudes in the pages of *National Review,* which he founded in 1955 with the financial and editorial assistance of a wide range of intellectuals and writers on the Right. Many libertarians, such as Frank Chodorov and Murray Rothbard, joined forces with *National Review* at first, then later severed relations with it to protest the increasingly hawkish and authoritarian coloration of Buckley's politics. It is interesting to look back at certain factors underlying the rising influence, at the time, of Buckley conservatism in right-wing circles, and the concomitant loss of influence suffered by the Old Right libertarians.

The Old Right with all its positive elements—its instinctive distrust of political power, its mind-your-own-business attitude on foreign policy—also carried with it a history of provincial anti-intellectualism and, in some quarters, a strain of anti-Semitism. These characteristics of the Old Right mentality were long a target of abuse for perhaps the most intellectual Rightist of the 1930s and 1940s, H. L. Mencken. "Booboisie" and "Boobus Americanus" were two of the choice epithets he used to describe such attitudes. By the late 1940S the term "Neanderthal" had all but become a synonym for "Right-Wing Republican," and, in many instances, with fairly good justification.

Buckley's rapid rise through the right-wing hierarchy must be seen against the background of this intellectual vacuum. The more sophisticated types on the Right—students, journalists, academicians—were desperate for a leader of sufficient stature to come along and do battle on their behalf. Buckley was tailor-made to fit the role. He was a Northeastern intellectual and a graduate of Yale, of all places, a major crucible for the formulation of the liberal point of view. He was urbane and eloquent; he had wit; he had charm; he was everything the conservatives had come to associate with liberalism in every respect except one: his ideology. On that point he was one of their own, a philosophical conservative. So great was the intellectual inferiority complex of the Right by this time that the average conservative could do nothing but hero-worship a fellow Rightist who epitomized, in most areas, the thing they themselves feared most—the image of the liberal intellectual. These Buckley qualities, combined with his timely entry into the public arena, were prime factors in his quick ascension to a position of prominence on the Right. Had he been a liberal, he would have been lost in the lines of candidates already forming up for the New-Frontier, Great-Society regimes of the 1960s. Once he had established himself as the Golden Boy of the New Right, it was then only a question of how he would maintain his pre-eminent position. By the end of the 1950s, William F. Buckley and *National Review* had come to be recognized as the major voice of conservatism in the United States. There was certainly no shortage of libertarian intellectuals attempting to subvert the mounting Buckley influence on the Right during this period. Through the late 1950s and early 1960s, they kept up a steady barrage of articles designed to reaffirm the decentralist principles of the Old Right and detour the New Right from its steady march toward a hawkish foreign policy. But with all the flak and all the intramural squabbles he found himself in, Buckley managed to build his base and increase his influence during a period beginning around 1953 and extending all the way through the next decade and beyond.

When you look back, the reasons are not hard to see. First, no one else on the Right was as successful as William Buckley in doing battle with the common enemy—the hated liberal intellectual. He could jab, feint, hook, and counterpunch with the best of them, and he had an uncanny gift for detecting an opponent's hidden weaknesses and driving in the shaft at the most opportune moment. For this ability he was rewarded with the unquestioning admiration of an appreciative right-wing audience—much the same as Adam Clayton Powell, once he had established himself as an expert gadfly capable of ruffling the white man's composure, could do no wrong in the black community.

It was also true that our religious traditions—particularly the Christian tradition—were of great importance to conservatives in the 1950s and the first half of the 1960s, and the Left was regarded as the major destroyer of religious morality in the United States, as it still is in the early years of the twenty-first century. Consciously or not, Buckley was able to parlay this fear of atheism and other "un-American doctrines" into a source of power for himself. He and his cohorts at *National Review* had seen this atheistic menace—exemplified in communism—for what it was, and they would do everything in their power to save the nation from it. William F. Buckley was, in fact, seen by his constituency as the final barrier between everything they considered holy and the barbaric reach of the anti-Christ (communism) which threatened to engulf the earth.

By the time Buckley emerged as a political candidate in the New York mayoralty race of 1965, his brand of conservatism was already unacceptable to a great many libertarians. And yet there simply was no one else to turn to. To libertarians, Lindsay and Beame represented an even more alien philosophy than Buckley. In the wake of the Goldwater disaster of 1964, you had given up almost all hope for libertarian reform within the system. Buckley was bad, but the others were worse. Maybe, just maybe, your candidate would rediscover some of his old libertarian principles of years before and implement them, even on a limited scale, in New York City. Maybe he would demunicipalize the Sanitation Department or decentralize the school system or decontrol the housing situation. Maybe. That would be something at least, wouldn't it?

There was nothing else to hope for, no one else to turn to. Your options were becoming more and more limited all the time.

5

Please Don't Kill Lenny Bruce

Buckley's defeat in the New York City mayoralty race of 1965 was considerably less traumatic than Goldwater's demise the previous year. For one thing, he had entered the contest more as a gadfly than as a serious candidate, and by his own admission he hadn't a chance in a million of actually being elected.

"If I win I shall demand a recount," was the way he phrased it himself.

And of course you had supported Buckley with considerably less enthusiasm than you lavished on Goldwater, who came much closer to personifying the ideal of freewheeling libertarian individualism. Still and all, the election of John Lindsay, the candidate whom Buckley hoped to defeat by attracting Republican votes to his own Conservative Party candidacy, left you with a new sense of abandonment and homelessness, not unlike the state you were in following the presidential campaign of 1960. A new vacuum had been created. There was no figure in the country who could qualify as a potential leader of a libertarian political movement with broad-based support. There was no political party or noteworthy organization, short of a few scattered discussion clubs, committed to the translation of libertarian principles into concrete political reality. The Republican Party was continually drifting further away from the quasi-libertarianism of the Old Republican Right Wing, and the Conservative Party of New York reflected for the most part the hard anti-communist conservatism of William Buckley and *National Review*.

For this reason your attention was caught more and more by the ubiquitous Young Americans for Freedom. YAF was the largest and best-financed conservative group on American campuses, and though it was most heavily influenced by Buckley-style conservatism, there had been a vocal libertarian minority within its ranks since its founding in 1961. Your alternatives, as far as right-wing political activism was concerned, had been reduced to YAF-Conservative Party organizing or a kind of Ivory Tower purism that left you without any political affiliation at all. And *so,* in the early months of 1966, you found yourself at some rallies and conferences sponsored by YAF.

Attending a Young Americans for Freedom function in the mid-1960s was like entering a time capsule and being transported ten or fifteen years into the past. People looked exactly the way you remembered them half a generation before. In an age of long hair, jeans, and love beads, it was a mind-blowing experience to enter a convention hall in, say, the Waldorf-Astoria, and find yourself surrounded by a brigade of Pat Boones. The white bucks had been stored at the back of the closet by this time, but those freshly scrubbed cheeks and porcupine hairdos with needle spikes sticking out in six directions, the horn-rim glasses with translucent lower halves, the charcoal-gray slacks and red vests, the blue blazers with political-slogan buttons on their lapels were all over the place. You immediately thought back to an age when the "other people," those degenerates in pegged pants, chartreuse shirts, and fuchsia socks were going at it hot and heavy with chains, bats, and homemade zip guns. You expected a battalion of them to invade at any moment, while Al Martino's "Here in My Heart" poured out of a jukebox in the corner; most urban neighborhoods had enjoyed at least one battle a week between Elvis Presley-style hipsters and charcoal-grayed Pat Boones.

Johnnie Ray and Elvis and the Four Aces! Where the hell were they anyway? Where were Dion and the Belmonts and Buddy Holly and Ritchie Valens and the Big Bopper and "Shaboom" and Frankie Laine and the Four Lads and the Shirelles and Tab Hunter and Moondog and Al Hibbler and Don Cornell and Hamish Menzies and Anne Francis and Aldo Rey and the D.A. hairdo and the twelve-inch peg and Holden

Caulfield and Grace Metalious and Debra Paget and Piper Laurie? Where were they all?

Why, they were right there in the Waldorf-Astoria, surrounding you at a YAF convention in the middle of the 1960s. And you loved every minute of it. Until that inevitable day when you learned for the first time that there were people in the world who had never heard of James Dean. James Dean! How could anybody never have heard of James Dean? Was there anything more important than James Dean in the 1950s? He was bigger than Sputnik, bigger than the Russian invasion of Hungary, bigger than the English bombs raining on Cairo. James Dean was a revolution all by himself. He was even more important than Marlon Brando. He stamped a lifestyle on an entire generation. A whole generation of teenage Americans walked around for years in red nylon jackets like the one he wore in "Rebel Without a Cause." Legions of red-blooded American high-school students with cigarettes hanging in the corners of their mouths were referring to their girl friends as "my friend," the way he'd introduced Natalie Wood to his parents. Legions more went on those school expeditions to the Planetarium and "mooed" out loud when Taurus the Bull came into focus on the ceiling.

James Dean was a way of life. James Dean was a teenage rebel before anybody knew what the Establishment *was*.

And so you found yourself in the middle of a convention hall in the Waldorf, surrounded by people who looked like Pat Boone and made you think of people like James Dean and Johnnie Ray—surrounded by people who *themselves* couldn't remember anything that happened before Peter, Paul, and Mary came along. More important than that, you felt a little sick with the understanding that if James Dean were to walk into the convention hall with his bright red jacket and his freaky lopsided grin, ninety per cent of the people there would consider him a Communist.

You knew now, suddenly and painfully, that this was not the way to Galt's Gulch after all.

With the first tremors of disillusionment, you started to take a closer look at the printing on some of those lapel buttons.

"Boycott Polish Hams!"

Why the hell would anyone in his right mind want to boycott Polish hams? Weren't we all supposed to be free traders? Didn't we all believe in the unregulated market place? What, in the furthest stretch of the imagination, did the Polish people have to do with Marx and Stalin? Were these poor bastards ensnared in a slave state by a tyrannical political regime to be further penalized by relatively free Americans who refused to buy their hams?

"Impeach Earl Warren!"

But Earl Warren could be good for you! We're individualists after all, aren't we? Isn't Earl Warren making life easier for individuals who find themselves locking horns with a gigantic State apparatus? Do we want to give the State even more power to hound its hapless victims every time they sleep around with the wrong people?

"Stop Lenny Bruce!"

Oh no! Please no, not Lenny Bruce. Wasn't it Lenny Bruce who said communism was a drag, just like a great big telephone company? Didn't Lenny Bruce say capitalism gives people a choice, baby, and that's what it's all about? So what if he used words like "fuck," "shit," "piss," and "rape," and even "come." Didn't we believe in free speech? Didn't we believe that an individual should be allowed to do and say anything he pleased as long as he didn't hurt anyone else? And Lenny was funny, goddamnit! He was saying things that had to be said. So what if he made fun of nuns and priests and said they were screwing one another? We found out later that they actually were, and not just other nuns and priests, but little children as well.

No, no. Not Lenny Bruce. Please don't kill Lenny Bruce!

It was through Young Americans for Freedom, whose founding in 1961 kept his right-wing coalition together, that Buckley exercised his greatest influence on campus intellectuals—those who would eventually take their place as speech writers, PR men, and other functionaries of the Republican Party. Buckleyite conservatives controlled most YAF chapters around the country, and with an adequate money supply and established organizational structure they were able to attract many

Rightist students to the traditionalist position. If Buckleyite conservatism characterized the great majority of the YAF membership, the second largest group, the libertarian faction, was most heavily influenced
by Objectivism. Objectivism was the logical home for most young people with a libertarian bent. And since the great majority of readers of
Atlas Shrugged and *The Fountainhead* had never visited the seat of
Objectivism in New York City, they had never come face to face with
the Randian idiosyncrasies that inspired so many New York libertarians
to make a more critical appraisal of Rand's ideas.

By the late-1960s, sufficient friction had developed within YAF
between the forces of William F. Buckley and those of Ayn Rand to
cause frequent battles for control of various campus chapters. Since the
YAF hierarchy was almost uniformly traditionalist, an attempt was
made to purge Objectivists from leadership positions on the nation's
campuses, which served only to escalate a situation of mutual distrust
into one of downright hostility.

Looking back to the late 1950s and the venomous assault *National
Review* made on *Atlas Shrugged* in the form of a book review, it seems
surprising that so many young Randians flocked to the YAF banner
when it was raised in 1961. Rand herself had denounced Buckley and
the New Conservatives as "immoral religionists," sharply criticizing
those of her followers who had lent their "sanction" to the conservative
movement. However, the shaky alliance between traditionalist conservatives and the Objectivists becomes less mystifying when you consider
that Rand, for all her intellectual impact, did not have a political base of
her own to offer young Objectivists. Many Objectivist students joined
YAF for the simple reason that they had no place else to go in order to
engage in political activities, and there is no question that most of them
joined with the explicit intention of transforming YAF into an Objectivist-oriented political institution.

Though Randians and Buckleyites differed strongly on questions of
religion, morality, and other key philosophical issues, they shared in
common a rhetorical devotion to private property and a free-enterprise
economic system. Tenuous though this bond was, it made it possible for

YAF to become a political base of operation for young libertarians and young conservatives, forced by the absence of alternatives to share one in common. According to the results of a poll conducted by the leadership of YAF and released in January 1970 in the *New Guard,* twenty-two per cent of YAF members considered themselves libertarian, naming Ayn Rand and Ludwig von Mises as their chief sources of influence. Seventy-two per cent cited William Buckley, Russell Kirk, and Frank Meyer as their intellectual leaders, and of this number nine per cent were Frank Meyer "fusionists" who stood somewhere between the libertarians and the traditionalists.

The remaining six per cent were "radical traditionalists," who might also be regarded as fervent American nationalists. The intellectual pillars of this faction were Buckley's brother-in-law, L. Brent Bozell, a fanatical convert to Catholicism who later founded the Sons of Thunder, a neo-Carlist paramilitary organization whose members, wearing red berets and rosary beads, invaded hospitals to baptize aborted fetuses; Henry Paolucci, an ardent American nationalist; Robert Welch, founder of the John Birch Society; and explicitly anti-Semitic followers of Willis Carto, whose extremist right-wing combine came to include Liberty Lobby, the new *American Mercury* magazine, and another campus organization called the National Youth Alliance.

All these forces at work on the American Right since the early 1950s had resulted in this rather shaky right-wing coalition. It was a combination of at least three elements: Buckley's appeal to the religious traditions of middle America, and his emergence as a "sophisticated" spokesman for the work ethic and the free enterprise system; Rand and Goldwater's impact on young Americans with a penchant for radically individualistic alternatives to the American Corporate State; and the creation of Young Americans for Freedom as a political base for the various types drawn to a libertarian-conservative frame of reference. A denouement of sorts was reached after the Goldwater campaign of 1964. The Right became disenchanted, to a large extent, with Goldwater's apolitical idealism and his "unrealistic" approach to power politics in the United States. Largely under the influence of Buckley, and later,

Kevin Phillips, who wrote *The Emerging Republican Majority*, the Right began to take a more "pragmatic" and less doctrinaire course over the next few years.

The logical end to this trend was, of course, the candidacy of that most pragmatic and fence-straddling political hack of all, Richard Nixon, in the Presidential campaign of 1968.

6

The Right Wing Joan of Arc

Standing out there in the rain, distributing campaign leaflets.

"Nixon is the One!"

Oh Christ! Is this what it had come down to? This shifty-eyed con artist? You could tell by looking at his picture that he would never have been allowed near Galt's Gulch. He was tall enough, all right. And lean, though in a dumpy kind of way. But in your heart you knew he wasn't right.

Nixon wasn't the one, and everybody knew it. And yet you stood out there in the rain on the West Side of Manhattan distributing this pack of lies to anyone with his hand out. A certain percentage of people would grab onto anything as long as it was free. And so all these liberals and wild-eyed West Side radicals would swarm on by, hatred spilling over their left-wing eyeballs, accepting their sheets of freebie propaganda even though they knew it reeked of fascism.

"Nixon is the One!"

This sleight-of-hand purveyor of shoddy goods from the heartland of America? This all-American carny barker? You told each other he'd worked his way through college selling worn-out French ticklers to pimply faced high-school boys. If Nixon was the one there was no hope for any of us. We might as well lock ourselves in the kitchen and turn on the gas jets. It was all over. It had all come down to this.

In your heart you knew Nixon wasn't the one, but in your heart you also knew that Hubert Humphrey was a freaked-out altruist on roller skates. Hubert Humphrey was a smiling kewpie doll. Hubert Humphrey was a left-over manservant from F.D.R.'s New Deal, a third-string water boy for J.F.K.'s Frontiersmen, who later choked on the table scraps from

L.B.J.'s Great Military Society. Hubert Humphrey was a nebbish, a nothing, a nonentity.

Hubert Humphrey was Wesley Mouch.

What a hoax on the American public. After all the idealism, all the years of frustration, struggle, and disillusionment, the American political system had degenerated to this: a contest between the two most thoroughgoing political hacks either party could possibly have come up with. Nixon and Humphrey. Walking personifications of the worst elements of the two-party electoral system. The worst of the lot. The dregs. The built-in weakness of our democratic republic was out in the open for all to see. For all to see who wanted to see.

I had joined the Conservative Club on the upper West Side of Manhattan thinking—naively, as it turned out—that the conservatives in this predominantly liberal area would tend to be more libertarian than they were, for example, in the Throgs Neck section of the Bronx with its heavy concentration of Birchers. And so I attended the weekly meetings expecting to join forces with local libertarians who, however obnoxious most of them might be personally, would at least be motivated by intellectual rather than prejudicial considerations. What I found instead, piling out of the ornate, thick-walled town houses along Riverside Drive and West End Avenue, was a collection of bejeweled dowagers and monocled relics who tended to claim blood relationship with virtually every crowned head of nineteenth-century Europe.

Then there were the older West Siders who remembered their area when it was predominantly Irish, with a scattering of German and Italian families. They were mainly low-income Law-and-Order types who had never achieved the wherewithal to move up to Riverdale or into the suburbs, and they resented bitterly the heavy infiltration of blacks, Puerto Ricans, Haitians, Dominican Republicans, Cuban refugees, and struggling artists, actors, and writers who had all but taken over the neighborhood by the early 1960s. Since I counted myself as a member of the last group, I had a difficult time adjusting to their notion of how a conservative society should be organized.

At the first few meetings I was somewhat startled to see several club members sporting George Wallace buttons on their lapels and dresses, but I dismissed them as a small, fringe element. The official policy of the club was to support Nixon, and except for a few pre-convention posters calling for the nomination of Ronald Reagan, the slogans on the walls and the campaign literature were strictly Nixon. But as the campaign progressed, the percentage of Wallace supporters grew in size and volubility until, by the early fall, Wallace campaign posters were appearing alongside the Nixon posters. When I first protested to the club leader, he told me not to worry.

"They're only a handful of kooks."

Later on he admitted that he couldn't be sure until he walked into the voting booth which way his vote would go, for Nixon or for Wallace. Nixon simply was not "strong enough," and was too much of an opportunist to be trusted. The high point of each weekly gathering usually occurred in the final minutes before adjournment. It was provided by an incredibly ancient woman, so old in appearance she could have been anything from a dissipated seventy-five to a well preserved one hundred and six. She was invariably groomed to the teeth, covered from head to foot with shining beads and baubles and gleaming silken gowns from an era long forgotten. She was referred to by everyone as "the Contessa," assumed variously to be of Russian, Slavic, Lithuanian, or Serbian nationality. It is doubtful that anyone ever knew her name or her true geographical origin.

The Contessa would sit quietly through the evening's proceedings, through the reading of minutes and the various courses of action proposed for the following weeks. By the end of each meeting she would have had quite enough. With the assistance of her neighbor on either side she would rise, infirm of body if not of purpose, to her feet. Quivering with rage like an infuriated peacock trimmed with Christmas ornaments, she would raise a knotty little fist at the assemblage and cry out in brittle, rasping tones:

"You Americans are zo ztoopid! So weak, and nai-eef, and ztoopid wiz all your talk aboud elections. You must *seize* power, *seize* power, *seize* power. Before it is too late!"

But this would-be Joan of Arc, ready to charge the steps of the White House if only she could find a dozen red-blooded stalwarts, was delightful compared to the Bircher who came down a few weeks before the election from, as I recall it, the "Douglas MacArthur Chapter" somewhere in the Bronx. He was eager to inform us that he was all in favor of a democratic form of government under present circumstances. Of course, such indulgences as campaigns, elections, and Congressional checks on the President were necessary only up to the point when you finally established "the right kind of people in power." From that moment onward, competitive elections would serve only to waste the taxpayers' money and create a climate of confusion. America had apparently missed its golden opportunity when MacArthur failed to seize command after being recalled from Korea. Popular support for him had been "overwhelming," and a takeover by the beloved general would have been an expression of the "will of the people." Now, of course, the military was so heavily infiltrated with Communists one could not be completely sure that anything beneficial would result from a military coup.

What were you doing with these people anyway? For almost ten years you had managed to avoid the more exotic fringe groups on the Right, and here you were, in 1968, sitting in a political clubroom flanked by relics of a long-past age of aristocracy, and slightly deranged recruiters for the John Birch Society.

Ironically enough, the form of fanaticism adopted by the John Birch Society's founder, Robert Welch, had led him in the middle 1960s to adopt certain positions that bore a strange similarity to those being espoused by the New Left. He was fond of referring to the United States government as "our main enemy," and to the war in Vietnam as a "CIA plot" to destroy the military strength of the nation. The New Left had, of course, designated the United States as the "most imperialistic" country in the world, while denouncing the CIA, years before the Pentagon Papers, as the main instrument behind the assassination of Diem and the conduct of the war itself. One important difference in these two views is that Welch saw the CIA as having been taken over by "agents of Moscow," while the New Left regarded it as a reflection of a deep-lying American sickness. Later in the 1960s, however, Welch began to join the traditionalist Buckleyite conservatives in their insistence on total victory in Vietnam.

It would seem that a simplistic view of world politics can have an appeal for the least intellectual elements on the Left as well as the Right. To those on the Right who found themselves totally mystified by the complexity of international affairs, Birchist theories offered a simple, easily grasped explanation for the continuing erosion of the American political system. How satisfying to blame it all on a "conspiracy"—the "Communist conspiracy," the "international Jewish-Communist conspiracy," the "world anti-American conspiracy"—it really doesn't matter what you called it. The more vague and preternatural the conspiracy, the better. And the more mysterious and satanically powerful these international forces can be made to sound, the better it is for the advocates of the conspiratorial view. The last thing in the world they needed was for the leaders of the conspiracy to be identified and brought to heel; they would then have been forced to invent a new conspiracy to explain the evils afflicting American society.

Similarly, there are anti-intellectual forces on the radical Left who were equally hard-pressed to understand the existence of poverty, hunger, oppression, exploitation, and privation in the world. Somehow, if these ills could be attributed to a single source, the whole political process is brought down to a level even the most confused can understand. Enter the reverse side of the anti-communist hysteria coin: America itself is inherently evil. The Enemy, for the unthinking Left, was *Amerika* with a K—K for Kill and Korruption. Right on, tiger! If only we can get that K out of Amerika, the peoples of the "Third World" would all be eating six meals a day. Just don't get too explicit about what that K really is. Don't deprive *them* of *their* conspiracy. K for racist-fascist-sexist-Kapitalist imperialism is quite specific enough.

In the years right after college, from 1959 through the middle 1960s, your affiliations on the Right had been limited to those groups whose libertarian principles were adulterated primarily by philosophical eccentricity or personal idiosyncrasies. The Randians and the Goldwaterites, whatever else you could say about them, were motivated by a hunger for a consistent, ethical individualism, which they could not translate into a viable political alternative.

Disillusioned with the hybrid libertarianism of Rand and Goldwater as a means toward the desired end—a free society—you had found yourself a fellow traveler on the traditionalist right of YAF and William F. Buckley, Jr. Leaving them, you had somehow ended up supporting Richard Nixon and consorting with ancient European ax-aristocrats and disciples of a right-wing Society that even Buckley had denounced as too authoritarian for his taste.

The facts were there and had to be faced. Your continuing Odyssey from faction to faction had only brought you further and further away from the America you wanted to reach.

Around this time I met the Galambosian.

"I am a Galambosian," he said.

A *what?* I was beginning to feel like a right-wing Yossarian. All these mothers were out to destroy every principle I believed in! If it wasn't square-jawed Southwesterners with mixed premises, or Ivy League intellectuals who mouthed off in public like truck drivers, or shifty-eyed carny barkers from the Midwest, it was an S. J. Perelman character with a pipe and an ascot, telling me he was a Galambosian.

"What the hell is a Galambosian?"

There was this individual, it seems, named Joseph Andrew Galambos who evolved a theory of "primary property rights." Apparently, as soon as someone came up with a new idea—whether an invention or an original philosophical concept—the prototype belonged irrevocably to him and was to be regarded forevermore as his primary property. Somewhere along the line Galambos picked up the notion that Thomas Paine had invented the word "liberty," whereupon he established the Thomas

Paine Royalty Fund, and every time he gave a lecture and used the word "liberty" he dropped a nickel into his fund box as a royalty payment to Tom. How he determined that a nickel was the proper measure of homage to Mr. Paine, I have no idea. Legend even had it that Galambos was still diligently searching for Thomas Paine's descendants so he could turn over moneys due their famous ancestor.

Sometime in the early or middle 1960s, Galambos decided that his name, Joseph Andrew, was actually the primary property of his father. In order to avoid giving his father a royalty payment every time he spoke the name, Galambos reversed the order and sent out notices to all his friends that henceforth his name was Andrew Joseph, and that he was to be addressed as Andy, instead of Joe.

"There are five legitimate functions of government," said the Galambosian.

"No kidding. What are they?"

"I am not at liberty to say. The theory was originated by Andy Galambos and it is his primary property."

The Galambosian also informed me that Andy had been introduced to Ayn Rand several years before, and that after five minutes of conversation they had pronounced each other insane.

"Of course, it is Miss Rand who is really insane," said the Galambosian.

"Why is that?"

"I'm afraid I cannot tell you. The reasoning behind that theory belongs to Andy."

The most peculiar thing about the whole Galambosian concept was the impossibility of finding out anything about it. Galambos's disciples were not at liberty to disseminate his philosophy without paying a royalty to their leader—who could not even *waive* payment, since primary property was an absolute good and could not be given away. You were stuck with it whether you wanted it or not, throughout eternity. Consequently, all the converts were those proselytized by Galambos himself—a time-consuming and self-restricting process, it being physically impossible to convert more than a handful of people at a time.

"If the rest of us were free to discuss his ideas," said the Galambosian, "there is no question in my mind that Galambosianism would spread throughout the world like wildfire."

There was no question in my mind by the end of the 1968 campaign that a brain-spinning lunacy was spreading like wildfire throughout my own world. If I saw just one more "Support Your Local Police" or "Nuke the Reds" sticker, I knew I would lock myself inside my clothes closet and assume the fetal position. I had seen enough protruding jaws, drilling eyes, and dollar-sign lapel pins to last a lifetime. There was only one proper response to anyone who firmed up his chin and talked to me of "second-handers" or international conspiracies—instantaneous violence. Whammo! Sock! Pow! Punch! Kick him where it hurts and then remove his tongue with a rusty fork. Rip off his "Bomb Hanoi" button and hammer it into his crazy skull. Draw and quarter the bastard and send the pieces to Ayn Barry Buckley Nixon Welch Galambos, Jr.

Sitting there in O'Neal's Saloon near Lincoln Center, staring through the picture window behind the bar at the great fountain across the street, you could get away from it for a while. Water jets shot in the air, fracturing into a billion parts, all on fire like gold coins under the still-bright November sun.

Ragnar Danneskjold! You were the only son of a bitch in the whole world who had a technique that worked. No more screwing around with slogans. No more shopping for compatible factions.

It's time to light up the sky with fireworks.

PART II
The Fracture

7

A New Kind of
Telepathic Imperialism

GOLDWATER AIDE JOINS THE NEW LEFT!

That's what the headline said as I sat there in my 1967 Chevrolet reading the Mamaroneck *Times*. What the hell could you make of a thing like that?

I had left the city earlier in the day to hunt for a new apartment for my pregnant wife and young son: the farther away from Galambosians and 106-year-old, right-wing Joan of Arcs, the better. Mamaroneck seemed as good a place as any. It was only forty minutes from Manhattan, right on Long Island Sound, and from the edge of town you could see the harbor where the boats with their white sails bobbed on the waves. Mamaroneck was as far removed from Upper West Side politicking in spirit as it was in miles, and still there was the headline in the local paper blazing as though it were written in fiery letters:

GOLDWATER AIDE JOINS THE NEW LEFT!

The sadists were following me!

Who *was* this one, anyway? Karl Hess, a former speech writer for Barry. Most of his face was covered by a black beard, so you couldn't tell a goddamn thing about the bone structure. That was one strike against him right there. He obviously had something to hide. His eyes looked all right, clear and direct without a trace of shiftiness. Chalk one up for Hess. He was a little on the hefty side, and his muscle tone looked as though it could stand a lot of firming up. There was no ques-

55

tion in my mind that he suffered from mixed premises and, probably, from some basic character deficiencies.

After working for the Republicans eight years or so, he was now calling himself an anarchist and a New Leftist. He was obviously trying to establish himself as a latter-day Ragnar Danneskjold, and I didn't like it one bit. Ragnar was mine, goddamnit, and I wasn't going to let his memory be dragged in the mud by a puffed-up ex-Republican who was ashamed to reveal the shape of his jaw.

On top of it all he had ruined a perfectly good day for me. It was impossible to concentrate on apartment hunting in Mamaroneck after coming across a thing like this. If I couldn't be left alone, if this Hess character insisted on hounding me like a driven rat, there was only one decent thing to do: stand up and fight back.

The career of Karl Hess as he evolved politically and philosophically through the 1960s was fairly well documented in a number of articles published after his defection from conservatism in 1968. Briefly, he was a major contributor to the Republican Party platform on which Richard Nixon ran in 1960. By 1964 he had emerged as Barry Goldwater's major speechwriter, and he accepted the number-two post on the Republican National Committee prior to the Goldwater nomination in San Francisco. Like Goldwater, Hess was semi-anarchistic on domestic issues, advocating the strict curtailment of government power to matters exclusively concerning national defense. Again, like Goldwater, Hess had caught the paranoiac anticommunist virus popularized in right-wing circles by Buckley and the *National Review* crowd in the middle 1950s.

As discussed earlier, the acceptance of dogmatic anticommunism by many on the Right divided the right wing into two broad camps: the libertarians who tended to be anarchistic on domestic issues and military noninterventionists in foreign policy, and the traditionalists who saw the existence of atheistic communism as a threat to the religious and cultural inheritance of the Western world. The most consistent libertarians, admittedly a small minority, rejected at the outset the notion that America had a moral obligation to maintain a strong military presence abroad to contain the spread of international communism, while the hard-line traditionalists supported Buckley's call for the temporary suspension of liberties at home until communism was defeated.

In the late 1950s a third force developed on the Right in an attempt to bridge the gap between these two disparate factions. The "fusionist" school—as it was later referred to—found its spokesman in Frank S. Meyer, an ex-member of the Communist Party who had become an editor of *National Review.* Meyer maintained that it is possible both to keep our strong, militarized, outward-looking nation-state *and* to preserve fundamental individual freedoms in the domestic arena.

Many libertarians, finding Buckley's "temporary suspension" attitudes totally unpalatable, jumped for the philosophical life preserver Meyer had tossed out to them. Here was a way to eat their cake and have it simultaneously, to hang onto their libertarian rhetoric and keep their conservative credentials at the same time. Hess, Goldwater, and others somehow managed to gloss over the inconsistency of a small, decentralized government that would be large enough to station nuclear-powered policemen in every potential hot spot in the world. The schizophrenia inherent in the very concept of "libertarian conservatism" was bound to erupt in a major conflict sooner or later. The chasm was simply too wide for anyone to straddle comfortably over an extended period.

Hess, of course, threw off his anti-communism for total anarchism in 1968; Goldwater went the other way, forsaking much of his libertarianism for the traditionalism of Buckley, Nixon, and Agnew around the same time.

Following the Goldwater defeat in 1964, Hess wrote a book defending Goldwater's philosophy and the conduct of the campaign itself, thereby reaffirming his own dedication to the cause of fusionist conservatism. The book, *In A Cause That Will Triumph,* was published in 1967. It is likely, however, that he was already starting to question some of his own political and philosophical positions, notwithstanding the passionate rhetoric contained in his book. For one thing, conservatives had started to repudiate the elements of libertarianism remaining in

Goldwater Republicanism, blaming the Senator's absolutist stand against the military draft and against every manner of social-welfare legislation for the landslide margin of his defeat. For another, Richard Nixon was resurfacing as the most likely candidate for the Republican presidential nomination in 1968, and Hess's estimation of Nixon, never lofty to begin with, had fallen substantially after Nixon's campaign in 1960.

And, finally, there was the issue of Vietnam. The horror of the war, combined with the conservatives' demand for total victory at any cost, managed to get through to him. James Boyd quoted Hess on this matter in his excellent profile article in the December 6, 1970, issue of *The New York Times Magazine:*

The immediate cause [of his defection] was Vietnam. Conservatives like me had spent our lives arguing against Federal power—with one exception. We trusted Washington with enormous powers to fight global communism. We were wrong, as Taft foresaw when he opposed NATO. We forgot our old axiom that power always corrupts the possessor. Now we have killed a million and a half helpless peasants in Vietnam, just as impersonally as Stalin exterminated the kulaks, for reasons of state interest, erroneous reasons so expendable that the government never mentions them now and won't defend them. Vietnam should remind all conservatives that whenever you put your faith in big government for any reason, sooner or later you wind up as an apologist for mass murder.

If Vietnam was the major issue causing Hess to plant both feet firmly on the libertarian side of the fence, the man most responsible for getting him across it was Murray Rothbard. Rothbard, along with Liggio and other libertarian purists, had maintained an independent presence on the Right through the early years of the 1960s. Rothbard enhanced his reputation as a leading Misesian economist with the publication of several books: a two-volume economic treatise called *Man, Economy and State; The Panic of 1819; and America's Great Depression.* He watched carefully when Leonard Liggio established ties with several organizations on the radical Left, which during this period were growing more active in their opposition to United States foreign policy. When the Bertrand Russell War Crimes Tribunal was founded in 1966, Liggio assumed a prominent role; his disillusionment with the evolving pattern of right-wing politics was leading him more and more into the company of New Left groups like SANE, SNCC, and SDS.

In 1965, Rothbard, Liggio, and a fellow named George Resch created Left and Right, Inc., in New York City, and together brought out a new journal which emphasized the common philosophical bonds uniting the anarchism and isolationism of the Old Right, and the instinctive pacifistic anarchism characterizing the New Left in the middle 1960s. Under the guidance of these Old Right libertarians, *Left and Right* was the first publication in the country to talk about a potential Left-Right political alliance, and it set the tone for the kind of articles on the subject that started appearing five years later in national magazines, from *Playboy, Penthouse,* and *Esquire* to *The Nation* and *The New York Times Magazine.*

But in 1965, the prospect of reaching a mass audience with these ideas seemed as remote as the most impossible of dreams.

The first important breakthrough for the concept of a Left-Right libertarian alliance came in June 1968, when Rothbard published his article "Confessions" in *Ramparts,* the most widely read magazine on the radical Left. In it he set forth the Old Right position with its twin themes of domestic decentralization and nonintervention in foreign affairs, while pointing out the similarities between his own free-market libertarianism and the cry for neighborhood government and neo-isolationism that had already surfaced on the New Left. It was this article that caught the attention of Karl Hess, who by this time had begun to drift further away from the *National Review* Republicanism now dominating right-wing politics. Hess flirted briefly with Objectivism, and then he serendipitously discovered the *Ramparts* article. In short, Rothbard reached him at the precise moment when he was most open to conversion.

Hess immediately called Rothbard in Manhattan, and for weeks they engaged in two-hour phone conversations, sometimes as frequently as two and three times a week, burning up the wires between Washington, D.C., and New York City with a veritable torrent of flaming anarchist rhetoric. When the time came for Bell Telephone to send its monthly greetings it became obvious that it would be far less expensive to carry on the dialogue vis-à-vis. Hess journeyed northward to stay with the Rothbards on those quiet summer weekends when most middle-class New Yorkers are out of town, deepening their suntans on Fire Island and at the Hamptons. By the end of the summer the radicalization of Karl Hess had been accomplished. He was now a free-market radical, an individualist-anarchist in the tradition of Lysander Spooner, Max Stirner, Benjamin Tucker, Stephen P. Andrews, James J. Martin, Murray Rothbard, and Leonard Liggio.

An interesting footnote to this summer episode in the sweep of American history is that while Hess was getting his head pumped full of anarchism by Rothbard and Liggio, he was also helping Barry Goldwater get reelected to the Senate. When the campaign moved into high gear in September and October, Hess did most of the speech writing for Goldwater, who was totally unaware of his principal aide's recent conversion. It is amusing to thumb through some of the speeches the Senator made that fall and pick out the little seeds of radicalism Hess managed to plant. Consider, if you will, the spectacle of Barry Goldwater informing a conservative student body in the Southwest that he found some overlapping areas between his own philosophy and certain "anarchistic elements in S.D.S." When you note the number of times Goldwater referred to himself as "anarchistic" rather than the more acceptable "libertarian," you begin to understand one of the fundamental weaknesses in the concept of representative democracy: most voters elect a candidate to a position of high power and authority for reasons other than the political issues involved, or the candidate's actual ideas. If liberal Republicans John Lindsay or Nelson Rockefeller had gone to Arizona and suggested that maybe some of the anarchists in S.D.S. weren't so bad after all, you would most likely have been able to tabulate their votes with a counting glass. Put the same words in the mouth of Barry Goldwater, conservative Republican, and you're riding the homestretch with a winner. The consequences are not so far-reaching when local citizens vote their politicians into a position where they can control and regulate only the lives of their constituents, but it is a different story when a president or Congressman decides on questions literally involving the life and death of the entire country.

Hess's revitalized libertarianism of a decade before, its conservative embellishments neatly trimmed off by Rothbard and Liggio, grew within him throughout the fall of 1968. In December he called a press conference in his office in Washington and announced that he was no longer a conservative, no longer a Goldwater Republican. He was an anarchist, and from this point on he would join hands with anarchist forces on the New Left with whom, he now discovered, he had more in common than he did with his former colleagues.

This was the story behind the headline that interrupted and then stopped my apartment hunting in peaceful Mamaroneck. At the time I knew only that the decision had already been made for me: I would have to annihilate the bastard in print.

8

Look What Happened to Kerensky

My anti-Hess article was published in *The New Guard,* the official YAF magazine, in April 1969. On the facing page, staring out defiantly at the reader, was Karl Hess's rebuttal, cleverly entitled "In Defense of Hess."

It was now apparent to me that this Hess fellow was the type of person who couldn't tolerate someone else getting in the last word under any circumstances. It wasn't enough that he had sent his message into Mamaroneck that day in December and upset me so much I was forced to head back immediately to Manhattan. Or that he had followed this assault with an article in the March 1969 issue of *Playboy,* which I discovered on my way to its centerfold and O'Neal's one afternoon. No, his lust for power was so complete he had even followed me into the pages of *The New Guard.* Where, just a short time before, Galambosianism had threatened to relieve me of my last vestige of sanity, now a form of left-wing Goldwaterism loomed on my horizon as the most formidable challenge I had yet faced. As much as I longed for a life of tranquility, I had no choice but to gird myself for all-out combat.

When Hess and I were asked by YAF to debate at a convention in New York City's Hotel Commodore, I looked forward to this opportunity to demolish him at close range. A week or so later, I received a copy of the flyer advertising the convention and discovered that what I had been led to believe would be a face-to-face clash with Anarchist Hess had now been scheduled as a four-way panel discussion among, besides Hess and myself, Frank S. Meyer of *National Review* and Professor Henry Paolucci, lately of St. John's University. Paolucci I remembered as a fervent nationalist given to wearing socks that never matched when he taught at Iona College ten years before. The YAFers, exercising their overkill mentality, had apparently intended to stage a three-to-one gang up on Hess. Having originally lined up Paolucci and Meyer to work him over, they'd decided as an afterthought to include me for additional security.

By the time I entered the convention hall for our so-called "debate," I had decided not to play the game. I was introduced to Frank Meyer and Henry Paolucci before we went up to the rostrum. Meyer seemed preoccupied, but Paolucci immediately launched into a twenty-minute monologue on his idea of the real hero of the Russian revolution, Kerensky, whose demise only proved that the Right could never establish political alliances with the Left no matter how much their immediate goals coincided. When I asked him why we shouldn't support the New Left on specific issues such as the anti-draft movement—since so many conservatives, theoretically at least, were also opposed to conscription—he rose on the balls of his feet and fairly screamed over the din in the hall:

"Look at Kerensky! Look what happened to Kerensky!" Paolucci called himself a "libertarian nationalist," a grotesque contradiction in terms if there ever was one. He had a mystical reverence for the American nation-state, attributing to it those divine characteristics which most people reserve for their religious institutions. How he ever reconciled an ethic of individual freedom with the concept of an elitist collective order intrinsically superior to all other collectives on earth was a mystery to me then, and remained so afterward even when I heard him go into detail on the subject on several occasions. He managed to blend St. Augustine, Plato, Thomas Aquinas, Adam Smith, and Mussolini in an eclectic grab-bag philosophy that defied reason—or, at least, *my* reason.

With it all, he had his own private following among young conservative students, upper-echelon YAFers who referred to themselves as "libertarian nationalists" with a look in their eyes that was an open challenge to argue with them on the topic. These were the uncompromising defenders of autocratic regimes at the time in Formosa, Spain, Portugal, Greece, Rhodesia, and South Africa. They had the ability to look you full in the face and tell you there was more freedom in those countries than you could find anywhere in the world except, of course, in the United States.

At the time the panel discussion was to begin, Karl Hess had not yet arrived. The three of us took our places on the podium, and moderator Arnold Steinberg, a libertarian-conservative who was then editor of *The New Guard,* decided to start without him. As Steinberg got set to introduce us to the audience, Hess, bearded and casually dressed, entered the rear of the hall with a long-haired hippie entourage—Rothbard's group of free-market anarchists, as I later learned. Rothbard moved down the aisle through their midst in his undeviating attire of rumpled suit, key chain draped from the belt, white shirt, and bow tie reminiscent of the bobby-sox era.

Here was an irony contained within an irony. Into the vortex of this vast sea of conservative, middle-class youth swirled a small school of bearded radicals whose love beads swung from their necks; at their center stood their leader, more middle class in appearance than the most conservative YAFer in the house. Rothbard's reputation as a Mencke-nesque, bumptious, curmudgeonly theoretician had preceded him, but the image was immediately dispelled by his conservative appearance.

Hess, on the other hand, had moved sartorially as well as politically to the Left. He looked a nicely balanced mixture of General U.S. Grant and Fidel Castro as he strode to the podium, his knotty black curls bunched behind his ears, a frizzy coal-black beard covering most of his face. He seemed outgoing and friendly as he shook hands all around. The basic amenities finally over, Steinberg called for order and got the meeting under way.

Frank Meyer was the first to speak. He gave a fifteen-minute presentation, criticizing Hess indirectly by condemning "unprincipled alliances" with the Left. It was his position that conservatives could never join forces with the New Left—even on such issues as the military draft, which he too opposed in principle—because the motivation of the radical Left was actually to weaken the U.S. military presence in Vietnam. Meyer would have preferred to see the Communists wiped out by

a "voluntary" and "professional" strike force, but since it was manda-
tory that we win in Vietnam, conservatives must take care to separate
their anti-draft sentiments from their position on the war. In other
words, the draft should be repealed eventually, but not until the war was
won. When he finished his address he announced that he was already
late for an appointment and would have to skip the question period.
This caused considerable consternation in the audience; the odds
against Hess were suddenly reduced to two to one.

Hess then rose to deliver a low-key, conversational synopsis of the
position he had set forth in his *Playboy* article. It was inconsistent to
preach individual liberty and local government out of one side of the
mouth while calling for a vast, centralized military complex through the
other. Anybody really against conscription should give more than just
lip service to the anti-draft movement. The New Left was doing something about it while the Right just talked. Motivation wasn't important;
the top priority was the attainment of a common goal regardless of
one's reasons for desiring it. Again, conservatives talked a lot about
decentralized power and neighborhood schools when the subject of bus-
ing came up, but they had reversed their positions rather dramatically
when the black communities of Harlem and Bedford-Stuyvesant
wanted the same policies for their own schools. In summation, Hess
was urging the Right to become more radical and more consistent in its
opposition to centralized power in Washington, and to reevaluate its
stand on military victory in Vietnam, which he considered immoral as
well as strategically disastrous.

The immediate reaction to all this was a smoldering quietude ema-
nating from the great majority of the audience. Rothbard and his anarchists did their best to take up the slack with applause and cheering, but
it was evident that their demonstration was strictly localized. From the
rostrum you could hear a few cries of "Get the Commies out of here!",
"They don't belong here!", and "Send them back to S.D.S.!"

Now it was my turn, and I rose to speak with a clear idea of exactly
what had to be done. Obviously, both factions were drifting farther and
farther apart into extremist positions. It was up to me to present a well-

balanced alternative, blending the best elements of conservatism and anarchism, enticing everyone back to the sane and solid center. Each extreme had become blinded by the light of its own dogma. If they could all just remain open to the voice of reason and sanity, there was every hope that moderation might win the day, and a final breach be avoided.

I spent the first few minutes talking about Hess's "wishful thinking" in expecting the Communist military threat to disappear simply because we didn't want to fight any longer. I said that anarchism could work only in a world in which everyone agreed not to try to conquer his neighbor by force. The crowd was warming to this theme and beginning to respond audibly when I suddenly shifted to the domestic area.

The federal monolith was now bureaucratized and rigidified to a degree that would have been unrecognizable twenty-five years before. Conservatives had been adamantly opposed to the expansion of the state-corporate system for more than forty years and it was extremely inconsistent, now that they were in the White House, to become such zealous defenders of the *status quo*. Conservatism was meaningless if it merely involved taking over a structure passed on by state socialists and somehow "trying to make it operate more efficiently." Working exclusively within the system was not sufficient to bring about the kind of changes that were called for. I was against violence, but nonviolent resistance to coercive state and state-supported institutions was justifiable on the grounds of simple self-defense.

I then catalogued a program of civil disobedience, advocating among other things active resistance to the military draft; refusal to pay taxes; boycott of the public school system in those areas where it was centrally controlled and the creation of storefront schools in the neighborhoods as an alternative; establishment of community police patrols to replace such municipal armies as "New York's Finest"; local control of streets and thoroughfares to regulate the flow of traffic and, consequently, automobile pollution; and neighborhood seizure of property that had been abandoned or condemned by the city for so-called "urban renewal."

The response was not at all what I expected. I had hoped that my dual message of qualified anti-communism and radical opposition to the impersonal corporate state would strike a responsive chord in just about everyone present. Not so. Hess, Rothbard and company, anticipating a crowd-pleasing denunciation of their position, were elated; YAFers responded either with inaudible hand clapping or outraged hostility. One young fellow, who stood on his chair to denounce me for failing to recognize the "Red menace" sweeping the nation's campuses (I couldn't be completely sure whether he was referring to Maoists or American Indians), was treated to a two-minute standing ovation.

More perplexed than anyone else was Henry Paolucci, bobbing up and down in his chair, turning red, obviously itching for the chance to get in his licks. Apparently, with the unexpected disappearance of Frank Meyer, the three-to-one gang up on Hess had suddenly become, in Paolucci's mind, a two-to-one assault on the "libertarian nationalist" from St. John's.

He fairly pounced on the microphone and, fists waving, sailed immediately into an anti-anarchist tirade. Arnold Steinberg attempted to readjust the microphone downward a foot or so to accommodate the speaker's height; Paolucci, trembling with evangelical fire, refused to relinquish his grip and continued his address. He had grown up in an anarchist household, he maintained, and had experienced firsthand the tyrannical fist of an anarchistic *patria potestas*. He had heard enough talk of "this brand of gradualistic anarchism" in his life to know that it was nothing more than a subtle form of subversion, a device to lower the guard of the nation while treasonous forces corroded it from within. All the beauty, wisdom, and truth of Western civilization had reached their apotheosis with the American nation-state, and it was the foremost duty of every loyal American to defend this heritage against the onslaught of barbarian and heretical alien forces. Individual freedom could be permitted only within the framework of an orderly preservation of the American religious and cultural tradition. (Buckleyites in the audience nodded their heads, perhaps recalling their leader's denunciation of those who rejected contemporary American values as "excommunicants" who automatically forfeit their right to freedom.)

Somewhere along the line Paolucci also condemned the "tyranny of voluntary association," which was somewhat unnerving since conservatives had always invoked the *freedom* of voluntary association as their reason for opposing neighborhood integration. He finished to a thundering ovation: the YAFers, to a man, rose and demonstrated their appreciation for a solid three minutes. This was the stuff they had come to hear. They wanted no wrist-slapping critiques of Hess's "naïveté": no wishy-washy speculations on the "impracticality" of anarchism. They wanted the body of the traitor strung on high for everyone to see, and Paolucci was stringing it.

During the question period Mario Rizzo, a Fordham economics major and a member of the Rothbard contingent, rose to his feet. Having acknowledged his willingness to accept questions from the "rabble in the corner," Paolucci listened patiently: Why, Rizzo wanted to know, shouldn't those who did not subscribe to traditional American values be allowed their freedom as long as they remained non-aggressive in their behavior toward those who did?

Now, Mario Rizzo at this time was a smallish, rather swarthy young man with dark, coarse hair and a long hooked nose. Paolucci sized him up for at least ten seconds and then finally replied:

"You! You of all people should be the last to criticize the concept of freedom within a stable religious order. Your people have been nomads for centuries, rejected by every society you ever lived under. Now your people have found a home, a home offering an opportunity to live in peace and freedom for the first time in history, and all this country asks in return is that you respect its traditions and express a little gratitude once in a while...."

Mario Rizzo stood there, stunned by this unexpected revelation of his family's nomadic past. For twenty years he had been living under the delusion that his grandparents had come straight over from Naples without being rejected by anyone along the way. It took a few minutes longer for him to take in the situation: there he was, a self-respecting

Italian-American from Queens, unaccountably being Jew-baited by a pro.

I left the convention later in the afternoon secure in the knowledge that Henry Paolucci was the most evil man who walked the earth. Looking back, I doubt it. My only regret, when I remember that day in April 1969, is my oversight in failing to check Paolucci's ankles. To this day I still don't know whether his socks were matching or not.

9

A Claque of Porcine Revolutionaries

My situation at this point had boiled down to this: after nearly a decade of contact with virtually every conceivable right-wing faction, from Objectivists to Birchers, I was now imbedded in the midst of all of them *at the same time.* Whereas before I could size up each faction individually and at close range before traveling on to the next, I was now caught in a maelstrom of ideological furies representing every conceivable point along the starboard political spectrum.

So far as the immediate future was concerned, I could retain my affiliation with the Right and attempt to libertarianize the conservative alliance from within; I could join forces with the right-wing anarchists and try to build a viable movement independent of all others; or I could drop out entirely and find some peace of mind away from any form of ideological or physiognomical coercion.

I eliminated this final alternative at the outset. In an age of electronic surveillance and telepathic authoritarianism, the earth had been reduced, in effect, to a global village. There was no patch of green, no valley, no glade, no grove of trees, no Gulch—I was sure of it now—that lay beyond the reach of space-age imperialists. Choice number three was out of the question. So was choice number one: libertarianizing the conservative Right. Elementary principles of self-defense, notably a concern for the preservation of my mental stability, required that I be removed as far as possible from square-jawed religionists, Ivy League Hegelians, Catch-22 Galambosians, or Paoluccian nationalists.

The debilitating influence of ideological osmosis was far greater than I had ever realized.

That left choice two: embracing free-market anarchism and turning it into a realistic alternative to traditional liberalism and conservatism—as well as rampaging adventurism on the Left. That meant making libertarianism the voice of the sane and moderate center.

The responsible anarchist center, so to speak.

This course would also afford me the opportunity to keep a close eye on Karl Hess, who was apparently determined to follow me through the news media no matter where I went. By aligning myself with him and his associates I could at least protect myself against the unnerving prospect of opening up a newspaper or magazine in my most private moments and finding his hirsute visage. It would also give me a chance to rein in his compulsive gallop toward extremist positions—indeed, to lend a moderating influence to the whole anarchist movement while it was still in the process of development.

Several days after the convention at the Hotel Commodore I received a phone call from Walter Block, a disciple of Rothbard. He invited me to join him and a few friends at his apartment on the upper West Side near Columbia University. My first reaction on walking into this den of anarchists was to decide immediately that there was no hope for a *detente*. Somehow, the spectacle of a half-dozen or so pudgy radicals sitting around on a Saturday afternoon, lapping up incredible mounds of ice cream and cake and talking anarchism and resistance, was not what I had anticipated. A barroom full of inebriated wire lathers taking time out from a football game on television could have wiped them out in a single encounter. This overweight crew would be lucky to find itself swabbing the deck on any ship of Ragnar's.

However demoralized by the sight of them, I had to admit as I listened that in theory, at least, this was my kind of stuff. Revolutionary capitalism. Uncompromising individualism. Free-market radicalism. Jeffersonian democracy revved up with a supercharge. State authority broken down to the minus n^{th} power—decentralization all the way to the level of the individual. The prospects were intoxicating. Their program was nothing less than the culmination, the absolute and final *logical reduction* of everything I had ever believed in.

I couldn't turn away at this point: Hess would never leave me alone anyway. These puffy, myopic revolutionaries had possibilities. With the proper kind of work—and exercise—they just might be transformed into a battalion of Ragnar Danneskjolds. They were raw clay ready to be molded and hammered into shape. The potential was fantastic—we could build a movement that would rock the nation.

How in Christ's name could anybody turn his back on an opportunity like that? Once I had decided to jump into the anarchist arena on the Right, the next step was to assess the prospects of creating a viable Left-Right political coalition. Under the broad umbrella of anarchism, the libertarian fringes of both sides ought theoretically to be able to join hands in an anti-state radical movement. Both the radical Left and the libertarian Right were opposed to the war; both favored the massive reduction of America's international military presence and a return to military neo-isolationism; both endorsed the concept of a volunteer army to replace the military draft; both opposed our state-corporate economic system and central planning by a ruling elite in Washington; both favored political decentralization and the control of essential institutions at the local level.

Where the New Left and libertarian Right differed primarily was in basic economic theory. The Left spoke the language of socialism and communism with a small "c." They talked a great deal about the "people" and a system of "humanitarian socialism" in which "people" would control the facilities of housing, education, police and fire protection, sanitation, health, and welfare in their own neighborhoods. The right-wing libertarians were committed to the rhetoric of *laissez faire* capitalism, free trade and open markets. Their decentralist theories went further than the New Left's; they spoke of "Freedom to the Individual" rather than "Power to the People." But the greatest obstacle by far to the realization of a Left-and-Right libertarian alliance was the issue of private property. Right-wing anarchists were ardent private propertarians, maintaining that there could be no real freedom for anyone outside a system of self-ownership and concomitant protection of the right to own land and other property; the radical Left, for the most part, still clung to the Marxist and anarcho-communist dictum that "property is theft."

Still, as serious as these divisions were, in actual practice there might not be so much difference between a system of decentralized neighborhood "socialism" and individualistic free market "capitalism." Both concepts reflected ideal positions, and the best either side could hope to achieve in the near future was a modified version of both. At the worst, if free-market radicals and neighborhood socialists did wind up locking horns over thorny issues like private versus community ownership, their battles would at least take place on a smaller scale than Washington, D.C.—or City Hall, for that matter. Instead of, say, disputes involving eight million New Yorkers representing six dozen private-interest groups, there would be thirty or forty thousand, and five or ten private interest groups. Weren't small problems theoretically more manageable than large problems? There would be less bureaucracy involved, less chance for power brokers and grafting administrators to hide inside a jungle of red tape. Fraud, graft, and corruption would be more visible to everyone, and the neighborhood Hitlers would be easier to lay hands on than the ones in City Hall or in the White House.

It was not utopian and not a panacea. It was far from perfect, but perfection was impossible when you were dealing with imperfect people. So long as some people insisted on attacking or cheating their neighbors, there would be a certain amount of violence and fraud in the world. Until the millennium arrived and everyone was a practicing libertarian, there would be people all over the place engaging in non-libertarian activities. All right, you'd have to have police protection and courts of arbitration. But the idea was to break down the power and break down the problems into smaller units, to diminish the measure of political power while increasing the measure of freedom and self-ownership for every individual. To keep the ideal in mind, so we'd at least be heading toward it instead of away from it, hoping to get as close with each step as was possible within the limits of human imperfection.

Even the most poverty-stricken neighborhood would be better off in a decentralized system. Take, for example, Harlem and Bedford-Stuyvesant in New York City—certainly among the poorest in the nation. We know that betting on numbers there is a billion-dollar-a-year enterprise. *A billion dollars a year in spare change spent on a daily numbers lottery in poor black neighborhoods!* At present, however, this activity is declared illegal by City Hall, which has in effect granted a monopoly on numbers running to racketeers who pay the police to look the other way. The billion-a-year is siphoned out of the community into the already affluent neighborhoods of Bay Ridge in Brooklyn or Country Club in the Bronx.

Why shouldn't this money be permitted to remain where it is needed? Why shouldn't all gambling be legal (it is a non-aggressive activity engaged in by consenting adults), and the numbers lottery be run by local groups with an interest in improving their own neighborhoods? It is not true that poor areas do not have the wherewithal to solve their own problems. They are prevented from doing so by centralized authority, which stifles local initiative and acts to grant monopolistic power to well-financed lobby groups such as those of oil, steel, the defense industry, and the Mafia. Anybody should be able to see that all of them, working hand in hand with the politicians, are what "organized crime" is all about.

My first exposure to any groups on the radical Left took place during a meeting at Columbia University. Several of us had gone there to hear Leonard Liggio and Ralph Schoenman, former assistant to Bertrand Russell, lead a discussion on the American presence in Vietnam. Left-wing groups of every description were swarming in, lining the walls after the last seats were occupied. They tended to cluster according to their affiliation, as did the groups on the Right. There were Wobblies with "IWW" buttons on their blue-denimed chests; YAWF-ers (Youth Against War and Fascism), many displaying "Al Fatah" buttons on their shirts or fatigue caps; Maoists; left-wing and right-wing Trotskyites; right-wing Marxists who favored the Soviet invasion of Czechoslovakia; and anarcho-Bakuninites who supported the Czechoslovakian rebels. The factionalization on the Left was, if anything, even more pronounced than that on the Right, and I remember thinking that Nixon need not lose any sleep if this was his opposition.

"These people are crazy," someone remarked to Walter Block when we had taken our seats.

"Of course they are," he said. "But right-wing crazies are crazier than left-wing crazies."

Maybe so, but I wasn't really prepared for this. My first inclination was to turn around and head back to more familiar terrain. After all these years of experience, I had at least grown accustomed to the vagaries of the right-wing mentality. This ideological jungle on the Left seemed impenetrable.

Ralph Schoenman began his talk, then went on to talk and talk some more until some members of the audience were calling for him to shut up. He went right on, pouring out an unpunctuated verbal cascade that seemingly had no ending. After a full hour of this ranting monologue, voices were being lifted from every section of the hall. One man in his middle fifties—dressed in steel-tipped boots and generally resembling the archetypical proletarian hero on a 1920s Communist Party wall poster—rose to his feet and raised his fist.

"I'm a worker!" he identified himself. "What are you? You're nothing but a goddamn bourgeois armchair socialist who never worked a day in his life!"

This sparked heated outcries from other factions in the room. A woman, fortyish and rather shopworn, as though too many years of inner turmoil had taken their toll on her once pretty features, was the next to speak. She identified herself as a member of the Communist Party and then proceeded to excoriate Schoenman for suggesting that the Soviet Union was guilty of anti-Semitism. According to her, the Communist State in Russia was a paradise of racial and ethnic tranquility. As proof she cited the fact that some obscure Jewish journal was still being published, unmolested, after more than forty-five years.

Next it was the Wobblies' turn. A young man in his thirties, built like a dockworker, his shirt sleeves rolled up to expose his forearms bulging with huge knots of muscle, got up and called everybody in the hall "a bunch of fucking fascists!" Apparently all of us except the Wobbly and his group had deviated years ago from the true Marxist-Leninist line. We were all "revisionists," if not "running dogs of fascist imperialism." Just when it appeared that he was about to throw himself on the nearest fascist, he unaccountably sat down and began to sob quietly. The moderator took this opportunity to praise the assemblage for their "democratic spirit" in allowing everyone to have his say. It was only at a socialist conference that one could find such a spontaneous outpouring of sentiment, and unsquelched sentiment at that.

"Socialism means peace or it means nothing at all!" was the way he wrapped it up.

By this time the crowd was too wound up to listen much longer and Liggio was forced to limit his remarks to a synopsis of what he wanted to get across. The infighting among the various groups continued on a more subdued level, but it threatened to break out of control at any moment. Liggio concluded quickly and the meeting was adjourned.

Reeling out of the hall later in the night, I found my sensibilities under attack once again. You don't leave the realm of right-wing eccentricity just to get yourself entangled in the corresponding area on the Left. The path to truth and sanity was obviously strewn with obstacles at every turn. You had to step gingerly and watch your footing, or you'd lose your balance at any moment.

The moderate anarchist center, now discovered, could be obliterated from both sides.

10

Deviationism Rides Again

It was during this period that the Radical Libertarian Alliance was formed.

In addition to Walter Block and Karl Hess, Murray Rothbard had gathered around himself quite a group of followers in the New York area. Most of them, college students and recent graduates, had been converted to libertarianism through the writings of Rothbard, Rand, Mises, and other libertarian authors. The concept of a Left-Right libertarian coalition had been Rothbard's dream from the early years of the 1960s, and he had been trying to involve right-wing anarchists in the anti-war movement as early as 1965.

The Rothbard circle had remained small and manageable throughout the 1960s, but the defection of Karl Hess and the ensuing publicity he received, particularly on the Right, attracted a good many more right wingers to the anarchist position.

By the late spring of 1969 Rothbard's apartment could no longer accommodate his followers, and so monthly dinners were arranged in certain West Side restaurants. To give these gatherings a semblance of structural formality, an organization was proclaimed and given a name: the Radical Libertarian Alliance. Hess and Rothbard decided that a publication would accelerate the proselytizing of further converts from the conservative Right, and under their joint editorship the *Libertarian Forum* appeared shortly after as the official RLA publication.

The first dinner attracted nearly a hundred people from New York City, New Jersey, and Connecticut. The libertarian "movement" had moved out of a living room and into the public arena. The next logical step was to take the offensive. We had to blitz the opposition before it could recover from the "debate" at the Commodore. YAF, as the most visible and symbolic conservative group on campus, was our most likely target. We would perform a surgical operation on the YAF membership and slice off the left wing—the twenty-two to thirty-one per cent ranging from moderate to radical libertarian. Almost everybody to the right of Meyer, and certainly to the right of William F. Buckley, could be dismissed at the outset. We could expect our highest scores among the Randians, Misesians, and the more libertarian of the Frank Meyer fusionists.

This was my kind of stuff. This was ballsy. The time for screwing around was finally over. It was time to get out in the ring and slug it out. No rules, no holds or punches barred. Whammo! Sock! Double him over, get him on his knees and kick him in the eardrum.

Nonviolently, of course.

Blitz, then rip away. We had our own paper organization now: The Radical Libertarian Alliance. We had a home for disaffiliated YAFers to turn to. They would need a way station when the rip-off was over, a place to get their wounds licked and their heads straightened out. A bed to recuperate in before going out on their own to establish local RLA chapters. All we needed was some cadre and we were off. A national political movement. Rip off, succor, build. That was the combination. A nation-wide Alliance, Ragnar-ready to knock the military-industrial-political complex on its ass. It was beautiful. It was even possible. If only it didn't bomb in New Haven. The *new* New Right. Climbing in bed with the *old* New Left, the disorganized and disillusioned New Left that was falling down on its back a little bit more every day. Didn't disheartened New Leftists need a home just as much as split-off Rightist libertarians?

We set our sights on the YAF national convention in St.Louis, Labor Day weekend, 1969. Buckley would be there. So would Al Capp. And Barry Goldwater, Jr., sporting a jaw like an upside-down anvil, a jaw that put even his father's to shame. And Buzz Lukens and Fulton Lewis and a whole array of right-wing luminaries—politicians, journalists, columnists, intellectuals, an entire gallery of sitting ducks lined up on the same podium. Hess was flying in from Washington, and I was going with some RLA people from New York.

It was shaping up to be one hell of a time.

And so it came to pass as planned.

Of a total of 1,200 delegates attending the convention, a full 350 were separated before the third day was over. The key wedge driven between the libertarian and conservative forces was, of course, the military draft. The conservatives had sponsored a resolution calling for a volunteer army to replace conscription. In opposition to this, the libertarians submitted a list of minority planks demanding immediate withdrawal from Southeast Asia, a repudiation of domestic oppression as well as the communist variety, legalization of marijuana, and *active resistance* to the draft.

The conservatives, predictably, were opposed to any measures that side-stepped legal channels. As libertarian planks were defeated one by one, the demoralization in libertarian circles became more and more evident. When it was obvious that the radical anti-draft resolution would also be hammered to extinction, the final polarization was achieved, and in the most dramatic manner possible: a draft-card burning incident.

The specter of a young rebel standing in the midst of a right-wing political rally, a burning card lifted over his head, was a truly breathtaking sight to behold. It was equivalent to reading an excerpt from *Radical Chic* at a Black Panther fundraising dinner; to singing the praises of a guaranteed annual income in Ayn Rand's living room; to calling the pope a Mafioso at a meeting of the Italian-American Civil Rights League.

At that moment the impending libertarian-conservative schism on the Right escalated from ideology to invective and, finally, to physical confrontation. After a few confused moments of punching and shoving and general commotion, the division was complete. There could be no turning back.

The libertarian conservatives had been radicalized, and in something like ten minutes.

They stalked out. They held their own caucus. They agreed to form a separate organization—the Society for Individual Liberty, as it was later named—independent of YAF and all other conservative groups. This new organization's founders, Don Ernsberger and Jarret Wollstein, further agreed to join RLA and other libertarian clubs in creating campus chapters for the express purpose of splitting away as many libertarians as they possibly could from the conservative right-wing alliance.

They said, "thanks but no thanks" to William F. Buckley and his conservatives; thanks for defending us from "heresy" all these years, but now we'd like to find some way of defending ourselves from our defenders, if it's all the same to you, old boy.

At first it appeared that we had taken on more than we could possibly assimilate. This libertarian herd suddenly inherited by RLA comprised a multifaceted assortment worthy of inclusion in anybody's gallery of American oddities. Most were Objectivists, whose leaders included a Randian super-hero with a penchant for showing up all decked out in a black stretch suit with an enormous gold dollar sign embroidered on his chest and a gold velvet belt cinching his waist. Someone remarked that all he needed to complete the image of a freaked-out capitalistic superman was a gold cape swirling from his shoulders—and he was immediately informed that the cape did indeed exist, but was kept for at-home wear lest its owner call undue attention to himself in public.

Then there were the Randian "heads," most of whom belonged to free-market anarchist organizations located in Southern California. I wondered if there wasn't something in the water of this region that transforms everyone who migrated there into a bizarre distortion of his former self. Here were devotees of Ayn Rand, disciplined to the restraints of Objectivist logic when in their native habitats, who emigrated to L.A. and points south and immediately began to blow their brains on acid, and turn in their business suits for beads, jeans, and shoulder-length hair while they talked about the "groovy," "outasight," "wild and funky" marketplace. Capitalists to the sixteenth power—joining communes, trading one another for cigarettes, pencils, candy, food, and pot in their own self-contained economic system—they were outwardly indistinguishable from the Jerry Rubin/Abbie Hoffman communal anarchists of the New Left.

There were the right-wing dropouts, retreatists who wanted to secede from the United States altogether and build an ocean platform, a seaborne Galt's Gulch beyond government jurisdiction where they could establish their own free and uncontrolled trading community. Others, who called themselves frogs, wanted to burrow under the earth and create an underground city—"Sink City," no less—undetected and undeterred by the restrictions of authoritarian political regimes. Some of these envisioned having their own atomic bomb for defense purposes, along with a private space program so they could homestead portions of the moon in the name of liberty "before the fascists gobbled it up."

There was an Objectivist Homophile League for young males who were more turned on by John Galt than they were by Dagny Taggart, or for *femmes* who dug Dagny more than John. There were radical entrepreneurs who wanted to remake the United States into a gigantic shopping center owned and managed by a single real estate concern, thereby eliminating the functions of the United States government; libertarian royalists who thought wealthy individualists should buy up large tracts of land and turn them into fiefdoms under a libertarian code of justice; anarcho-Minute Men who wanted to take to the mountains ala Che Guevara and organize a revolutionary guerrilla movement for intransigent free enterprisers; radical reformists who favored moving all the libertarians in the country into a single state, Nevada or Wyoming perhaps, and taking over the political structure through the elective process.

Some were disciples of Robert LeFevre, a self-styled educator in California who refers to himself as an Autarchist. He coined this title, translating literally as "self-rule," to distinguish himself from the anarchist tradition dominated by collectivists such as Proudhon, Bakunin, Kropotkin, and the anarcho-syndicalists of the 19th and early 20th centuries. LeFevre was a raw individualist whose enterprises include a private school called Rampart College and a quarterly magazine through which he disseminated his credo of uncompromising capitalism. LeFevre is equally contemptuous of liberals, conservatives, socialists, communists, and collectivists of the anarchist school with whom, unlike other free-market anarchists, he sees no hope for an eventual Left-Right coalition.

Autarchists are also called radical private propertarians, since they maintain that an individual is entitled to all the land he can see from any given point. This was bad enough when people were limited to mountain peaks with a visibility of thirty or forty miles, but in an age of space travel it is conceivable that a particularly self-centered individualist might orbit the earth and claim the whole ball as his personal domain. Presumably, according to the Autarchist code of ethics, this space-age landlord (earthlord?) would then have the right to charge his six billion tenants rent under the threat of being shuttled off into unclaimed space. One can envision a society in which the poorest tenants are confined to the cheaper plots in Antarctica, while land in the temperate regions is rented at a premium to the wealthy.

Still others were advocates of the philosophy of Max Stirner, a nineteenth-century individualist. Stirner, who has been described as Ayn Rand in a bad mood, promoted a kind of rampaging individualism that maked Nietzsche look like a Germanic version of Wesley Mouch. He recognized no moral code whatsoever, and in fact considered any talk of moral restraints on human behavior to be an intolerable abridgment of individual liberty.

And so the list went, on and on, boggling the most stable and well-fortified of imaginations. As likable and human as many of these students might seem when compared with the specter of an army of Objectivist slaves marching in orderly precision to the beat of Randian drums, they were hardly the stuff to offer as a viable political alternative to the most dictatorial of political regimes.

"What are we going to do with these screwballs, these morons, these cretins?" Professor Murray Rothbard was practically vibrating in his armchair, his bow tie on an angle.

"To know them is to hate them," offered Walter Block.

"They're deviationist creeps!" said Rothbard.

Oh no! Not again. I heard enough of that crap when I was an Objectivist. I didn't deviate from conservatism to start denouncing other people for deviationism!

"Not deviationism," I said lamely.

"The right-wing deviationists are walking around with their goddamn dollar signs plastered all over the goddamn place, and the left-wing deviationists are destroying what's left of their brains with acid and pot."

Let them. Let them do anything they want to as long as they don't hurt anybody else. Let's not start the bullshit all over again. There's room for everybody who's non-aggressive, who's nonviolent: the weak, the insane, the lame, the strong; those with square jaws and receding jaws, those with no jaws at all—even those with two jaws; those with dollar signs on their foreheads and gold-plated pricks; and those who blow their minds on acid six times a day.

"We're too small to start worrying about deviationists," said Block.

"We aim for quality, not quantity." Rothbard's mind was made up. "We can't accept all the shit that walks in off the streets."

There it was, but there *we* were. Now that we had fractured the right-wing alliance there was room for everybody in the responsible anarchist center. We were in the process of building a home, a resting place, an organization big enough to squeeze in everybody in the whole goddamn world if only they agreed not to hurt each other.

The sane and moderate anarchist center was already under attack, it seemed, more from within than from either the Left or the Right.

PART III
The Coalition

11

Greed is What Makes the World Go Around

Columbus Day Weekend, 1969: a libertarian convention, the first of its kind, was sponsored by the Radical Libertarian Alliance. Now that we had all these homeless right-wing radicals on our hands, we had to give them a place to rest their heads. If we waited too long a sense of alienation might set in and drive them back to the motherly arms of Bill Buckley or the fatherly caress of Ayn Rand.

We couldn't waste a moment. We had to move while everyone was still in a state of shock, still trying to figure out exactly what had happened. The RLA convention at the Hotel Diplomat in New York City, coming barely a month after the YAF affair in St. Louis, would serve as a rallying point for our homeless legions. There we could begin the process of molding them into good libertarian radicals, unyielding free-market rebels. A battalion of Ragnars charging en masse against the state. A hundred thousand revolutionary individualists tearing away at the American eagle feather by feather, claw by claw. Christ Almighty! It was so beautiful I couldn't stand to think about it.

"We'll get the right-wing and left-wing deviationists in the same room and chop off the fringes. We'll drive them miles apart."

"Not *apart*, Murray! *Together*, for Christ's sake. We'll weld the fringes into a solid anarchist center. A moderate and responsible libertarian middle. Leave the polarization to Nixon and Agnew."

A giant Left-Right libertarian coalition: left-wing anarchists and acid-dropping love children; middle-class tax resisters and blue-collar hardhats; right-wing free traders and intransigent individualists. We had to make them know each other and respect each other. Love, maybe even understanding, was too much to hope for. As long as they respected one another and agreed to leave everybody else alone. That was the ticket. Anything else was doomed to failure.

They hitchhiked in from Canada, they bummed rides from the West Coast, they drove up in Morgan Plus-Fours and new Chryslers from Florida and the Deep South.

We had business executives from the Midwest whose vest pockets bulged with cash and credit cards. We had twenty-year-old Objectivists from campuses all over the country. We had love children, real live love children with beads and sleeping bags and a serene gentility glazing their eyes. We had some giggling teenyboppers from Washington, D.C., and at least two matrons from Atlanta, Georgia. We had communal anarchists from Pennsylvania and Maryland who devoted all their time to arts and crafts, and hard-eyed profit mavens from Minnesota who got horny reading *The Wall Street Journal.* We had three hundred of the most unlikely and most diverse types imaginable who had traveled clear across the continent to learn how anarcho-communists and private enterprisers could live together harmoniously in a libertarian society.

That was the idea, anyway.

The first sign that things might not proceed exactly according to plan occurred about a half-hour before the opening address. People were filing in, buying their tickets at the door and fastening name cards on their shirts and jackets—an orderly procedure all around. People who hadn't seen one another in six months or a year were shaking hands and getting re-acquainted; others were being introduced to strangers. Everyone was smiling and talking pleasantly, long hair and jeans chatting with stiff collars and business suits. A truly happy opening.

Until, suddenly, a voice rang out: "Mary's destroying the coalition!"

Who? What? What the hell was going on? We hadn't even gotten *started* yet! Don't let anybody wreck the coalition before it even gets off the ground.

People were running out into the corridor. Necks were craning as everyone rose on his toes to get a better look at what was going on. For

Christ's sake, it was true. The coalition was in jeopardy. Mary, the sociopathic bitch, was beating the shit out of a love child!

Mary was all the worst aspects of women's liberation rolled up into 180 pounds of flaming terror. Mary wasn't big, she was gross. She had a pair of shoulders on her that made a linebacker look like a ninety-pound weakling. She had thick black hair that stuck out fourteen inches in all directions. If she stared too long at you with those fiery red eyes you could feel your nuts roasting between your thighs. She was Ayn Rand on a two-week binge. She was a super-heroine shot through with 1,600 volts of electricity.

To complete the image, she had dressed herself all in black.

Her wide shoulders and broad-beamed back were covered with a shiny, jet black shirt, and she wore an arm band with a clenched red fist along her biceps. She had on a pair of tight black jeans that revealed every contour of her muscular thighs, and her black calf-high boots were polished to a mirror shine, as were the dollar-sign brooches that adorned her collar tabs on both sides. I was willing to concede that she might even qualify as a "right-wing deviationist," although I had come to despise the term.

There was Mary, over in the corridor with this emaciated love child from Pennsylvania, slamming him back and forth against the wall and screaming at him. It seemed this dreamy-eyed communalist had been regaling some Objectivists with stories about his "extended family" in Pennsylvania, telling them how it was out there in the countryside, away from all the factories and automobile exhaust. Everybody loved everybody, and they all spent their days making sandals and weaving straw into backing for rocking chairs. They swam together in the raw in a pond behind the farmhouse, and wrote poetry in the evening before climbing onto a big mat on the floor and fondling one another. They had loved being off in the woods by themselves, away from technology and civilization and greedy profiteers.

Greedy profiteers! Mary's eyes lit up and hatred shot out of her eyes the way sparks do from a toy machine gun. This anti-life collectivist was attacking greed?

"Profiteers?"

This puny little altruist was badmouthing the *profit system?* Mary could contain herself no longer. It was at that point that she stepped forward and grabbed the anti-mind second-harder by his bony shoulders and started to slam him back and forth against the wall.

"Greed! Greed! Greed's what makes the world go 'round, you degenerate altruist son of a bitch, you filthy little whim-worshiper, you collectivist creep!" she screamed over and over while she punished his body again and again.

Somebody knock her down and sit on her, goddamnit!

Tape her mouth and throw her out in the street! Damn it all, she's destroying the coalition! Don't let her get away with it!

"Quality, not quantity. We have to skim off the cream and throw out all the rest."

"Consolidation, Murray. There's room for everyone in the moderate center"

Maybe the retreatists had the right idea after all. Drop out. Get away from it all. Build your platform out in the ocean and run your own system the way you like. Dig into the ground or stake out a cave and find happiness in Sink City. Away from all the nonsense, away from all the bullshit. Maybe lunar homesteading was the only real alternative after everything else was said and done.

Now an apparition in olive-green battle fatigues materialized in the corridor, surrounded by a personal entourage of sartorial imitators. What the hell's going on this time around? Necks craned once again as people swarmed to greet the olive-green apparition. Who the hell is it now?

"It's him. He's arrived," a voice called out.

"Who's arrived?"

"The Field Marshal of the Revolution."

The what? The bloody what? Has the whole world gone insane? The Field Marshal of—I looked, then choked before I could get it out.

For Christ's sake, Karl. Give us a break, will you? You can't mean it. Say you're not serious, will you for God's sake? There he was, the funkiest looking revolutionary in fifty states, with a wardrobe fresh off the rack of Abercrombie & Fitch. Combat boots laced to the top with rawhide strips; olive-drab pants cinched in at the waist with the biggest, knobbiest, most outasight belt buckle you ever saw; khaki shirt opened to the third button so his chest hairs stuck out; sheepskin hunting jacket to ward off the October chill; and, *piece de resistance*, a green Fidel Castro fatigue cap with a black and red Wobbly button pinned over the peak. All in all, a week's pay worth of proletarian garb.

Karl, you crazy son of a bitch, say you don't mean it! Oh, but he's not even smiling.

The college kids from Fordham, Rutgers, and points west were flipped out, goggle-eyed, and you knew, you just knew that before the week was over they would scrape together every dime they could lay their hands on and get themselves a revolutionary outfit just like it.

The matrons from Georgia and business executives from Kansas just stood around self-consciously, shifting from foot to foot. Was this the same, was this really the same gentleman who used to write speeches for Barry Goldwater? One could not be quite sure with all that facial hair and those knotty curls that stuck out like grapes underneath his cap.

The olive-green satellites stood to the side, smiling, talking about their "outasight" trip up from Washington. They had all ridden in the back of Karl's jeep, they said.

Jeep?

Yes, of course. It had to be a jeep. A dark-brown or olive-green one, no doubt. You didn't expect them to drive up like that in a brand new Cadillac, did you?

"Lop off the fringes and keep a good purist libertarian center. We can't accept any deviationists and we don't need any crazies. Let everybody else keep the crazies. We'll build a good, solid, *quality* movement."

You can't lop off the fringes, Murray. You can't drive the crazies away because *everybody* is crazy. If we polarize all the deviationists, there won't be anybody left in the goddamn center!

There were banners on the wall to please every faction imaginable. On the wall behind the podium was an enormous black one with red letters: POWER TO THE PEOPLE!

That was a grabber for the Left.

Slightly to the right of it was an equally large black banner with gold lettering: LAISSEZ FAIRE! A natural turn-on for the profit mavens in the crowd.

To the right of this, just as large and just as prominent, was the final banner: SOCK IT TO THE STATE!

This one was for everybody, Left, Right and in between, since they were all radically opposed to the liberal-conservative *status quo*. We had all the props, all the psychological ploys and P.R. bait laid out like a spider web. This was the rallying point. We had built our rest home, our way station, in the Hotel Diplomat, right in the middle of Times Square.

Joe Peden was calling for order. Everybody take their seats. The conference is about to begin. Rothbard, Liggio, and 1 were on our way to the podium when 1 saw him.

1 saw *him!*

It was the Galambosian. He had followed me from the upper West Side of Manhattan all the way down to West 43rd Street. He was probably right behind me that day in Mamaroneck for all I knew. He was looking at me now, he was smiling at me. He *recognized* me.

"I am now an anarcho-Galambosian," he said, shaking my hand.

Leave me alone, I don't want to hear about it. Now I know why Lenin needed his Cheka. That's what we need now more than anything else, a libertarian Cheka. A secret police to take care of all the goddamn deviationists.

"The anarcho part of my philosophy is my own primary property. I'd be glad to discuss my modifications to Andy's system whenever you have the time."

Never! I don't care about it. I don't want to hear your modifications now or at any time in the future. Just leave me alone before I start lopping off the fringes right this minute! "Sure," I said. "I'll be glad to hear about it later, when the first panel discussion is over."

From the podium you could get a good overview of the crowd.

The business executives and the Southern matrons were huddled together front and center, fidgeting nervously in their seats after having witnessed the pre-convention activities in the corridor. Mary and her anarcho-Objectivists were just behind them, unfurling their black flags embellished with red fists and gold dollar signs. The hippies, long hair matted under sweaty Indian head bands, blue-denim shirts limp and soiled after several weeks of wear, sat across the aisle from Mary and her friends, understandably wary.

The leader of the Objectivist forces in St. Louis was in the balcony, where he had set up a table to advertise his organization and offer paperback copies of Rand's novels and other right-wing literature at a discount. Although he was wearing brown slacks and a glittering shark-skin jacket, I expected him at any moment to disappear inside a phone booth and resurface in black leotards, predictably emblazoned. He was not yet twenty-five years old, but there was no question in my mind that he would have a novelty store in Times Square offering black-and-gold whips to sex deviates by the time he was thirty.

The olive-green revolutionaries, the Field Marshal situated in their midst, were at the opposite end of the balcony casting sour glances toward the shark-skinned profiteer and his display table. Between them, and scattered randomly throughout the orchestra seats below, was a sampling of quieter libertarian types, including the lone Galambosian. All of a sudden the Galambosian was beginning to look like a purist middle-of-the-roader.

When the discussion finally began and the first condemnations of the state-corporate system echoed through the hall, a horrifying roar rose from the audience. Mary and her troop were on their feet, black flags waving wildly over their heads, right fists lifted straight up in the air.

"Strike! Strike! Strike! Strike!" their voices rang in a loud, paralyzing chant, sending shivers down the spines of the industrialists in front of them, and an ominous chill throughout the entire audience.

One could only sit back in awe, wondering what kind of hellish fanaticism had suddenly been released at this conference, which was supposed to be devoted to the principles of justice and individual liberty. The whole world *had* gone berserk.

That night it was Hess's turn. The Field Marshal of the Revolution poured forth a message to match his attire. Strike! Assault! Direct action against the state!

How could you keep up with a guy like this? His swing from the Goldwater Right to the oxygen-deprived Left was breaking the ideological sound barrier. The matrons and business executives were riveted to their chairs, too dumbfounded to move. Mary and her friends were beside themselves with ecstasy, on their feet once again, waving their flags and fists.

"Strike! Strike! Strike! Strike!"

"Which side of the barricades will you be on when the chips are down?" Hess asked hard-eyed from the podium, menacing the profit mavens and other right-wing libertarians in the audience. He had perfected a way of asking questions so that they sounded like threats. "There is no neutral ground in a revolution," Hess continued in his best *Cause That Will Triumph* manner. "You're either on one side of the barricade or the other," he said, cleverly paraphrasing Eldridge Cleaver's "You're either part of the problem or part of the solution" ultimatum.

At that precise moment the polarization was complete.

Mary and her friends were joined by the love children, left-wing anarchists and adventurists, and other cultural New Leftists, all of whom were on their feet shrieking!

"To the barricades! Shoulder to shoulder with our brothers and sisters of the revolution! To Fort Dix tomorrow morning!" The last exhortation represented a spontaneous collective decision by the Leftists to join the war-protest march on Fort Dix the following day.

The other half of the crowd remained in its seats. The division was clean down the middle. The right-wing anarchists, moderate Objectivists, and business types sat in stone-faced opposition to the radicals singing and chanting maniacally around them. The emotional release was almost sexual. The revolution was here and now, you could feel it all around you. Tension! Violence! Instant action! At that moment, there was no question in the minds of the radicals that the government would be in ruins by tomorrow afternoon and that they would be occupying the seats of power. All were caught up in the intoxicating delusion of collective invulnerability. Troops? Tear gas? Bayonets? With a determination and solidarity of purpose such as this, how could anything stop them?

Sunday morning the conference reopened to an audience of fifty. The Leftists were all off in the wilds of New Jersey, singing and chanting as they marched on Fort Dix. Most of the right-wing libertarians, including the Midwestern industrialists and the garden-variety Objectivists, had gone home in disgust. Out of an original crowd of over 300, fifty "centrists" remained who were determined to hold their ground and salvage what they could of a splintered movement that never really got started in the first place. The fringes were lopped off, the corners rounded—although in a way not anticipated. The deviationists had been driven off in different directions to parts unknown. We were left with fifty middle-of-the-road anarchists.

Informal speeches and panel discussions continued into the middle of the afternoon. Along about three o'clock in the afternoon, while somebody was droning on about nonviolent resistance and constructive alternatives, the quiet of the hall was interrupted by a loud commotion in the corridor. Fifty heads whipped around to the rear, one hundred ears strained to hear what was going on. A loud bellow resounded in the corridor and then a crash as the doors swung open.

It was Mary, of course. Standing at the rear of the hall, a vision straight from the flaming depths of hell. Her black shirt and arm band were in tatters. Her feet, her bare dirty feet—where the hell are your boots, Mary?—were planted squarely on the floor in the manner of a slugger ready to trade you blow for blow.

Finally she started her slow approach down the center aisle toward the rostrum, her shoulders and arms swaying heavily with a power all their own, her eyes shooting hatred in all directions as she moved. Now she reached the front of the hall and mounted the podium steps, her heavy bare feet slapping loudly against the wood.

"Where the fuck were you?" her voice, amplified through the speaker system, zapped the hall.

"Do you know what it's like to be tear-gassed?"

Well, no we don't, Mary. And we had no desire to find out; that's why we didn't go charging down to Fort Dix with you yesterday.

The Fort Dix demonstration, it seemed, had gotten out of hand. Instead of marching in orderly fashion along the prescribed route to protest the war, the demonstrators had formed an assault force and gone charging toward the stockade where some G.I. dissenters were being held.

"Do you know what gas does to your eyes? Do you know what it's like to feel your guts on fire and your lungs clamped in a vise?"

We're sorry it happened, Mary. But you must have known they would retaliate before you did it. What did you expect from them anyway? Those soldiers out there, all dressed up in helmets and fatigues, all just as frightened as you are, all trapped in the system just like anybody else.

"Where the fuck were you?"

And then it was all over. She caved in on herself and fell over like a rag doll. Jets of salty tears issued forth from the fiery coals, and rivulets ran down her cheeks onto her lapel pins.

Don't cry, Mary, we'll get the ones responsible for it one of these days. But you don't fight atom bombs with knives and sticks, Mary. David and Goliath was a fluke. Nixon, Agnew, and LBJ, and all the rest of them are the enemy, not some bunch of weekend soldiers who'd rather be anywhere else, doing anything else but guarding a military base on a Sunday afternoon. We'll get the real enemy, Mary! But not with knives or rocks or stones. That's *their* way. That's what they're hoping for. Nothing drives the middle class into the arms of the administration faster than violence, and the politicians know it better than anybody else. There's a better way than that. A radical and revolutionary way, but a nonviolent way. Do you understand, Mary? Nonviolent revolution is the only way to get back at them.

Now the rest of the Fort Dix contingent was storming back into the Hotel Diplomat. Back to the center. Back to their home.

"Hurry!" they were yelling. "We have to get out of here. The place will be alive with feds in no time flat! They're after us, they're after Hess. They're after everybody." Rumors spun around the hall, a new one every second.

The first libertarian conference was over.

12

Ragnar Lets Me Down

It was a beautiful day in the middle of fall of 1969. How long had it been since I last set foot on the Fordham campus in the northeast corner of the Bronx? Ten years? Fifteen years? Oh my God, could it possibly have been *fifteen years* since I strolled across the Quadrangle in white bucks, red corduroy jacket, shirt and tie, and the spikiest crew haircut you ever laid eyes on? Now I was back again, though in a new role: to address a group of Fordham anarchists.

It was an eerie feeling, walking the concrete walks past Hughes Hall half a generation later. The gray stone buildings wrapped in vine, the neat rectangles of lush green grass were exactly as I remembered them. As was the huge field across from Hughes Hall. I remembered the way it used to be: every spring they'd erected a giant statue of the Virgin Mary in a corner of the field and smothered it with tons of flowers. May was the month of Mary, and every day after lunch the entire student body of Fordham Prep would be compelled to mass out in the field for a community rosary service. Fifty-five or sixty hapless freshmen were drafted to represent the Hail Marys and Our Fathers in the five decades of the rosary, which meant forming a chain of human rosary beads around the statue of the Virgin and leading each prayer when your turn came. It was usual for the token black kid accepted at Fordham each year to be appointed the Apostles' Creed; he had to stand apart from all the others, a black island alone in a sea of white and pink. Intended as an honor, this designation no doubt served only to remind the Apostles' Creed of his ethnic uniqueness at a time when he wanted more than anything else to blend inconspicuously into his surroundings.

Mary, Mother of Our Master, Just a Statue Made of Plaster!

Several hundred pink-and-white faces with sports jackets, shirts and ties; one black thumb in the midst of them all nervously reciting the Apostles' Creed.

Jesus, Jesus, come and Squeeze Us!

The field of grass was cut to a quarter-inch to match the haircuts of the students.

Mary, Mary, Dressed in White, will I Go to Hell Tonight?

Mary, Mary, Dressed in Blue, I'm a Pig, I Love to Screw.

For a few minutes there you're sixteen years old in the early Eisenhower years, the years when the most exciting campus demonstrations were the weekly football or basketball rallies. Of course, you strained your throat screaming Rah! Rah! Go! Go! and maybe even blackened someone's eye at the inevitable beer bash that took place in a neighborhood saloon after the game. At sixteen you were already learning to guzzle with the best of them.

But the illusion of recaptured youth lasts only as long as it takes you to make a closer examination of your environment. The grass and trees and gray stone buildings cloaked in ivy were still the same, all right. But not the people swarming by—these students were different, these students don't belong here. Oh my God, Fordham's campus has been invaded by legions of heretics and nihilists. They chased the white bucks and crew haircuts off the premises and filled it with blue jeans and long hair. And black people, too. Not just a token black kid or two from Pelham Bay or Jackson Heights. But a battalion of wild-eyed militants with electrified Afros and variegated dashikis. That's okay for Berkeley or Columbia. But *Fordham?* It's subversive.

It's also ruining my nostalgia.

But who're you kidding, anyway? White bucks? Charcoal grays? Johnnie Ray? All in the past. There's a war going on now, and these kids are its victims. Innocent lives are being destroyed and you've already decided to take your stand with the innocent. You grew up in an age when the National Guardsmen on campus were there to recruit new members, not shoot down students. Nobody who grew up in an age of peace has any right to resent the presence of the victims on his campus.

So a renegade from the Pat Boone era, himself now stepping along in denims and boots and granny glasses and a mustache where last he trod in white bucks and a needle-spike hairdo, returned to the campus of his youth to spread the message of anarchism and resistance. You see him moving by, an ex-conservative and ex-writer of articles for right-wing journals of opinion, hurrying along a concrete walk where once he ran on his way to class, to address a gathering of students who want to know the best way to overthrow the government of the United States. The same government he swore he would defend when he joined the Marines at twenty years of age; the same government he thought was the freest in the world when he blackened someone's eye at a beer bust back in 1955.

But all that was so terribly long ago, so very, very long ago.

For a minute it had seemed like yesterday, when you saw the trees and grass and ivy-covered gray stone buildings. For one long second you *felt* sixteen again.

But it was really so terribly long ago after all. My, my, how the times have changed. All that was before the war; all that was before the riots; all that was before the napalm and the bombs; all that was before they shot Fred Hampton and Mark Clark at four o'clock in the morning; all that was before they killed the kids at Kent State and Jackson State; all that was before they murdered James Rector at People's Park; all that was before My Lai and Song My; all that was before the Bay of Pigs and the Gulf of Tonkin; all that was before the Conspiracy-to-Commit-a-Conspiracy trial in Chicago; all that was before surveillance and dictatorship by dossier; all that was so terribly long ago.

You knew now that your government wasn't the freest in the world after all. You knew now that your government was a bloodthirsty tyrant, an anachronistic claque of imperialistic lunatics who could kill civilians with abandon today and listen to Billy Graham talk about Jesus Christ the following morning in the White House.

You knew now that whatever the cost, your government would definitely have to be stopped.

Just as I anticipated, the Fordham contingent had fitted itself out with revolutionary outfits to the last man. Many wore olive-green and khaki, carbon copies of Hess at the October convention right down to their Wobbly buttons. Others opted for blue jeans with dark blue T-shirts under light blue work shirts open at the collar. And most of the clothes were crisp and spanking new, still smelling of camphor from the neighborhood Army and Navy store.

These were my Ragnars, my revolutionary individualists, separated now from YAF and ready for combat. Legions of libertarian radicals straining at the bit, itching for the chance to lay their hands on Nixon, Johnson, and a few others, and trade them to Hanoi for American POWs.

It was going to be so easy. Organize! Strike! and bring him down! One, two, three, and it's all over. Swift and surgical. A minimum of bloodshed—you just emasculate Goliath and drop his carcass in the middle of the Atlantic. There was no doubt in anyone's mind that by the beginning of the summer of 1970 at the very latest, the government of the United States would be out of the catbird seat never, never to return again.

But wait! Something was wrong. All was not going according to script. I listened, not sure I could believe what I was hearing.

"Comrade _____ has the floor now. As you all know, Comrade _____ has been working with the Student Progressive Labor Party to unionize the workers in the cafeteria. He ..."

"Comrade _____ has been busy these past few weeks building a bridgehead with representatives of the Socialist Workers Party. We're planning to join them in their Campus Radical Front to keep local merchants from purchasing California grapes...."

"Comrade _____ has been organizing neighborhood welfare workers to set up picket lines around ..."

Enough! Have you all gone mad? We're supposed to be building *strategic* alliances with the Left, not turning ourselves into a bunch of goddamn Marxists. We're trying to create a Left-Right *tactical* coalition and convert the Marxists to libertarianism, not the other way around. You've all become a bunch of crazy left-wing deviationists!

Mind you, these were the same students who had traveled out to the YAF convention in St. Louis, filling the chartered buses with their short-hair, horn-rimmed glasses, regimental-ties, drip-dry suits, and oxblood-brogans while they shouted things like "Nuke the Reds," "Bomb Hanoi," and "Impeach Earl Warren." Now, three months later, they sat around a conference table at Fordham University in proletarian shirts and combat boots, calling each other "Comrade" and talking about their "brothers and sisters" in the Maoist-oriented Progressive Labor Party. Instead of "Nuking the Reds" they now wanted to "Off the Pigs," neatly transferring their fanaticism from one object of hatred to another.

"Comrade _____ is organizing a group of brothers and sisters to hold open the doors of subway cars during morning rush hour and distribute leaflets to exploited workers."

Clever. That one will really go over big. Some poor bastard who's going to be docked an hour's pay because he's ten minutes late is really going to be radicalized by that tactic. Sure you'll get converts that way. You'll get a kick in the nuts and a punch in the teeth, that's what you'll get.

"I really believe in doing my own thing," said Comrade ____. "The only problem is, when I feel like doing my own thing nobody will do it with me."

That's the point of doing your own thing in the first place, numb-nuts. If everybody did the same thing, it wouldn't be *your* thing any-more, it would be everyone's thing.

It was clear to me that the moderate anarchist center was being blitzed from all sides. Apparently, everybody in the whole world had become a deviationist.

Were these my *free-market individualists* sitting around a conference table in prole garb and calling one another Comrade?

Ragnar, you son of a bitch, you let me down again!

13

I Fail to Make a Citizen's Arrest

After Fordham, we decided to launch major assaults on both our flanks. There was no question that we were beginning to get a bit paranoid about our developing "movement." For the first time since I could remember, libertarianism had a decent chance to become something more than an intellectual pastime, and we had become a little hypersensitive about having our prospects destroyed by our extremist fringe elements. There was only one proper thing to do at this point: we had to thin our ranks.

Rothbard kicked it off in the November 15, 1969, issue of the *Libertarian Forum* with a flaming attack on ultra-Left adventurism. While the Left was reeling with the aftereffects of the first blow and the Right was feeling comfortable in its own brand of heresy, I drove in the first shaft on our starboard flank with a blistering swipe at the Objectivists. Rothbard followed with a second blast at anarcho-communism, indirectly criticizing Karl Hess, whose swing to the Left was still accelerating at a breathtaking rate.

Now that we had the left- and right-wing deviationists on the ropes, I cold-cocked our right-wing libertarians with an attack on lingering conservatism in their ranks. In March 1970 Rothbard annihilated the entire New Left with a headline article entitled "New Left, Rest in Peace," which was followed by another piece called "Farewell to the Left" and, finally, by my own swipe at Rightist extremism,

By this time we knew our campaign was a huge success: our circulation was falling off like crazy.

"We're driving them away by the hundreds, Murray. We lost another fifty subscribers last month."

"Fantastic. Pretty soon we'll be down to eight or ten stalwarts. An even dozen purist middle-of-the-road anarchists firming up the center."

"The Galambosian is still hanging in there. He's getting better all the time."

"I don't know about him, he's a little too right wingy. Besides that, he's crazy. He gives me the creeps every time I see him."

"I'm keeping a close eye on him. He's not a bad guy, long as he keeps his mouth shut."

A Left-Right Festival of Mind Liberation was sponsored by the California Libertarian Alliance, featuring Leftists Paul Goodman and Carl Oglesby as well as spokesmen for the libertarian Right. Harvey Hukari, an ex-YAFer who admitted openly that profit was his supreme motivation in life, saw nothing wrong with informing on campus radicals to the FBI if the price was high enough. The warm response he received from the so-called Objectivist "anarchists" in the audience was a startling and horrifying experience for libertarians of the Left. Phillip Abbott Luce, formerly connected with the Maoist Progressive Labor Party before turning informer for the Right, was also calling himself a "libertarian."

As was Jeffrey St. John, a conservative, pro-war journalist with Objectivist underpinnings, based in New York City. Just when we were starting to get something going, charlatans of every description were squirming out from under rocks. The people we'd left the Right to get away from were now chasing after us, tracking us down in the streets to hop aboard our overburdened band wagon. The inclusion of people like Hukari, Luce, and St. John in libertarian ranks would inevitably destroy any potential Left-Right coalition in the gestation stage.

Next thing you knew, Lester Maddox and the Reverend Carl MacIntyre would be calling themselves libertarians. We had to squash them before they ruined us altogether.

In the spring of 1970, *Nation's Business* published an article in which libertarianism was identified as "the fastest-growing ideological movement on American campuses." Obviously, the piece would only serve to attract more deviationists to the fold. Just as obviously, we were waging an uphill battle. The more publicity we received, the more screwballs and oddballs would flock to our banner. It was a thoroughly demoralizing situation to be faced with.

And then, something happened that made us forget—temporarily, at least—our internal problems. Richard Nixon invaded Cambodia.

NIXON'S THE ONE!

That slogan was beginning to take on greater meaning every day. What could you do about a man like this? He had eked out a narrow victory in 1968, partly on the promise that he would get us out of Southeast Asia as soon as possible. You'd remembered what happened in 1952 when Eisenhower defeated Stevenson and managed to bring our involvement in Korea to an abrupt conclusion, and you'd naively thought history might repeat itself when Eisenhower's ex-Vice President assumed command. Why the hell else had you bothered to pull the Nixon lever in the polling booth?

Now here it was, almost a year and a half since he had taken the oath of office, and not only had the man made no real attempts to end the draft—another campaign pledge—but the war was actually being expanded under his administration. Whatever reasons he gave for the escalation, he clearly was still clinging to the old anti-communist paranoia that had so influenced his politics from the late 1940s throughout the 1950s. He just couldn't get it through his head that American "traditions" weren't being threatened here, that communism wasn't the monolithic bogeyman it was made out to be under John Foster Dulles, that in any case the peasants he was hell-bent on bombing out of existence were the greatest victims of the war, and not its progenitors.

Nixon, always fancying himself as a man of crisis (six? seven? How many?), saw himself rising to the national emergency and saving the country, possibly the entire globe, from extinction. Having lived in the shadows of other men all his life, he was determined at all costs to go down in the textbooks as a president who achieved greatness: Vietnam would be his Finest Hour, no matter what. Lincoln had his Emancipation Proclamation; John F. Kennedy had his Cuban Missile showdown;

and Richard M. Nixon would be remembered as the man who brought us Peace with Honor in Vietnam. It wasn't enough for him to stop the damned war and bring the troops home, you see. It had to be done to coast-to-coast acclaim as the banner of Victory flew high.

For those of us who had supported him it was impossible to feel anything but disgust once we realized exactly what he was up to. For the country at large—Left, Right and in between—it was a time of great despair, frustration, and then outrage with our own inadequacy, under a system of government that was theoretically of, by, and for the people, to do anything that would make him reverse course.

Not all the disgust was directed toward the mediocrity in the White House. *We* were the ones—the ones who had given this man more power than any other living human being on earth!

And here he was, raining bombs on people who were still living in a seventeenth-century agrarian society.

How much longer could we let him get away with it?

This was a time to put politics aside. Left? Right? Libertarian? The distinctions suddenly seemed unimportant. Only one thing mattered at this point: somehow or other the carnage had to be stopped. People everywhere, disgusted if not radicalized by this most recent escalation, felt compelled to make some gesture of protest against the war policies of the government.

I drove down to Washington for the demonstration against the Cambodian invasion, thinking all the while how nice it would be actually to lay hands on the man. How sweet to snap on the handcuffs and perform a citizen's arrest! Was it not our right to apprehend those caught in the act of committing a criminal offense? Why should a criminal have immunity merely because he happened to be the President of the United States? No amount of votes in the world could give any man the authority to operate with the moral recklessness of a Raskolnikov.

I had heard in advance that government agents would be taking down the license numbers, for future surveillance, of all cars heading into D.C. Since I was driving a machine owned by an insurance company, my employer at the time, the idea of J. Edgar Hoover's lieutenants surrounding the main office in Hartford only filled me with joy. Most likely the rumor was based on paranoia, but the spectacle of an upper-echelon crook in our state-corporate insurance system finding his house surrounded at three o'clock in the morning was a lovely one indeed.

Arriving in Washington in the late afternoon, I went directly to Karl Hess's houseboat on the Anacostia River. He had been living there with his girlfriend over the past year, since abandoning his suits, ties, apartment, and all the trappings of his right-wing past.

The marina was a community of houseboat-dwellers inhabited by Hess, his son, and a wide assortment of their friends and disciples. Hess's leftward swing had continued on through syndicalism—which was where he was during the October conference—and into the headier realm of anarcho-communism. He proudly referred to his waterfront group as his "little commune," and he wore his new mantle of voluntary collectivism as openly as he once had waved the banner of Goldwater conservatism.

Karl had split from the *Forum,* feeling that Rothbard's criticism of the radical Left was a bit too personal and directed more at him than anyone else. He was no longer interested in the concept of Left-Right coalitions, and since he was working exclusively with the Left, he felt that Rothbard's attack on the Left would undermine the overtures he was making in that direction.

Stepping aboard the *Tranquil,* my eyes were drawn immediately to the wall poster of Che Guevara staring watchfully toward the deck. The bulkheads were papered with radical slogans and various kinds of revolutionary graffiti. Karl emerged from the vessel's dark interior dressed in heavy jeans and a denim jacket with the sleeves cut off, worn like a vest over a navy work shirt.

The look in his eyes cut me short. There was that glaze that had become so common with the kids of this latest generation, from love children to paranoid Yippie subculturists. Could it be? Had he actually opted for that route? What are you trying to prove, anyway? Sure enough, the paranoia was there.

"Did you hear about the hardhats beating up the kids in Manhattan last week?" I asked.

"How do you *know* they're really workers?" came the unsmiling response.

Come on, now. Don't give me that nonsense, will you? That working-man-can-do-no-wrong line you used to laugh at two years ago. You don't really think J. Edgar Hoover infiltrated the trade unions with agents to create a pro-war demonstration, do you? Anybody who believes that doesn't know the American working man from his Dutch uncle. I went to school with them, friend; I drank with them on weekends. You tell any self-respecting sheet-metal worker that it's OK to spit on the American flag; you just show him your Che poster and ask him what he thinks of it! You're lucky if he doesn't throw you into the Anacostia in your denim jacket with the red fist stenciled on the back.

How do I *know* those were really hardhats who beat up the dissenting students in the spring of 1970? Because I heard them *laughing* about it in the Blarney Stone the day after it happened.

We spent the rest of the evening in the boatyard watching Richard Nixon address the nation on television. From the way he moved his hands to emphasize a point; the way he flashed that toothy smile after delivering one of his deft witticisms; the way he furrowed his brow and stared directly into the camera when he told you how much he hated to kill people but how he had to do it to preserve the sacred institutions of the Western world; and the way his voice became low and solemn when he asked for the support and the prayers of his "fellow Americans"—you could tell that our leader was just oozing with sincerity.

"He's got to be offed," said Hess, glaring at the screen.

I had never believed in capital punishment, but I was almost willing to make an exception in Nixon's case. At the very least he should be traded to Hanoi—along with Johnson, Rusk, and a few others—for American POWs and have his fate decided by a North Vietnamese tribunal.

It was good to see that Karl's mind was still functioning clearly after all.

I got a few hours' sleep aboard someone's sailboat and rose early the next morning before anyone else was up. The river was gray and calm in the new dawn, and for a brief moment it was hard to see the filth and sewage that floated past the marina on its way to join the Potomac further south. The houseboats, side by side, bobbed quietly, almost in slow motion, on the gently heaving Anacostia. It was graveyard still out there on the catwalk reaching out over this strange river in Washington, DC, with the boats rocking gently all around and not a flutter of human activity anywhere.

Driving through the early-morning streets of Washington, the only signs of life came from squads of patrolmen already anticipating the marchers that would appear over the next hour or so. Almost without realizing it I found myself heading for the Ambassador Hotel on K Street. This was my first visit to Washington since the summer of 1957 when I had been stationed at Quantico, Virginia, as a candidate for officer training with the United States Marine Corps. The weekends, when I could get away, were invariably spent at the Ambassador in the company of a honey blonde from Mississippi. How transient the nonessentials are—I had forgotten her name, but could still recall the drape of her silky hair across those smooth shoulders, the firmness of her stomach, the unsilky hair below. It was a fine summer if you counted the weekends and forgot about those long hours of brainless drill on the sun-bleached wasteland that was Quantico, Virginia.

On checking into the Ambassador I experienced for an instant the same kind of nostalgia that had engulfed me when I visited the Fordham campus after an absence of fifteen years. The corridors of this hotel, once crawling with Marines and other servicemen from nearby camps, were now teeming with long-haired hippies and others who had traveled from scattered regions to protest the war.

After breakfast I left and walked slowly down 16th Street toward the triangular hub of the day's activities bounded by the Washington Monument on the south, the Lincoln Memorial on the west, and the huge field off the southern wall of the White House on the north. It was unreal watching thousands of marchers decked out in everything from business suits to beads and blue jeans, moving along the broad Washington streets in orderly fashion toward the meadow near the White House. The cops stood by nonchalantly, billy clubs and side arms well displayed, conversing easily with the wildest looking hippies from San Francisco and New York and all points in between.

Kids were smoking pot openly and the air was heavy with its cloying aroma. Patrolmen turned their heads the other way, apparently under orders to avoid confrontation at all costs and to react only to violence should it break out. At one point I saw a gang of Yippie and Weatherman types, their faces smeared with war paint and FUCK NIXON spelled out in block letters on their foreheads, circling around a squad of police chanting, "Off the Pigs! Off the Pigs!" The cops chatted among themselves or with other passers-by until the scurvy pack finally departed, ignored by all.

Dave Dellinger's voice, amplified through the speaker system, rang out across the meadow. The meadow itself was literally carpeted with people, contoured over the sloping grass as far as the eye could see. The sun raged high above, red and pulsating in the naked sky, making your shirt stick to your back and chest no matter how slowly you moved. After a while, when you'd had your fill of speeches and sun, you moved further south across another thoroughfare and up the grassy stretch toward the Washington Monument. Here, thousands more were lying about, eating their lunches on the grass, or turning on, or strumming guitars and entertaining one another with well-known songs or songs of their own creation.

An hour later, you left the vantage point of the Washington Monument with its bird's-eye view of the river to the south and the White House to the north, and you walked the quarter-mile or so to the Reflecting Pool in front of the Lincoln Memorial. Things were livelier here. Hundreds had stripped down to their skins and jumped into the cooling water of the pool. Dozens more were divesting themselves of shoes and pants and making ready to join the fun. A ring of cops stood

in the shade along the grassy knoll to the sides, some observing the fes-
tivities with a grin, others looking grim behind the anonymity of their
wraparound sunglasses.

The kids were circling bare-assed in the pool, sitting on the various
jets of water and deflecting them toward the spectators on the perimeter.
There were hefty female students from Hunter College frolicking in the
middle of the pool, their pendulous breasts flopping about like punching
bags; there were scrawny college dropouts with boils on their backs and
gigantic erections plowing through the water in a diligent search for
receptive apertures. After a while, the grabbing and touching and grop-
ing was universal. By the time they starting jumping up and down,
splashing one another with water yelling, "One, two, three, four! We
don't want your fucking war!" you began to tire of this a little and
worked your way back to the crowded meadow and the speeches that
were still droning on beneath the indomitable sun.

Later that night, high on grass yourself, you stared up at the Washington Monument, which shot like a streak into the pitch-black sky. It
seemed to quiver with an inner life of its own out there in the blackness
with the moon spilling silver all over its sleek sides. The air was thick
and heavy with the sweet-sick smell of marijuana, by now a seemingly
permanent admixture to the atmosphere. For a while you could enjoy
your high and listen to the guitars and forget about the war and the kill-
ing and all the devastation it had wreaked on the lives of so many
human beings, and on your country.

For a moment at least, out there near the Washington Monument, it
was possible to get away from it.

The following morning, before you left the city that was the capital
of your country, you read in the newspaper that Richard Nixon had
made a personal appearance in the early dawn of the previous day,
speaking to students near the Lincoln Memorial. Your biggest regret as
you directed your car northward out of town was that not a single one of
those students had the presence of mind to make a citizen's arrest; and
you weren't there to do it yourself. An opportunity like that comes
along only once in a lifetime, if ever it comes at all.

14

Left, Right, and In-between

"This is a movement to be proud of, Murray. A good, purist, middle-of-the-road revolutionary movement."

"All the crazies are gone for good. It's a nice feeling to know you can hold your head up high and call yourself an anarchist at the same time."

"No more crackpotism to worry about. No more Neanderthalism. Murray, I haven't slept this well since Al Martino made a comeback in the middle sixties."

"All the weirdos have gone over to the extremists by now."

"You don't know how great it is to be able to finish a meal without running for the Bromo-Seltzer. My digestive juices are staging a comeback. By the way, what ever happened to Hamish Menzies?"

"I don't know, 1'm a Bach man myself. How many copies of your book have been sold to date?"

My first book, *Radical Libertarianism,* had just been published. "Six or seven, last I heard. I don't have the exact figure yet."

"It's pushing up into two figures already. You don't know who these people are, do you?"

"No way of knowing. People can buy books all over the country without showing identification. You don't believe in registering books like guns, do you, so we'd have a record of who's reading what at any given time?"

"As an anarchist I'm opposed to all forms of licensing and registration. It's a dangerous practice. The authorities would be able to lay their hands on every book and magazine in the country any time they wanted to."

"Still, there should be some way of finding out who's reading my stuff. I'd like to know if it's getting into the wrong hands."

"Shouldn't be too big a problem if the book sells less than twenty copies. If the figure goes much higher than that, we may be in serious trouble."

"And we don't know who's passing the book around, either. Or who's reading my column in the *Forum* and passing *that* around. There should be some sort of rule keeping people who buy books and magazines from showing them to anyone else."

"Too Galambosian for me. We may have to get rid of him, by the way. His brand of heresy seems to be making inroads into the center."

"He's only free to talk about his modifications to Andy's system. Long as nobody knows what Andy's system is, we're safe."

"If you say *so.* You know, it's been a peaceful summer so far."

"It really has. I think we've finally got things under control, Murray. After years and years of struggle we seem to be on top of the situation once and for all."

It was hard to come up with an accurate estimate of how many individualist libertarians there were in the country at this time. The circulation of the most wide-ranging libertarian journals was somewhere around 50,000, but we knew that a sizable portion of these readers were really Buckley-style right-wingers with a strong fondness for *economic* libertarianism and political *conservatism* in other areas. Of the radical libertarian journals, all of which had purged any traces of conservatism from their pages, none was reaching more than 10,000 or 15,000, at the outside. How many conservative hangers-on remained on those subscription lists was anybody's guess.

As far as active libertarian cadre were concerned, the leading organizations were the Radical Libertarian Alliance, the Objectivist-oriented Society for Individual Liberty, and a plethora of independent libertarian clubs operating on a local level. Both RLA and SIL counted their membership as ranging between 5,000 and 8,000 but, again, no one could estimate the overlap. It is probably reasonable to assume that by the end of the summer of 1970 there were 5,000 active libertarian radicals in the

United States. About half of them were Leftist deviationists who followed Hess, while close to half were Rightist heretics under the influence of Ayn Rand and splinter groups in California.

Raising the banner of the moderate center were Rothbard and myself and a dozen or so middle-of-the-road anarchists whose task it was to hold the fringes in abeyance and keep the center from being overwhelmed. If we opened the floodgates too wide on either side, we'd be swept away in a tide of extremist propaganda. The price of freedom is eternal vigilance. We had worked too hard to lower our guard for a split second in these crucial late rounds.

Of course, like the lull before the storm, this state of affairs couldn't last indefinitely. It was only a question of time before somebody broke the dam and inundated us with problems once again.

The dam broke in the early fall of 1970.

Someone noticed us. Someone discovered us in our anonymity, in our saneness and our moderation, and began writing stories about us. They had gotten tired of writing about the Black Panthers and the Weathermen and the Chicago Seven. They needed copy and so they started to zero in on us. This could be disastrous. If they found out about our extremists we were finished; no group in the world had extremists like ours.

They found out. In September, *Esquire* ran an expose of libertarian nomads and troglodytes—the ocean-platform claque and the cave-dwellers. Stop it now, will you? We're responsible; we're middle-of-the-road anarchists. What do you want, picking on a bunch of crazies like that? Have you no sense of proportion?

Then *National Review* blasted us from the Right, with a full page attack on *Radical Libertarianism*. Why are *they* making waves, anyway? Ivy League Hegelianism is getting out of hand again. Who do you think you are, Bill, Jr.—H. L. Mencken?

Other right-wing journals fell immediately into line. First the *New Guard,* the YAF monthly, bombed our rightist flank; then *Triumph*, L. Brent Bozell's Sons of Thunder publication, dropped one on the radical center.

We had to consolidate our forces. The right-wing deviationists were being driven back to Buckley by the hundreds. They were exposed out there. They had no protection, no air cover, no nothing. We couldn't just abandon them, we had to take them back. There was always the danger that once they were back in the moderate radical center we'd never be able to get rid of them again. But we had no choice.

In November a surprising development took place. We suddenly found ourselves gaining support from an area where we least expected it: the liberal Left. The assistance came in the form of a favorable article on free-market anarchism in the November 16, 1970, issue of *The Nation.* Can you beat that? *The Nation* found some kind things to say about free-market radicalism. The only problem was that they tied the individualist anarchist tradition to the far Left: anarcho-Bakuninism, anarcho-collectivism, anarcho-syndicalism, wobblyism, anarcho-communism. They saw individualist and collectivist libertarianism as cut from the same bolt of cloth. Total voluntarism was their line.

In effect, they had reunited the center with the fringes on the Left.

"It's a bloody Leftist avalanche. Everybody wants in now!"

"I can't stand it, Murray. My digestive system isn't strong enough."

"Next thing you know, Arthur Schlesinger and John Kenneth Galbraith will be embracing anarchism."

"At least we've got no appeal for Lawrence Welk or Bob Hope."

But all that was nothing compared to what happened when *The New York Times* decided it wanted in on the act. Not *The New York Times!* Please! *The Nation, The New Republic,* the *Progressive,* even *Newsweek* I can handle. But once the *Times* starts in, you might as well put a lock on the door and close up shop. You'll never build a sane movement and keep out the crazies once you're discovered by *The New York Times.*

They started it with a December 1970 article on Hess in the Sunday magazine section followed by a January 1971 issue with a cover story, no less: "The New Right Credo—Libertarianism." That one really did it.

Within days, I began to understand the charge that the New Left, the Black Panthers, Ecology, Women's Lib, whatever, are all creations of the media. In the brief span of five months, from September 1970 through January 1971, libertarianism emerged as the Movement of the Hour. From an underground discussion club comprising twelve moderates and 5,000 deviationists, libertarianism had suddenly become a major political and philosophical force that threatened to sweep the nation off its feet.

Why were the liberals doing what they were doing? We didn't know at the time. Maybe they just wanted to embarrass William Buckley. Anyway, they did it. They made waves. Our center was inundated, not only with left- and right-wing deviationists but with legions of people who had never heard the word *libertarian* before *The New York Times* printed it. They would come up to you with copies of the articles in their hands.

"Hey, man. What's this libertoonism I been readin' about? Sounds like an outasight philosophy, man."

"We been hearin' about this groovy new movement. How do we join?"

The New Left was floundering on the ropes. Women's lib was last year's issue. Ecology was being co-opted by the politicians. The anti-war movement was in a temporary state of limbo. These kids wanted a cause, any cause, to turn them on. They needed a movement. There was a vacuum to be filled and we were there at the right moment. The timing couldn't have been better had the whole production been staged by Cecil B. DeMille. Libertoonism was the Movement of the Hour.

"Where do we sign up for this outasight movement of yours?"

There is no movement, goddamnit! The movement has been disbanded. Go on home and do some reading if you're really interested. Try to find out why private property isn't theft. Don't take our word for it—convince yourself logically and then we'll talk. If you want to call yourself a libertarian, you've got to be able to defend certain positions that have been under attack from a hundred different quarters for a hundred years. You can't go around telling people that free trade and individualism are "groovy" and "outasight" and expect them to *believe* you. They'll just think you're un-American, some kind of Communist. Convince yourself and then come back. If you're really that interested when all the hullabaloo dies down, we'll be glad to talk to you.

By now we were engaged in some serious speculation as to why the liberals were showering us with so much convert-gaining publicity. The most obvious conclusion was that they saw libertarianism as a handy weapon to use against the conservatives, particularly at a time when a right-wing administration was in power. Divide and conquer.

But we were already divided, and had been on a large scale, since the summer of 1969. True, giving national publicity to the fracture on the Right made the libertarian-conservative rift take on a broader meaning. It was easier to discredit the policies of a conservative administration when a large percentage of disillusioned right-wingers were joining the attack.

Another possibility was that a major philosophical and political splintering on the Right just happened to make good copy. The whole idea of a group of free-market individualists and disaffiliated right-wingers joining the radical Left on peace marches and antiwar demonstrations—all the while criticizing the domestic policies of the conservative establishment—was a fresh phenomenon in this era of polarization. It was a newsworthy development and may have been viewed as deserving of attention from that standpoint alone.

Then there was the undeniable fact that the liberals themselves were in poor enough shape politically to seek out allies and sympathizers wherever they could find them. As vulnerable as Nixon was, liberal Democrats were saddled with as sad a cast of characters as they'd ever seen. It was almost as though the Republicans had selected their presidential hopefuls for them. Muskie; Humphrey; Jackson, an old-time hawk who sometimes made Barry Goldwater sound like a peacenik; McGovern, the best of the lot from a libertarian point of view, but too low key to stir up enthusiasm—he had even less chance of making it all the way than Eugene McCarthy had; Ted Kennedy, somehow lacking the personal magnetism of his older brothers and, for the time being at least, still under the cloud of Chappaquiddick. At this point, libertarians had been making overtures to the Left for several years, especially since the traumatic break with YAF in the fall of 1969, and now that they had finally gotten a response that they weren't quite sure how to handle.

Tied in with this was the fact that the rhetoric of decentralization had suddenly become respectable again. During the years when liberals had been busy creating technocratic central planning boards in Washington, they'd had little patience with anyone who tried to tell them people had a right to run their own affairs. Decentralized power, particularly in the form of Old Right radical individualism, was quickly dismissed as "reactionary" or even "Neanderthal." But by the late 1960s it had gotten through to all but the most stubborn of old-line liberals that their gargantuan technocratic machine in Washington somehow wasn't functioning properly. All of a sudden a new cast of characters was calling for decentralization and military isolation, the twin themes of the pre-Buckley Right. Now it was the radical Leftists who were criticizing their corporate-liberal mentors—their parents, in many instances—for having established a heavily centralized state that stripped individuals and localities of basic freedoms. Now it was Charles A. Reich—hardly a conservative by anybody's standards—who was lambasting the New Deal state-corporatism of Franklin D. Roosevelt in *The Greening of America*. Now it was Gabriel Kolko, another leading spokesman for the New Left intelligentsia, who was saying in *The Triumph of Conservatism* that it wasn't *laissez faire* but the state that had led to monopoly capitalism by the turn of the twentieth century. Now it was Norman Mailer, the Black Panthers, and a wide array of people with impeccable left-wing credentials who were calling for neighborhood government and local control of all basic institutions. Now it was *Times* columnist Tom Wicker who was writing about Left-Right coalitions in articles for *Playboy* magazine.

Suddenly, the basic tenets of libertarianism didn't frighten liberals so much anymore. How could libertarian principles be totally "reactionary" when some of the leading intellectuals of the radical Left were espousing them?

Whatever the motives behind the liberals' sudden publicizing of the libertarian cause, at least it was a beginning. An alliance of sorts, however shaky, was now a possibility for the first time in history.

The idea of a new political coalition is always intoxicating whenever it arises. As time passes and a society's political climate evolves from one stage to another, the shifting and realignment of various factions becomes all but inevitable. The old labels quickly become obsolete.

"Liberal" and "conservative" had certainly lost by 1970 the definitions they had in the early part of the 1960s. In the wake of the old divisions, the distinction between centralist and decentralist was becoming more relevant. Totalitarianism and voluntarism were at polar ends of the political gamut; the choice between dictatorship and individual freedom was becoming more of a reality in the lives of all Americans now living in an increasingly polarized society with barricade situations erupting from day to day.

It was not surprising that, for many, these concerns should take the form of choosing between an increasingly authoritarian government and the libertarian ethic.

What we needed to do now was to build libertarianism into an independent third force in American society. We had to set ourselves up in opposition to the centralizers, no matter what they called themselves. Anyone who wanted to accumulate more and more power in Washington was the enemy. The liberals would spend your money on public housing projects and welfare for the "needy"; the conservatives would spend it on "welfare" for the oil industry and the Pentagon. Liberal or conservative, it really didn't matter any more.

It didn't make any difference, because no matter who got into office it was all the same for people paying the taxes. The only thing that could make a difference for *them* would be what libertarians were working for—decentralization and an end to the whole concept of nation-states. Which meant an end to the particular nation-state in which all of us—liberals, conservatives, libertarians, whatever—were now living.

15

The Center Is Big Enough For All

The Freedom Conspiracy at New York City's Columbia University was possibly the largest single libertarian chapter in the country. Surprisingly enough, the Conspiracy was also the largest student organization on campus—a novel situation for any group with libertarian underpinnings, and one that was unduplicated anywhere else in the nation as far as anyone could tell. If this could happen at Columbia, hardly a citadel of philosophical individualism, could West Point be far behind?

The first libertarian conference in 1971 was scheduled for the weekend of March 13 at the Columbia University Law School. Its sponsors—in addition to the Freedom Conspiracy itself—were the Society for Individual Liberty and the New York Radical Libertarian Alliance. Conferences over the past year had included such Leftist spokesmen as Paul Goodman and Carl Oglesby; this one would be more individualist in orientation, with no spokesmen for the collectivist-anarchist point of view even invited to attend.

Before the conference began, word came down from Boston that Noam Chomsky was concerned about the sudden burst of publicity surrounding the free-market libertarian movement. While he welcomed the libertarian-conservative split as a healthy development on the American political scene, he was apparently afraid we might succeed in toppling the federal government before Leftists could demolish the private-property system in the United States. Although we didn't share Chomsky's optimism about the imminent collapse of centralized government in America, we chose to interpret it as prophetic, and thus we were able to face the beginning of the conference in high spirits.

They paraded in from various corners of the country the way they had for the first gathering at the Hotel Diplomat. The same diverse types were here again, though hopefully their penchant for extremist positions had been modified in the intervening year and a half. In addition to these we had managed to attract a group of Jeffersonian decentralists who journeyed by subway from Greenwich Village with a suitcase full of their own literature. All told, about 350 Americans, and a few Canadians, came to Columbia University in March 1971 to find out what was going on in the moderate anarchist center.

The Law School forum at Columbia University was large and bright and airy, in sharp contrast to the dark, narrow conference hall at the Hotel Diplomat. The crowd was orderly and quiet, with everyone in his seat well before the conference had officially begun. There was a sobriety about the audience now that was lacking in the past, a reflective, open-minded mood in place of the raucous hostility that factionalized the first conference before it even got under way. There was another change too, subtle at first, but more and more discernible as your eyes swept back and forth over the crowd.

The audience was integrated this time.

Whereas before it was compartmentalized into factions ranging from Leftist to the outer reaches of the Right, now you saw random groupings all over the hall. Now you noticed business suits and blue jeans, capitalists and communalists, potheads and martini guzzlers talking to each other, seated together throughout the conference hall.

The super-Randian was there, but no longer would he be selling black-and-gold whips in Times Square by the time he was thirty. Already he had modified his attire to a black jumpsuit over a gold turtleneck sweater, and while this may seem weird by conventional standards, it represented a marked change from midnight-black leotards and huge gold dollar signs.

Right on, young hero! You're doing just fine.

Missing, too, were the slogans and banners—the "Laissez Faire" and "Power to the People" and "Sock It to the State" clichés that characterized the first convention. Nowhere to be seen were the waving black flags and the clenched red fists of October 1969. This time the slogans, fists, and dollar signs were limited to private lapel buttons, something else to be grateful for. This was a time to collect your wits and reflect on what you were going to do. This was a time to figure out where the hell we went from there.

Now the moderator called for order and introduced the first speaker of the day. You saw him rising to address the crowd.

"Your theories on private judicial tribunals to replace the state law courts are very interesting, sir, but I don't see how they're going to work. Do you mind elaborating on that point a little more?"

Enough, I was tired already of talking about private tribunals. I had to take a leak. Would you let me get off the stump for five minutes so I can go to the goddamn men's room?

"Your anarchist monetary philosophy sounds all right in the abstract. But before it will work in practice, you've got to do something about the international banking conspiracy."

Well, we know you, boy, don't we now? Our Man from Birch is here. Just *whom* are you referring to when you talk about banking conspiracies? You're not talking about Eskimos, I'm sure. No, there aren't too many Eskimos mixed up in banking circles. How about Venezuelans? Wrong again. Indonesians? I'm not even warm now, am I? I've got it. Corsicans! Everybody knows that the international banking community has all but been taken over by those sneaky Corsicans during the past 200 years.

"Sir! Do you realize that at this very moment your life is in danger?"

Hold it now, pal. In danger from whom? From you, maybe? What are you talking about, anyway? You say I need an organization to help me hide out when the authorities come after me? What organization did you have in mind, friend? Anything I've heard of before? Oh, I see. Or, I will see if I just read this magazine called *American Opinion*, the Birch Society rag.

Infiltrated again! The center besieged by whim-worshiping hair splitters, gray-flannel anti-Semites, and bearded Birch recruiters. What could we do about it? Purge? Purify? Drive out the deviationists?

As it turned out, the conference ended smoothly this time around. The deviationists proved to be a small—though unnerving—minority, while the center could now count a hell of a lot more moderates than ever before.

Sunday night we all departed in high spirits and with a feeling of togetherness. The various factions were still there, but for the first time they seemed willing to discuss differences in theory without flying at one another's throats.

And anyway, I was tired of worrying about deviationists.

They can worry about me for a change. I'm not nuts, I'm a libertarian. I'm a sane and moderate middle-of-the-road anarchist.

And I'm going to knock this government on its ass some day. Ragnar and I are going to blow the whole system sky high. Just like that! You wait and see.

PART IV
The Campaign

16

Ayn Rand Strikes Again

On a rainy Thursday night in the early part of April 1971, I went off to address a class of left-wing anarchists at Hunter College in New York City. It would be the first time 1'd gone before such a group at its invitation.

Perhaps the whole thing might have come off a little better had I been alone. I don't know; it's easy to speculate with the benefit of hindsight. Anyway, there to lend me moral support was a small group of right-wing libertarians, including a radical Objectivist follower of Mary's, complete with lapel pins, LAISSEZ FAIRE buttons, and a whole grab bag stocked with right-wing bric-a-brac. While a classroom full of hairy anarcho-Communists sat around in their love beads, head bands, brocaded vests, and walrus mustaches, the anarcho-Objectivist set up shop in the corner selling capitalist literature and LAISSEZ FAIRE buttons at twenty-five cents a throw.

Somehow, I had this premonition that all might not go according to plan.

Beginning somewhat apprehensively, I emphasized the areas of agreement between free-market anarchists and anarchists of the Left. We were all against the war, against the draft, against the American state-corporate economic system, against legislation regulating sexual practices and abortions, against censorship of literature whether "pornographic" or not, and against any other curtailment of basic civil liberties; we were all in favor of local self-determination, control of civic institutions at the consumer rather than the managerial level, a maximum amount of individual freedom and expression.

So far so good.

The great barrier between us, of course, was the formulation of economic principles, most especially the question of property rights. Here you had to step a bit more carefully.

"Hey, man. What do you mean by free-market economics anyway?" a voice called out through a furry beard in the back of the room.

"Free exchange of goods and ideas in an open marketplace."

"You don't mean that if some pig wanted to own his own factory and hire other people to work for him, he could get away with that, do you, man?"

"The only way you can stop private ownership and the exchange of labor for capital is by state coercion. If you're serious about anarchism you have to accept the possibility of all forms of voluntary exchange whether you like them or not."

"Like, that's exploitation! How about private property, man? You don't believe in private property, do you?"

"There's no such thing as freedom without a private property system. There's no way you can divide the earth equally among all people even if you wanted to."

"We don't wanna divide, man, we want everybody to use anything he needs. The earth belongs to everybody."

"It's impossible for everybody to use everything in common. Unless you acknowledge the concept of individual autonomy and individual ownership, there can be no freedom, no privacy."

"Fuck privacy, man! We all gotta love one another. I mean, like, we're all brothers, you know what I mean?"

"If some people want privacy, they have a right to it. You can't force people to share everything if they don't want to, not in a voluntary society. That's not anarchism, you need a dictatorship for that."

"You can't have some pig ripping off the land from the people and let him get away with it. That's exploitation, not freedom. Some greedy fuckers are gonna have more land and more money than others under your system."

"The only way you can guarantee complete economic equality is with a dictatorship. And if you destroy individual initiative, you'll only be able to guarantee equality at the lowest level. If you want to eliminate greed in a libertarian society, you have to do it through education. If you try to out-law it you'll have to create a state all over again."

"*Greed is what makes the world go 'round!*" the radical Objectivist screamed, bringing the classroom to silence. "The profit motive is part of human nature. You people are denying human nature. A is A. A thing is what it is. You can't deny reality. Collectivism is a philosophy for psy-chotic, anti-life whim-worshipers."

"Who is that creep anyway?"

"Like, what's he saying?"

"Who the fuck you talkin' to, baby?"

"I came here to hear a lecture tonight," the right-wing deviationist con-tinued. "Why don't you have the courtesy to keep quiet until the speaker has finished his presentation?"

"He's a pig!"

"He's a goddamn male chauvinist!" shrieked a hefty feminist in the first row.

Now the Objectivist was on his feet.

"I just want to know one thing. If we were living in an anarchist society and you people had your commune organized the way you wanted it, what would you do about private property owners who didn't threaten you in any way? Suppose there was a capitalist community five miles away that left you alone and minded its own business. Would you coexist with it or would you try to suppress it?"

Perhaps it was a reaction against the anarcho-capitalist and his little marketplace, perhaps they really meant it; I have no way of knowing for sure. But to this question there was a universal outcry from the class at large:

"We'd come in and kick the shit out of you, man!"

"We'd beat your ass in!"

"We'd rip you off, baby! Just like that!"

I slowly started to gather my paraphernalia. The meeting was clearly out of control. By the time I left there were at least ten or twelve people standing on chairs, shaking their fists, and shrieking simultaneously at the top of their lungs.

Richard Nixon and Spiro Agnew had no reason to lose any sleep over us that night.

Nor did they several weeks later when a right-wing group at the State University of New York in Stony Brook, Long Island, invited me out to talk about the long-range possibilities for a Left-Right libertarian alliance.

I drove out on a Tuesday night and found myself overwhelmed by the bleak, Kafkaesque nightmare of the university grounds. You drove on through vast stretches of flat, undeveloped wasteland punctuated now and then by ultramodern dormitories or administration buildings rising in lonely isolation in the middle of nowhere. What an incredible waste of the taxpayers' money! Here was an enormous tract of land claimed by the state for purposes of education, its multimillion-dollar buildings scattered miles from one another. The very look of the place was the antithesis of Paul Goodman's concept of a Community of Scholars. Students were trapped in expensive modern buildings styled like upper middle-class housing cooperatives, separated literally by miles from other student dorms and areas of cultural activity. There was more feeling of community in a prefabricated army barracks than you could ever find in a place like this. Ironically enough, the area I was headed for was Lenny Bruce College, a designation that would have caused the now-departed satirist to sue for libel.

The talk was scheduled for 8:30 and I found myself facing a group of students and some professors representing every conceivable point along the political spectrum. There was the leader of the campus YAF chapter with several of his membership; Objectivist anarchists who had invited me out; some middle-of-the-road Edmund Muskie types; a few Left-liberals in the vein of Eugene McCarthy and George McGovern; and radical Leftists under the influence of Mike Zweig, a syndicalist-anarchist who taught a course in economics at the university.

I started off with general principles, giving them basic libertarianism as concisely as I could, and then moved into practical alternatives such as police, courts, sanitation, education, and other institutions in a stateless society. It was interesting catching flak from all directions—Left, Right, and Center—at the same time. It was a lively group, imaginative and sharp and not unruly like the claque I'd faced at Hunter. After touching as many bases as I could and spending a solid two and a half hours on the stump, I finally prepared to leave. It was then, after all was said and done for the night, that I found myself confronted by several Objectivists with worried lines creasing their foreheads.

"How can we trust anybody who doesn't have a proper philosophical foundation for the concept of liberty?"

"Can we be sure of anything when we're dealing with people who fail to understand that A is A?"

"... That a thing is what it is?"

"... When you're dealing with people who are anti-life and anti-mind?"

At the first break in this flurry of questions, one of the Left-liberals interrupted to make her own point.

"You libertarians don't seem to be concerned enough about spastic children. How are you going to guarantee that spastic children and cripples will be provided for? How do we know they won't go starving in the streets under your system?"

"See what I mean?" said an Objectivist. "Left-wingers are philosophical altruists."

"They're anti-self-esteem."

"All collectivists are inherent totalitarians under the surface. That's all there is to it."

"If *freedom* doesn't work, we're all doomed," was the best I could muster at that point. And so I left.

Objectivists were just as hopeless as knee-jerk liberals. The final straw for me as far as any iota of patience with Ayn Rand's philosophy was an interview she gave on the subject of pollution. On a Sunday afternoon in May 1971, she appeared before a nationwide television audience and denounced the ecology movement for being anti-life, anti-man, and anti-mind. Among other things she said it was a last-ditch effort to destroy what remained of the capitalist system. I've long forgotten her actual words, but my supercharged memory and her position on the ecology movement would suggest something like this:

All of you out zere beyond ze age of twenty-nine should get down on your knees every time you zee a smokestack.

Ayn sweetheart, say you don't mean it. I know you can't mean what I just heard you say.

Pollution is ze symbol of human achievement. Wizzout technolochy and pollution, man would still be living in ze stone age.

Don't tell me fresh air and clean water are anti-life, Ayn. What kind of *rational double-think* is this?

Trees, rocks and mountains are nonproductive elements. Zey just sit zere occupying space, creating nozzing of zeir own.

But trees aren't very intelligent, Ayn. You can't expect them to produce anything.

We are locked in a life-and-death struggle between nature and tech- nolochy, between mindless rocks and trees and ze boundless genius of ze human mind.

Forget this either-or crap, baby. Nature *and* technology. We can have both. We'll *recycle.* You know? Pump the filth back into production so it doesn't get into people's lungs. Pollution is an act of aggression for Christ's sake!

We'll build factories on ze beaches and highways over ze oceans. We'll build a smokestack to ze moon.

Ayn, you sweet, lovable, crazy bitch! Don't tell me it usually *ends* with you too!

How the hell could you forge an alliance with anyone? Put three people on a desert island, and two of them will gang up on the third one and steal his loincloth. That was it for me. Politics was a fool's game. I decided to drop out for good … or so I thought. My retirement from politicking lasted three years, until I got a call I couldn't possibly anticipate three years later.

Early in 1974, I received a phone call from Roger Eisenberg, a member of the fledgling Free Libertarian Party of New York State.

"I'm calling to ask if you would consider running for Governor of New York this year as the Free Libertarian candidate," he said. His request was so incredible, it almost floored me.

"Ayn Rand put you up to this, didn't she?" I joked.

"No, she had nothing to do with it. The whole thing is my idea," he said, not getting the irony. After the publication of *It Usually Begins With Ayn Rand*, Rand had denounced me and other libertarians as right-wing hippies and moral degenerates.

"I'll tell you what," I said to Roger, trying to put him off. "Why don't you report back that I'd rather run for the Senate against Jacob Javits? He's a Republican incumbent who could be vulnerable right now in the wake of the Nixon disaster."

"We need a gubernatorial candidate to realize our goal of getting fifty thousand votes in the statewide election."

"So what's the big deal?"

"It has to be in the gubernatorial race to give the party official stature in the state, along with the Republicans, Democrats, Liberals, and Conservatives. It doesn't count if it's for the Senate."

"But why me, Roger? I'm anything but a politician."

"Well, Murray Rothbard says he won't do it, and Karl Hess is kind of crazy. He's gone off the deep end. You're one of the only other libertarians with any kind of a name. You've got books behind you."

Yes, three books that had sold a combined total of about 16,000 copies. At the time there were only about five libertarians in the *entire* country with any known accomplishments at all. There was Rand of course, who wanted nothing to do with us. Milton Friedman, the future Nobel Prize winner in economics, was equally famous, but he was more closely affiliated with the Republican Party than the independent libertarian movement. Rothbard and Hess had raised their own profiles during the past few years. And then there was me with three books in print.

"I don't know, Roger. This sounds kind of nuts to me. I need some time to think it over."

"Well, I wish you'd consider it. A bunch of us here at the FLP think you'd be great at the top of the ticket."

Fifty thousand votes seemed like nothing in a state with the population of New York. How hard could it be to rack up one percent of the vote, which is what it would come to? In my naïveté, it seemed to me that anyone who got his name on the ballot as an alternative to the two major party dorks was bound to get at least one percent of the votes cast. That magic number guaranteed a New York gubernatorial candidate's party a permanent place on the ballot. No more petition drives with hordes of eager, scruffy, idealistic volunteers manning tables in the streets to gather signatures. The last party to make it into the major leagues of New York politics was the Conservative Party in 1962. That made four recognized parties in the state. The Republicans occupied line A, and the Democrats were second with line B. Since the Conservatives had outpolled the Liberals in 1966, they took over line C and pushed the Liberals a notch down the ladder to line D. A dozen or more parties had made their bids for permanent ballot status over the decades, but none had come anywhere near the goal.

New York at the time was host to a staggering lineup of left-wing splinter groups, so exotic in their ideological underpinnings that they constituted the very, very, very, *very* neurotic fringe group in a lunatic asylum. There were the Socialist Labor, Socialist Worker, U.S. Labor, and Communist Parties, all of which accused the others of being front organizations financed by the CIA. They hated one another more than they detested their common enemies on the right. The finer points of their philosophical differences were lost on everyone to the right of Leon Trotsky.

Against the backdrop of this ideological quagmire, the Libertarian Party was cobbled into existence in 1972. The party's presidential candidate that year managed to come in not too far behind the Democratic candidate, George McGovern, in terms of electoral votes. McGovern had garnered all of seventeen electoral votes, and a Republican elector named Roger MacBride defected and cast his vote for the Libertarian. Toni Nathan, the Libertarian vice presidential candidate, went down in the record books as the first woman in U.S. history to receive an electoral vote.

This was an auspicious start for a brand new political party with less than 2,000 members on its roster. In 1973 the Free Libertarian Party of New York (the word *Free* was added to avoid confusion with the state's Liberal Party) ran another woman, Fran Youngstein, for mayor of New York City. In its New York political debut, the Free Libertarians succeeded in outpolling the four minor party candidates, all representing various shades of the oxygen-deprived left, with a bit more than 9,000 votes.

By December 1973, riding high in the wake of Fran's encouraging showing at the polls, a few Free Libertarian leaders began salivating at the prospect of getting the magic 50,000 votes in the 1974 gubernatorial race. Their brashness proved to be infectious and irrepressible. They had raised $18,000 for Fran's campaign, and it remained to be seen if they could come up with a significantly larger amount for a realistic statewide effort such a short time later. In addition, a long and grueling petition drive would be needed on the heels of one that had taxed the strength of party members almost to the breaking point. It took 7,500 signatures to put Fran on the ballot, and 20,000 had been collected to withstand any challenges. In the statewide race a minimum of 20,000 signatures would be necessary, which meant twice as many would need to be gathered to be on the safe side.

Could a tiny party already drained of volunteer energy and capital mount the kind of effort necessary to make a serious bid for major party status in New York? A few diehard optimists believed it could, and so began the search for a suitable gubernatorial candidate to spearhead the drive. The party elders had laid all this groundwork prior to my phone call from Roger Eisenberg at the end of December 1973. Determined not to take *no* for an answer, Eisenberg called me again a month later.

"I'm calling to see if you're interested."

"I'd rather run for the Senate. Can't you get anybody else to run for governor?"

"I told you already that the only other people we'd be interested in are either crazy or out to lunch," he said, his voice rising a notch higher than he intended it to.

Why the hell would I even consider running for public office in the first place? Governor? Senator? Without even a million-to-one chance of winning either race? Who needed the grief? Why was I tempted? Rage? Hostility against the status quo? An urge to stand up in public and make some waves? All that was there. But the more I thought about it, the more I realized how simple the answer really was: I just happened to be between books at the time. I was *bored* without any idea about what kind of book I wanted to write next, and without the high of an illicit, dangerous adventure to keep my adrenalin flowing.

Why run? Quite simply, it would give me something *exciting* to do, something worthwhile to keep me out of trouble while I plumbed the depths of my psyche for a new book idea. Or so I thought. I never entertained the possibility that even a minor party run for office would land me in *more* trouble than I had ever thought possible.

My biggest fear was of making a fool of myself. The gaggle of political parties jockeying for a ballot position in 1974 extended from the plethora of socialist splinter groups on the exotic left all the way over to the Courage Party, which was three steps to the right of Mussolini. The Courage Party was a kind of blue collar, head-cracking, law-and-order, white supremacist social club that disagreed with the libertarian positions (legalized marijuana and other drugs, elimination of victimless crime laws, less government, lower taxes) on everything but taxes. How could any minor party candidate raise his profile and make his voice heard in this raucous zoo? It would not take long to find out.

After talking to Roger Eisenberg the second time, I called Gary Greenberg, a lawyer who was one of the founders of the Libertarian Party, and told him I was thinking of running for the Senate.

"Personally, I'm happy," he said. "But it doesn't mean anything without a viable candidate for governor."

"Anybody else in mind?"

"We're talking to Thomas Szasz as well as you."

Szasz was a libertarian psychoanalyst who had written several books, including *The Myth of Mental Illness*, and he had been leading a virtual one-man campaign against the involuntary confinement of nonviolent patients in mental institutions.

"Excellent. He's well known and he's got a big following."

"I've got my fingers crossed," Gary said. "I'm surprised you want to run for anything, though. I figured that was the last thing you'd want to do."

"That's what I thought too," I said. "At least it wasn't even on my radar screen a few months ago."

One of the major concerns we had, assuming that we secured enough signatures in a petition drive, was a challenge to our right to be on the ballot from one of the major parties. This was more than mere paranoia, which has always been my first line of defense. Two years earlier Congressman Ed Koch, who was later elected Mayor of New York City, had successfully kept Gary Greenberg from running against him for Congress, and columnist Nat Hentoff had taken Koch to task for doing so in the *Village Voice*. Koch later admitted he was worried that Greenberg's civil liberties platform might have nibbled away his margin of victory in a close election.

On February 16, 2004, I received word that Szasz had decided not to run, dashing all hopes of a Szasz for Governor/Tuccille for Senator ticket. *Well, they'll find somebody else* I figured. Meanwhile, I would keep my options open.

The Republican incumbent, Malcolm Wilson, had replaced Nelson Rockefeller as Governor of New York in 1973, when Rockefeller agreed to become President Gerald Ford's vice president. Malcolm Wilson personified that grim, gray streak in the American soul like no one else since Richard Nixon. The Democratic hopeful was Hugh Carey, a party hack from the Madison Club in Brooklyn who resembled a side of beef. I talked to Murray Rothbard about him running for governor on the FLP ticket, with me running for the Senate, but Murray just laughed it off. "I'm an anarchist," he said. "What the hell kind of a platform does an anarchist run on?"

"How about 'Stamp Out Idiocracy!'"

"Idiocracy?"

"You know, government by idiots."

"No thanks. It's catchy though. I think you should run with it yourself."

"Thanks, Murray. But that's not much help."

17

Taking the Candidate for a Test Drive

Three weeks before the FLP convention in Manhattan, I discussed the possibility of running for the Senate with Jerry Cullen, a Republican Party operative who had been working in party politics for more than twenty years. Cullen was a shaggy man in his late forties with thick, graying hair, bushy sideburns, an unruly mustache, and a fondness for beer and scotch that instantly endeared him to me.

"I question the advisability of running on a broad libertarian platform," he said to me over drinks one evening. "You'll appeal to the kids with your stand on legalized pot, but how many of the little fuckers bother to vote in the first place? On the other hand, the middle class bread-and-butter issues are taxes, taxes, taxes, the economy, the economy, the economy—do I have a job or not?—and that's where you have to come on strong.

"Also, you'll have to figure out a way to make Javits attack you personally to get some visibility," Cullen continued. "I've known the man and watched him maneuver for years, and he's impossible to pin down on anything specific. He's a political chameleon with no redeeming principles whatsoever. He'll ignore you as long as he thinks he can get away with it."

"Does he have any weaknesses?"

"He has one tragic flaw you'd have to work on relentlessly: his ego. He can't stand to be made fun of. He married an attractive, cultured woman who's provided him with all his social contacts and smoothed down his rough edges. She introduced him to the theater, the opera, fine arts. Beneath his white tie and tails, though, lurks the soul of a gutter fighter. He's a working class shlub like Louie Lefkowitz, but with a shine on his shoes. The difference is, Lefkowitz likes what he is while Javits has been trying to become Nelson Rockefeller from the time he figured out how to tie his shoes."

Cullen's advice made sense if Javits and I would be competing on an even playing field. But why would a slick political operator like Javits pay any attention at all to a minor party provocateur unless he was in a tight race for reelection? The latest polls, however, indicated that Javits would beat any potential Democratic opponent in a landslide—even against the backdrop of the Watergate scandal mounting in Washington, which was putting most Republicans on the defensive.

The Free Libertarian convention took place from March 29 to March 31, 1974, at the Williams Club in New York City. My wife Marie and I went down together and were impressed by the party faithful. Previously we had grown accustomed to a libertarian "movement" peopled largely by disheveled, obese, unemployed neurotics dressed in black—black for the anarchist flag of no colors. The people at the Williams Club in late March looked *normal*. The men wore jackets and ties, and the women slacks and dresses. Dozens of party stalwarts were in attendance, laissez faire capitalists to the nth degree who actually had jobs and were otherwise gainfully employed. The convention was getting off to a promising start.

Marie was titillated by the prospects that lay ahead while simultaneously harboring doubts about my sanity. Simply put, what business did a young writer with a wife and two kids to support, and virtually no money in the bank, have even *thinking* about embarking on such a treacherous path? But I would not be deterred.

A key figure behind the scenes, who was one of the FLP's main financial supporters, was a wealthy young real estate developer named Howie Rich. Over the ensuing years Howie would go on to sponsor many libertarian political causes, including term limits for politicians, since he didn't think anyone should be allowed to hold public office for longer than six or eight years—hell, six or eight *months* if you pressed him hard on the subject. When Howie heard I wanted to run for the Senate instead of for governor, he pulled me aside and explained the facts of life to me.

"Here's the story," Howie said. On the surface he was low-key and not overtly threatening, but underneath he was made of steel and he had a computer for a brain. "Without a gubernatorial candidate, there's no campaign. You won't get on the ballot, there won't be any money or volunteers. But if you agree to run for governor, we'll do the whole bit: mailings, telephone lines, an organization, and a real effort to raise major bucks and make a run for it."

I took a deep breath and said, "Let me review my options. If I agree to run for governor, I've got a viable organization behind me. If I don't, I'm fucked."

Howie chuckled good-naturedly, truly magnanimous when tightening the screws in anticipation of a victory he knew was his. "Bottom line: that's it," he said.

"I know I'm crazy, but I'm not stupid," I replied. If you're going to cave in, you might as well do it with a smile on your face. "I guess I'm your man."

Andrea Millen—the future Mrs. Rich and the chairwoman of the FLP—had also urged me from the beginning to run for governor, not for the Senate. Another major player behind the scenes with deep pockets like Howie was Leland Schubert. Lee was a Lincolnesque, pipe-smoking capitalist who was forever spewing black lung disease through his pipe in sympathy with the benevolent tobacco magnates extolled by Ayn Rand. Howie and Lee cemented the deal by writing checks for substantial amounts to my campaign chest as soon as I had officially secured the nomination.

"I think you're crazy," Marie said on the way home after the convention. "How are you going to run for political office and hold on to your job at the same time?"

"It's only a third party effort," I said. "I won't be out campaigning fulltime like a major-party candidate. A few TV and radio spots, some newspaper interviews, that's all it'll be." The company I worked for was headquartered in Lincoln, Nebraska, and I ran an office for them close to home with little supervision from the main office. I convinced myself that I would be able to organize my time without anyone finding out what I was doing.

"You're going to get yourself fired."

I didn't realize at the time just how prophetic that statement would turn out to be.

I suddenly felt as though I were living in the middle of a Marx Brothers comedy crossed with a farce starring W. C. Fields.

On a warm day in early April, the leaders of the FLP decided to take their gubernatorial candidate out for a "test drive," as it were. My idea of campaigning was to go on radio and television and deliver the libertarian message to lobotomized human couch potatoes perched on the edge of their sofas with pillow-sized bags of chips and five-gallon vats of Coke. I never realized I would actually have to pound the pavement and shake hands with the great unwashed multitudes out there.

Javits was a pro at it. He was capable of oiling his way through a crowd with a plastic smile *stitched* on his face, nodding at everyone he encountered and saying nothing to offend anyone. Hugh Carey and Malcolm Wilson could do it; they had been trained for it all their lives. But the very thought of campaigning in person among the voters was terrifying for me.

My campaign advisers led me on a tour of Greenwich Village, with an entourage of about twenty FLP volunteers trailing behind. This should be easy. Greenwich Village was full of hippies and stoned-out radicals. All I had to do was talk about legalizing marijuana and they'll love me. Right? Wrong.

Our first stop was in a small park on the Avenue of the Americas, occupied by a platoon of nursing home residents. The entire park was a sea of white heads that looked like giant cotton candy cones. Their faces were giant prunes ravaged by decades of exposure to the blistering sun. Half of them were sleeping when we entered the enclave. I wanted to let them rest in peace and wander off to a more convivial assemblage, when suddenly Lee Schubert called out, "Meet Jerry Tuccille, the Free Libertarian candidate for Governor of New York!"

Damn it, he woke them up. Thirty pairs of hostile eyes skewered me. They hated me before I so much as said a word. They grabbed their canes as though to defend themselves against an assault, and I immediately stepped back out of striking distance. What the hell was I supposed to do now?

"Say something nice," Marie suggested, squeezing my hand.

I reached out and shook hands with the first one on the bench. "Hi, I'm Jerry Tuccille, the—"

"What are you going to do for us?" The eighty-year-old crone asked without a hint of a smile.

"I er, um, I want to, um, turn New York State into a Free Zone. No more taxes, no more laws against—"

"No more taxes? Who's going to pay for our Social Security benefits?" she barked.

"Well, actually, I, um, have a plan to privatize Social Security and—"

"You're like all the rest of the politicians. We worked hard all our lives, and now you want to take away our benefits."

"She doesn't *pay* taxes anymore," Marie whispered. "And you're running for Governor of New York not the U.S. Senate. Talk about *state* issues."

"Drugs should be legalized," I said, the beginning of a sneer curling my upper lip.

"Ahh!" the crone shrieked as though I had just cold-cocked her between the eyes.

"Brain rot has already set in," one of the volunteers said to Marie, who began to giggle helplessly.

"All victimless crimes—drugs, prostitution, gambling, pornography—should be decriminalized!" I shouted at the old woman on the bench.

"Oh my God, Jerry's snarling at the voters," Lee Schubert said to Marie. "Can't you *do* anything with him?"

"He's always like that when people disagree with him," said Marie.

"Let's get the hell out of here!" said Andrea. "They're *all* getting agitated now."

"Hey, this is great!" one of the volunteers yelled out from behind me. "Our candidate's telling it like it is."

"He's right on," said another. "He just needs a little work. Smooth down the rough edges a bit, that's all."

By the time we got back to party headquarters I was hyperventilating. Walking the streets and shaking hands with strangers was one of the most horrifying things I had ever done—including such life-threatening activities as skydiving and rappelling down the side of a cliff with nothing but a pair of thick gloves and a harness around my waist.

"Why can't I just go on television?" I asked Howie Rich.

"Television costs money. We'll do that later."

Well, sure, if I didn't have a nervous breakdown beforehand. It was too late to back out now. The FLP newsletter had already trumpeted the results of the convention in a headline: TUCCILLE FOR GOVERNOR! STAMP OUT IDIOCRACY! In addition to me at the top of the ticket, we had a full slate of candidates for U.S. Senate and various state and local offices. I was committed whether I liked it or not.

It didn't take me long to realize that the candidate—at least one who was not raising his own money—was the least powerful person in a campaign. The major power struggles took place behind the scenes: campaign strategy, fund-raising activities, scheduling, even ideological emphasis. The candidate was told only as much as he needed to know to get the job done.

I felt like a wind-up doll. *Speak, candidate, speak! Give them speech number five tonight.*

"I feel like Mongo in 'Blazing Saddles,'" I complained to Gary Greenberg, referring to the oafish character played by former football star, Alex Karras. "Remember his line? 'Mongo is only a pawn in the game of life.' My ego's being crushed."

"Don't worry," Gary laughed maliciously. "We've got your ego on tape."

Encouragingly, volunteers trekked in by the dozens, droves and droves of them from all over the country. There were young hippies willing to sleep on the floor in somebody's apartment and lick stamps during the day. There were buttoned-down, middle-class business types anxious to staff tables on street corners and collect signatures.

And then there was the murderer.

A demented young fellow named Charles Yukl, who had been working on our petition drive, was arrested for murdering an aspiring actress named Karin Schlegel. Yukl had been released from prison in 1973 after serving five years of a seven-to-fifteen-year sentence for a previous murder, just in time to join the FLP for Fran Youngstein's mayoral race. Youngstein was a gorgeous brunette who had been hounded by shoe fetishists and other stalkers throughout her campaign, but Yukl—unknown to everyone in the party—was by far the most dangerous of them all. Now here he was in the middle of my campaign.

"That's it," I said to Greenberg, my innate paranoia at full boil. "I'm too exposed. I'm fair game for any lunatic."

"Relax. He seemed to like you."

"We need to screen people better. Do some sort of a quality check. Make them fill out an application."

"We need all the warm bodies we can get. Besides, look at the bright side."

"What bright side?"

"Yukl collected thirty signatures before they carried him away."

On a warm Sunday morning the party leaders dragged me out to a school in Forest Hills, Queens, to speak at a rally protesting high-rise, low-rent projects in the neighborhood. The City of New York had already built three structures against the will of the community, and the local citizens wanted the new building earmarked for senior citizens only. No welfare recipients whatsoever, with all their drug-related crimes. This was a no-brainer for us since the FLP was opposed to publicly financed housing for any purpose. All I had to do was oppose the project on principle and everyone would love me. Right? Wrong.

All the political bigwigs were supposed to be there: Mayor Abe Beame, Congressman Mario Biaggi, Senator James Buckley, Queens Borough President Donald Manes who would try to commit suicide years later by stabbing himself in the chest with a steak knife, and others. But nobody showed up except me and a gaggle of enraged Orthodox rabbis who were spoiling for a fight. One of them was up on the podium screaming when I arrived. He was positively horrific with his long black coat, long black beard, and wide-brimmed black hat. He quoted from the Torah and equated the construction of low-income projects in his neighborhood with the Roman destruction of Jerusalem and the temple in 70 A.D.

"It's nothing less than genocide!" he bellowed. "It's an assault on American Jewry. Where's Abe Beame today? I'll tell you where he is. He's up in Harlem with his real friends! He's a traitor to his own people!"

Uh oh. I didn't want any part of this. New York City blacks and Orthodox Jews had been at one another's throats since the 1960s, and here I was in the middle of their squabble. Now I understood why the other candidates had skipped this event. I was the only one stupid enough to show up. "Let's get the hell out of here," I started to say, when Lee Schubert suddenly called out, "Meet Jerry Tuccille, the Free Libertarian candidate for Governor of New York."

"Lee, are you crazy? You're going to get me killed."

"Who are you?" The head rabbi skewered me with his coal black eyes. "Which side are you on?" he demanded. "Are you with us or *them*?"

Now what was I supposed to say? I couldn't come out in favor of public housing for the elderly any more than for welfare cases since I was opposed to the whole concept of public projects in the first place. I didn't want to alienate this man, but I didn't want to come down too solidly in his corner either. Already I could see tomorrow's headlines:

FLP GUBERNATORIAL CANDIDATE SIDES WITH RABID RAC-
IST RABBIS

"Do you join us in our demand for housing for the elderly?"

"Not exactly. Actually, I'm opposed to—"

"Not exactly!" the rabbi shrieked. "Not exactly means *no*. It means you're in favor of genocide, in favor of crimes against the Jewish people, in favor of bringing in more crime and hatred into our community, in favor of launching a new *Diaspora*!"

"I'm opposed to public housing for low-income groups," I fought back gamely.

"So you're with us?"

"I'm also opposed to public housing for the elderly."

"So you're against us?"

"I've got a different approach to the entire question."

"There is no middle way!" the rabbi yelled, pointing at me accusingly. "There can be no talk of compromise. Compromise is genocide. It is tantamount to a declaration of war on our people, on our culture, on our whole way of life!"

There was no way to win this debate. Whatever I said, I was either a racist or an anti-Semite. I was caught up in a Talmudic conundrum. "Get me out of here now," I hissed at Lee, "before this man calls down the wrath of God on my head. I'm superstitious enough as it is."

The FLP team agreed that a tactical retreat was the best course after all. When we got back to party headquarters I pleaded with Howie once again, "Why can't I just go on television and deliver the message?"

"Don't worry. The money's starting to come in. Just be patient a few more weeks, OK?"

"I'm begging you, Howie. Just get me off the fucking street."

18

Marvin the Exterminator Loves Porn

On the way back to White Plains Marie and I passed my father Salvatore's house on East Tremont Avenue in the Bronx. I looked up at the wall on the side of his building and received another shock that chilled me to the bones. Stretched across the brick wall was a banner with huge black letters that read:

MARVIN THE EXTERMINATOR
VOTE TUCCILLE FOR GOVERNOR OF NEW YORK

"What's that all about?" asked Marie.

"Fucked if I know." I was truly stunned by what we were looking at.

A pest exterminator named Marvin Mendelsohn rented the storefront on the street level of Salvatore's house in the Bronx and also had advertising rights on the side of Salvatore's building.

"Why is Marvin promoting your campaign?" Marie persisted.

"I have no idea. I'll have to talk to my father about it tomorrow and see what's going on."

"It looks horrible," said Marie. "It looks as though you're being endorsed by a hit man for the mob."

The next day I visited Salvatore at my aunt's apartment in Parkchester, where he was recuperating after surgery. They spent every waking moment sitting around the kitchen table, drinking coffee and munching on something. Evidently neither of them ever left the apartment to take a walk or go for a drive to breathe some fresh air. Salvatore was notorious for getting in his car to drive half a block to buy a pack of cigarettes, and Molly hadn't walked more than ten steps to the refrigerator since she was twelve years old.

"Look who's here," Molly said, a big smile on her face as she opened the door. "What a nice surprise."

"My son the governor," Salvatore said to someone else in the kitchen whom I couldn't see clearly from the doorway.

"We were just having some pastry from Arthur Avenue," said Molly. "Georgie brought it over."

I could see my cousin Georgie sitting at the table next to Salvatore when I entered the kitchen. On the table in front of them was a huge platter of Italian pastries. Salvatore and Georgie were drinking espresso with a bottle of anisette on the table between them.

"How's the governor today?" asked Salvatore.

"Couldn't be better."

"Hey, cuz," said Georgie.

"Make yourself comfortable, sugar," said Molly. "Have a canoli, some sfogliatell. Arthur Avenue makes the best."

"Don't mind if I do." I took a seat at the table and decided to make myself at home. Molly had succeeded in fattening Salvatore back up to his pre-hospital weight, complete with the heavy paunch he had sported for most of my adult life. The sweet, intoxicating aroma of the Italian delicacies and strong espresso filled the kitchen, whetting my appetite. Georgie eyed me warily from the corner of his eye and pushed the bottle of anisette toward me after I poured myself a cup of coffee. He made a few comments about his cousin the next governor and laughed a bit too loudly at nothing in particular. I waited a few moments and then said to Salvatore, "I drove by your place yesterday and saw Marvin's sign. Did you know he put a sign up there endorsing my campaign?"

"Oh?" He looked genuinely surprised.

"You didn't know about it?"

"He didn't say nothin to me."

"But … why would he do it then?"

Georgie laughed. He evidently knew something I didn't know.

I looked at Salvatore who just shrugged his shoulders and smiled back at Georgie.

"Marvin runs an exterminating business, right?" I asked both of them.

"Among other things," Salvatore said, loosening up a bit more.

"Among *what* other things?"

"Marvin's a pervert," said Georgie. "He runs porn outta the back a the store."

"Porgnography?"

"You know, beaver shots, tits an ass an a lot more. He makes more money sellin that shit to teenage boys in Throgs Neck than he does killin cock-a-roaches." Georgie pronounced the last word as though it had three syllables.

"Jesus, Dad!" I said to Salvatore. "You found yourself another creep for a tenant?"

"He pays higher rent," said Salvatore. "You're like your mother for chrissakes. You think I'm made outta money. I'm an old man on a fixed income. I need the extra cash."

"I give up. You're unbelievable. But I still don't get it. Why would he put up a sign telling people to vote for me?"

"You're askin me? You're the one who's in favor a legalizin that shit. Maybe Marvin thinks you'll call the cops off his ass when you're the next Governor of New York State."

The three of them laughed uproariously, and all I could do was stare back at them in silence. It hardly seemed worth the effort to point out that decriminalizing an activity didn't mean you were in favor of it, and certainly not when it came to underage children. People interpreted things to suit themselves, and there was little you could do to change their perceptions.

"Have another canoli," said Georgie. "You need to keep your strength up on the campaign trail. Tell him, Sal."

"My son the governor," said Salvatore. "He thinks I'm made outta money, just like his mother did."

Howie Rich decided it was time to ramp up our campaign effort. He called a meeting in Gary Greenberg's apartment for July 1 to announce the formation of a new campaign team. "Laura Wertheimer will be your campaign manager," Howie said. "She's a real pro. She worked with F. Clifton White on the Goldwater campaign and really knows what she's doing."

(In one of life's little ironies, Clif White, who orchestrated the Goldwater movement in 1964, called me up in 1991 and asked me to coauthor his political memoir, *Politics As a Noble Calling*, which was published in 1995, six months after Clif died. I had not met him personally until I worked with him on his book.)

"Someone else will be at my apartment too," said Gary Greenberg.

"Who?"

"It's a secret. We can't mention his name."

"Why is it a secret?"

"He was way high up in CREEP, Committee to Re-elect the President, Nixon's reelection committee. He was so important he was almost arrested with G. Gordon Liddy and the others."

"That's reassuring. What does he want with us?"

"He's a close friend of Laura Wertheimer. She says he's really a closet libertarian."

"A closet libertarian who worked for Nixon?"

"Nobody's perfect. Anyway, this guy's a genius and he's agreed to coach Laura as a personal favor, free of charge."

"I can't wait to meet him."

Thirty people were crowded into Gary's apartment by the time I arrived. Laura seemed pleasant enough, and I figured we could get along just fine. Then she guided me toward a man sitting deep in shadow in the corner of the room.

"Meet Art Finkelstein," she said.

Finkelstein looked like an unmade bed. His hair hadn't been combed in a month and he had his stockinged feet tucked under his buttocks like a rumpled Buddha. He stared at me without blinking, as though he were sizing up a germ specimen under a microscope. It wasn't until years later that I learned of Finkelstein's strange, reclusive behavior even as he directed some of the most important Republican campaigns in recent history. Every now and then someone would report a Finkelstein sighting, but no one could actually swear to having seen him in the flesh in several years. He was like Christ after the crucifixion, as rumors of his disembodied appearances made the rounds for some months afterward. Finkelstein was the Republican Party equivalent of Karl Rove at the time—except that Rove didn't mind being seen in broad daylight.

"You're the candidate?" he asked me.

"That's me."

"Don't say anything," he said.

"I beg your pardon."

"During the campaign, I mean. The public is stupid, so your campaign strategy should be to say nothing of substance."

"You're kidding."

"I'm serious. Just appear in public … with a suit and tie." He pointedly took in my turtle-neck sweater and safari jacket. "If anyone asks what you want to accomplish as governor, say, 'Let's send them a message they can't ignore.'"

"That's it? Let's send them a message they can't ignore."

"That's perfect."

"That's going to get us fifty thousand votes? Suppose people ask me what libertarians believe in?"

"Tell them to write to campaign headquarters for details if they want to know what the message is."

"I can't believe this."

"Don't confuse the voters. Most of them are imbeciles. Just remember to attack your opponents every opportunity you can, smile at the camera, and tell everyone, 'I'm running to send them a message they can't ignore!'"

"I can't believe that's going to translate into fifty thousand votes."

"*Nothing* you say will get you fifty thousand votes. If you want to get fifty thousand votes, you have to raise three hundred thousand dollars."

"How come?"

"It costs six dollars a vote. It doesn't matter what you say or do, whether you're the smartest or most articulate candidate out there. It still costs six dollars a vote. If you take a position on *any* issue, roughly half of the voters will agree with you and the other half will hate you. The votes you lose just cancel out the votes you get."

For this kind of advice mainstream politicians paid Finkelstein a fortune. And it worked! The man had an enviable track record. After the election in November I divided the amount of money we raised by my vote total, and it worked out to *six dollars a vote*. Art Finkelstein was a diabolical genius. At the time of our first meeting, however, I thought he was the most cynical person I had ever met. I had decided to make this run to stand on principle—a commodity sorely lacking in politics—and I was not about to be swayed.

19

Wonder Woman Kicks Butt

It didn't take long for the FLP leaders to start referring to Laura Werthe-imer, my campaign manager, as Wonder Woman. A tall, leggy, statu-esque redhead, Laura took charge immediately. "First we need a family portrait," she said. "You, Marie, the two kids, and a pet."

"A pet?"

"I'll lend you my Doberman Pincher if you don't have one. Better yet, we can rent a Collie. Collies are less menacing."

"We have a cat."

"A dog would be better, but a cat will do."

Then she printed up thousands of posters with our campaign slogan, "Send them a message they can't ignore: 50,000 votes!"

"That sounds trite," I complained.

"It has a nice Italian ring to it." This was supposed to be the Year of the Italians, according to her, after the success of *The Godfather*. That assessment turned out to be premature; Mario Cuomo would stumble around for a few more years before he finally got elected Governor of New York.

Next she assigned jobs to everyone. A fellow named David Grant would handle public relations. Gary Greenberg got up early at her behest for meetings with campaign contributors. "She's spending money faster than I can bring it in," he lamented.

"Set your alarm earlier, Gary. Mug people if you have to."

Laura set up an org chart with thirty different areas of responsibility covering press relations, scheduling, youth and campus advance work, position paper communications, and other aspects of the operation throughout the various counties and regions of the state.

"Did you leave anything out?" I asked Laura when I reviewed her chart.

"We'll make up positions if we have to," she said, impervious to my sarcasm. "The idea is to find something to do for everyone who wants to get involved."

Then Laura pulled off her biggest coup of all when she convinced Roger MacBride to sign on as an aerial chauffeur.

"He's flying up from Virginia in his private plane to take you around the state."

"How did you convince him to do that?"

"He wants to run for president in 1976." Her cynical smile said it all; he would need all the help he could get to secure the nomination.

MacBride was the Republican Party elector who had cast his vote for the Libertarian candidate in the 1972 presidential election and was an outcast in his own party as a result. He was a portly man with thick glasses that made his eyes look as though they were peering at you from under water. He lived on an estate in rural Virginia and, most important, was wealthy enough to fund a credible third party run for the presidency if he was able to get the nomination.

Our first road trip outside the city was a tour of upstate New York on July 25. Once again I pleaded with Howie and the other financiers to just let me go on television. "I can't take any more nursing home voters on park benches."

"Don't worry. We'll do the media stuff when you get back."

"I can't handle any more violent rabbis either."

"There aren't any north of the Bronx."

"If I have to go out in public again, let's stick to college campuses. Kids love it when I talk about legalizing marijuana."

"We're going there too, but you have to talk to grownups also. The parents are the ones who vote."

"Yeah, but they won't vote for me when they hear what I'm saying to their kids."

A group of us met Roger MacBride early in the morning at Westchester County Airport north of White Plains. Roger was affable and encouraging, although his face was so beet red from high blood pressure that I feared for his life—and mine—as I boarded his airplane. Our first stop was Poughkeepsie where the local radio, television, and newspapers reporters were waiting for us as we landed. We posed for pictures with the local FLP Congressional candidate, and then I made a terrible blunder: I actually started to talk about issues we believed in.

"We want to turn New York State into a Free Zone," I said to a reporter from the *Poughkeepsie Journal*. "We want to roll back taxes step-by-step and abolish all laws on the books against victimless crimes, including gambling, pornography, prostitution, and drugs."

"Oh my God! What's our candidate saying?" asked an FLP volunteer off to the side.

"He's telling it like it is," answered another.

"He's not supposed to say anything except 'Let's send them a message they can't ignore.' Somebody's got to stop him before he gives away the whole platform."

It was too late; the damage was done. The next day the newspapers reported that libertarians wanted to do away with taxes and empty the jails of pornographers and drug addicts. It was clearly a case of diarrhea of the mouth—*my* mouth. I knew Laura and Art were going to be terribly annoyed, but it was too late to do anything about that now.

"You told them what the message is," Laura scolded me with a scowl.

"Why can't I do that?"

"Art told you why. You'll just confuse people and get them upset. Most of the people who agree with us don't bother to vote anyway."

"Well, damn it—"

"If they really want to know what the message is, they can write to campaign headquarters and ask about it."

We were up the next morning at five o'clock to fly to towns I never knew existed. Plattsburgh, Ogdensburgh, Watertown. They were so far north I was afraid I might get a nosebleed on the way. One Manhattanite I knew told me that he got nosebleeds every time he traveled north of 96th Street in New York City. Plattsburgh would have given him the bends.

The towns rushed by like a blur beneath us, with Roger at the controls of his flying station wagon—a twin-engine Aztec. Ithaca, Rochester, Jamestown. We did eight interviews in three different cities *before* breakfast on July 28. When we landed in Buffalo a bunch of FLP volunteers were waiting for us. They all jumped into various cars and went off to lunch—everyone, that is, except Roger and me. They stranded us. They forgot the fucking candidate and his aerial chauffeur. This was outrageous.

"To hell with them," Roger said. "Let's take a cab and have our *own* lunch." Which is exactly what we did.

With the two of us seated in a roadhouse not too far from the airport, Roger said, "I vote we start with an extra dry martini." He echoed my sentiments exactly, but I was a bit disconcerted with the knowledge that we had a whole afternoon of campaigning ahead of us.

Roger liked to eat and drink in style, as I would learn during the ensuing months of the campaign. Whenever we went out to a Chinese restaurant with a group in New York City, Roger insisted on having his own dish instead of sharing all the entrees with everyone else. His culinary attitudes gave him away as a country squire from Virginia.

Halfway through his first martini, Roger's face took on a royal purple flush as his blood pressure soared into the ionosphere. Whenever we checked into a hotel at the end of a long day on the stump, the first thing Roger did was crank up the air conditioning to full blast. He was not comfortable until ice began to form on the insides of the windows. Roger was unmarried at the time, the single father of a young girl, but I did not see who would be able to cohabitate with him other than a penguin. If his first wife hadn't divorced him, she would most likely have died of pneumonia. I only hoped he lived long enough to secure the Libertarian Party presidential nod in 1976, if that's what he wanted.

By the time the others caught up with us I was half in the bag myself. "Cancel all my afternoon interviews," I felt like telling them. "The candidate's not responsible for anything he says this afternoon."

No such luck. The show went on as planned, and once again I gave away our entire platform without skipping a beat. Laura and Art were definitely going to be in a monstrous snit by the time we headed back to the Big Apple.

Wonder Woman was optimistic about the prospect of getting conservative leader, William F. Buckley, Jr., to endorse my candidacy.

"You're a miracle worker if you can pull that off," I said to her. In 1971 I had attacked Buckley in a *New York Times* Op Ed piece about his support for the war in Vietnam, and since then he frothed at the mouth whenever my name was mentioned.

"I have a call in to him," said Laura. "We'll know in a few days."

The rumor that Buckley might support our campaign buzzed around headquarters for the next week. Not that he was such an intrepid campaigner himself. His New York City mayoralty bid a few years earlier was less than a smashing success. Buckley himself was moved to declare, before the vote was in, that if he were elected he would demand a recount. Still, he was a right-wing superstar, the only conservative at the time who could string three sentences together worthy of publication. Alas, not even Wonder Woman could pull that one off. Buckley's reply was short and to the point when it arrived.

"I do not think that anyone much cares about Mr. Tuccille's candidacy," he wrote. That was it: one sentence.

Aside from a Buckley endorsement, the major concern we had as the summer of 1974 wore on was getting the major media to pay attention to our platform. The small dailies and local radio and television stations in upstate New York were not a problem; they all carried stories on our campaign every time we visited, happy to have *something* to cover other than the latest Rotary Club meeting. But cracking the Big Apple was difficult, if not impossible. Unless you were covered by the major networks, as well as the *New York Times*, *New York Post*, and *Daily News*, you were in political No Man's Land. You might as well have been running for chief apparatchik of Siberia. Milton Friedman's son David had been writing position papers for us on every issue conceivable, to no avail. We could have been launching them into space for all the attention they garnered on Planet Earth. Playing it straight with the issues was clearly not working for us. We needed an event, a *cause celebre*, a *stunt* to put us on the map.

The first media breakthrough occurred in September in a manner no one could have foreseen—or welcomed. Albert Ellis, a well-known psychoanalyst at the time, had received a letter, which he shared with us, containing a death threat. Some screwball who lived on West End Avenue in Manhattan had written to Ellis, threatening to shoot him and Free Libertarian gubernatorial candidate, Yours Truly. Another psychopath was on the loose. One murderer was bad enough, but now we had two crossing my path in the space of a few weeks. *Stop the campaign! I want to get off.* But where I saw danger, Wonder Woman saw opportunity.

"We'll go right to the press with this," she said.

"You want to publicize it?" I said. "Suppose he gives somebody else the same idea?"

All she could think about was a headline. Free publicity! "It could be good for a thousand votes," she said. "Only forty-nine thousand to go. We'll contact the FBI as well. The FBI doesn't do anything without the cameras rolling to capture their derring-do for posterity."

She made her call, and within twenty-four hours the *Daily News* carried the headline she was looking for:

FREE LIBERTARIAN GUBERNATORIAL CANDIDATE TUC-CILLE THREATED WITH ASSASSINATION
FBI Called In

As it turned out, incredibly enough, there was little the FBI could do about the situation except to keep the letter writer, who was actually demented enough to sign his name and give his address, under surveillance for a week or two.

"What he did is not illegal unless he comes after you," one of the FBI agents explained to us. "This guy's got a history of institutionalized psychosis. He's forty-seven years old and he lives by himself. A complete loner. Don't worry though. He's been threatening people for years and he's never taken action against any of them."

"How long will you keep him under surveillance?"

"A week. Maybe two. Don't think we're taking it lightly. We're not. But we can't spare the resources to stake him out longer than that."

The only people who were delighted about the situation were Wonder Woman and the man from CREEP. "We're on a roll," she said. "We've got to come up with some stunts now that you're in the headlines."

"Stunts?"

"Yes. Stunts designed to deliver our message in a way that captures the public's imagination."

So it came to pass that we sent out a press release announcing that I would be "fishing for votes" on Lexington Avenue, in front of the building where President Chester A. Arthur had been sworn into office ninety-three years earlier. On September 20 a group of us showed up at 123 Lexington Avenue near 28th Street to honor Arthur, a president who was famous for spending more time fishing than he did governing the country. No issue or cause was too great to be ignored, as far as Arthur was concerned.

I felt more than slightly foolish, still dressed in a safari jacket despite Wonder Woman's attempts to dress me up, sideburns down to the bottom of my earlobes, holding a fishing pole with a four-and-a-half pound fish dangling from the end of the line. Campaign volunteers paraded up and down Lexington with signs that read, "Lower Taxes, Less Bureaucracy," "Tuccille, the Un-politician for Governor," "Send Them a Message They Can't Ignore: 50,000 Votes," and "Politicians, Go Jump in a Lake." I stood stupidly in their midst with the rotting fish swinging back and forth, wondering what type of lunacy had brought me to this sorry state of affairs. Wonder Woman stalked pedestrians on the sidewalk, practically tackling them as they tried to scoot by, pushing them in my direction.

"Say something pleasant," said Marie as a few people approached.

"I'm, um, fishing for votes. I want to lower your taxes and legalize free enterprise in New York State."

"You've got to do better than that," Marie said as she watched them scurry away in fear that I might assault them.

Finally, the media arrived.

"They're coming!" Wonder Woman shrieked.

Three television vans braked to a stop almost simultaneously: ABC, NBC, CBS. The three big networks had come to our party. So did Leslie Maitland, a reporter from the *New York Times*, with a photographer at her elbow. Suddenly we had a crowd around us, attracted to the presence of the media like flies to a putrefying peach on the sidewalk. Maitland, an attractive young woman with dark hair and flashing brown eyes, strode up beside me already scribbling in her notebook. I gave her the sound bites she was looking for, a tidbit about how the country would be better off if politicians went fishing instead of going to work, and an offer to give my fish as a gift to Democratic candidate Hugh Carey if he embraced the fishing line and abandoned the party line. But just as things seemed to be going smoothly, a well-dressed businessman who had been listening in said he agreed with almost everything I said, but added that he would probably vote for Carey anyway.

"I can't stand Malcolm Wilson, Rockefeller's flunky, and I don't want to waste my vote," he said.

Maitland, of course, quoted the gentleman the next day in her generally upbeat article, effectively neutralizing whatever appeal I might have had for independent voters.

By this time the fish was beginning to smell a trifle gamy, driving some of the onlookers away holding their noses. Maitland crinkled her own nose and suggested we get rid of it.

"Where?" asked some elderly woman. "It's illegal to just throw away a dead fish in a city trash can."

"What else am I supposed to do with it?" I said. "The fish is from the Hudson River, which is half mercury anyway."

"You can't throw mercury away either," the woman said, scowling. "You need a special toxic waste permit. You libertarians don't care anything about the environment."

"It's the same old story," said another bystander. "Everyone wants to get rid of toxic waste, but no one wants it buried in their neighborhood."

That was it for me. I had had enough campaigning for one day. Pandering for votes was starting to get tedious. Thomas Jefferson had the right idea: just let it be known that you are available, and if the people want you badly enough they will vote for you. He refused to demean himself by actively campaigning for political office. The man from CREEP also made sense despite my original skepticism: raise as much money as you can, smile inanely, say nothing to offend anyone, and spare yourself a lot of grief.

The television crews packed up and got ready to leave, and the crowd dispersed. Our stunt was over. We had gotten what we came for, free publicity, but I seriously doubted that I had won a lot of votes with our day in the limelight.

20

Stuntism Runs Amok

Wonder Woman summoned Roger MacBride from Virginia for another tour through upstate New York. "We're rolling now," she said. "We've got the debates lined up, which will get you good exposure on television across the state, and I've got plans for a few more stunts."

The next few weeks leading up to the election went by in a blur. Roger and I landed at the airport in Buffalo on a Sunday morning at the end of September. The local libertarians had organized a motorcade through the downtown area on the way to the campus of Buffalo State College. This time I was accompanied by Thomas Poster, a reporter for the *Daily News* who laughed uproariously as, once again, I was left behind by my entourage. Poster's article the next day said it all:

> Jerome Tuccille went to Buffalo this week to push his campaign as the Free Libertarian candidate for governor. A motorcade was set up and Tuccille got into the last car in line, shouting "Let's go!" to the woman driver. The woman, looking shocked, shouted back, "Get the hell out of my car or I'll call the police!" Tuccille, realizing the car was not part of the motorcade, explained quickly that he was running for governor.

> "When she had that explanation the woman started screaming. Tuccille leaped from the car and raced to a safe place until others in the motorcade realized that the head of the ticket was not among them and returned.

The only thing Porter left out was that there was a red brick mental institution along the route where I had jumped into her car, and the startled woman was surely convinced that I had just escaped from it.

Back in New York City on September 26, Wonder Woman rented a hotdog stand for forty dollars in a stunt she devised to protest the city's recent eight percent sales tax on meals under a dollar. We set up shop near City Hall on the corner of Broadway and Murray Street, where I took my place at the wagon and started to give frankfurters away with their ends nipped off to symbolize the inflationary impact of the "hotdog" tax. As though by magic, word spread quickly that someone was giving away free food. Within minutes a swarm of hungry citizens poured into the streets from blocks away to get their fair share of the circumcised hotdogs. A group of FLP volunteers paraded around the wagon with signs reading, "Repeal the Tax!," "Frankly We Don't Relish the Idea of a Hotdog Tax!," "The Hotdog Tax Just Ain't Kosher!," and similar witticisms.

Once again the media showed up en masse. The formula was working: dream up a stunt, send out press releases, and watch the TV camera crews and print reporters trip over one another in a race to get the story first. What they got, however, was a story we had not anticipated. A *real* hotdog vendor whose territory we had invaded, a seventy-three-year-old Bulgarian-born Greek named Constantine Macatsoris, charged up to me and screamed in broken English, "If you give a them away for free I'm a not gonna sell nothink all day!" We had not planned on being sandbagged by a hard-working entrepreneur whose livelihood we were threatening, even if only for an hour or so.

The media captured the confrontation well in imaginative, craftily worded headlines:

HOTDOG HASSLE IS MUSTERED UP
JERRY TUCCILLE TRIES TO CUT POLITICAL MUSTARD WITH
FRANK PROTEST AT CITY HALL

The *Long Island Press* probably cost me more votes than I ever hoped to win with the following description of the moment:

> His arms flailing and apron flapping, Macatsoris vigorously complained about the competition. Leaving the cart in the custody of his press agent, Tuccille retreated into City Hall telling reporters, "Our little demonstration is not going to cut into his income."

I do believe the reporter made that quote up. The story in the *Daily News* merely stated that I ignored the Greek Bulgarian when I realized that I had lost his vote forever. In truth the entire episode remains a blur to me. All I remember is that I couldn't wait for my hotdogs to run out so I could get the hell off the streets before I completely humiliated myself.

A few days later I was back touring through upstate New York, with Roger MacBride at the controls of his flying station wagon. Disaster struck while we were still airborne, and Marie broke the news to me when I called her from the airport outside Albany. "I knew this was going to happen," she said.

"You knew *what* was going to happen?"

"You lost your job. Your boss came in from Nebraska and saw one of your campaign posters on a telephone poll. He called here and asked me what was going on."

"It was inevitable," I said.

"He sounded genuinely pissed off, as he had a right to be. He said he'd send you your severance check in the mail. He's already hired a replacement for you."

"This was supposed to be a part-time lark," I said. "I didn't realize it would grow into a fulltime effort."

"I knew I shouldn't have agreed to go along with this. What are we going to do now? That's what I'd like to know," said Marie.

"What can I do?"

"You have to quit the campaign and get another job."

"I can't do that. I'm committed to see this through. Do you know how many people have contributed money and volunteered their time and services? How can I just walk away from it?"

"What about us, me and the kids? We have no money. How are we going to pay our bills?"

"Something will turn up." I knew that sounded feeble, but it was the best I could come up with at the moment.

"I'm very upset about this," she said. "I'll have to quit college and get a fulltime job and Christine's only five."

"I'm upset about it too." Marie had been working part-time and had returned to college to get her degree, but now she would need a fulltime job. I felt awful about the situation. "Look, the campaign will be over in a few weeks and we'll work things out then. We'll be fine, you'll see."

There was silence on the end of the line.

"I love you," I said.

Marie grunted. "I'm so sick with worry now I can't think straight," she said, and then she hung up.

Roger was waiting for me when I got off the phone.

"Everything all right at home?" he asked.

"Everything's fine thanks. Where are we off to now?"

"We're off to the state capital. It's time to take the governor's mansion by storm," he said.

The remaining weeks of the campaign became a surrealistic blur. We arrived at the Mall in front of the State House at 3:30 in the afternoon on October 11, where we erected a Monument to the Taxpayer in the form of a replica of an Egyptian pyramid. The idea was to protest the expenditure of billions of taxpayer dollars for the construction of the Mall, which was nothing less than a monument to the egos of state lawmakers in Albany. "The method used to build the Mall does not differ in principle from that used to construct the pyramids of ancient Egypt," our statement read in part. "Both were built as monuments to a few big shots at the expense of the average citizen. Thousands of years ago slaves were forced to build pyramids. Today people are still coerced into building grandiose public projects via taxation. By the time the Albany Mall is completed, more than $2 billion of taxpayers' hard-earned money will have been wasted on it."

This was another one of Wonder Woman's stunts. If we had just come to read a statement, nobody would have showed up. But our tottering, cardboard, three-dimensional triangle turned the statement into a media event, and the networks turned out in force once again. Click, click, click, the cameras captured our makeshift pyramid for posterity. Was it humiliating? Well, sure. But at least it diverted my attention from my pressing problems back home.

"We better get the hell out of here!" yelled Roger with a look of alarm on his face. We all looked up just as our pyramid started to come unglued. One strong gust of wind was all it would take to send it toppling down on our heads.

"How symbolic," said Roger. "A house of cards, just like all boondoggles."

"Are you getting it on film, guys?" I yelled at the photographers. "The governor's monument to his ego is tumbling down like Humpty Dumpty."

Too late. They had already left to file their stories.

"It's time to leave," said Roger, more insistently this time. "I think I'm going to need an *extra* dry martini after this."

The next day we went to Ithaca where I was scheduled to deliver a speech to the student body at Cornell. Roger and I were both half-drunk by the time I arrived on campus. With a wine glow on my face, I faced an audience composed of the usual assortment of scruffy students and a smattering of professors, most of whom looked like clones of Leon Trotsky. I had moved well beyond political diplomacy at this point and decided to let it all hang out. Forget about Jefferson, Paine, and Madison. Forget about high-blown political philosophy and moral principle. I went right for the jugular.

"Vote for me and my first act as governor will be to legalize drugs. Not just marijuana, but all kinds of drugs including LSD, heroine, cocaine, and opium."

They jumped to their feet instantly, shrieking like a chorus of demented banshees. "Right on, man!"

I had an auditorium full of degenerates in the palm of my hand. If only I were running for Governor of Cornell University instead of Governor of the whole state. The only problem was that none of these brain-dead zombies bothered to vote. Unfortunately, this particular plank in the FLP platform didn't go over too well outside of a few universities scattered throughout the state and Greenwich Village in New York City. What could I possibly say next that would top my opening line? I had shot my load in the first fifteen seconds of my speech. I was on safe ground with drugs, sex, sodomy, perhaps even bestiality. There was no point talking about lowering taxes because only capitalists paid taxes, and this audience thought capitalists should be paraded before a firing squad let alone be forced to pay confiscatory taxes. Come to think of it, I didn't pay taxes myself anymore now that I was jobless. I ended my talk quickly and walked off stage with the audience roaring. All I wanted to do was go back to my hotel room and sleep off the buzz I had gotten after drinking five glasses of cheap red wine with dinner.

On October 18, Channel 13 sponsored the first debate of the campaign among the minor party candidates for governor. I took my place on stage alongside the only other candidates who showed up: Courage Party candidate Wayne Amato and Communist Party candidate Jose Ristorucci. Amato was a short, slick, dapper fellow, a street-smart blue-collar type who could barely restrain himself from grabbing Ristorucci by the throat and slamming his head against the table. Ristorucci was easy to hate on first sight. He looked like a stereotypical Commie, complete with unkempt hair, pock-marked skin, foul breath, and a genius for sloganeering. He began his opening statement in a high-pitched shriek, spouting the party line about capitalist exploitation of the meek, the humble, the downtrodden, and imbeciles like himself. I kept staring at Amato who looked as though he were ready to rip out Ristorucci's vocal chords if only there were no TV cameras present to record the mayhem. For his part Amato's hatred of the Communist Party candidate was his most endearing quality. Aside from that he wanted to throw everyone in jail—users of mind-altering substances, pornographers, and prostitutes, along with murderers, rapists, and common thieves. I felt like a duck out of water featured on Zoo Parade and prayed for the so-called debate to end quickly so I could beat a hasty retreat.

A high note of sorts took place a few days later when, unexpectedly, my candidacy was simultaneously endorsed by two well-known political columnists: New Leftist Nicholas Von Hoffman and Conservative George F. Will. Von Hoffman called us "the great, great grandchildren of John Locke and J.S. Mill" and said we were "the only people worth voting for." George Will found merit in our defense of Chester A. Arthur and cited Mark Twain's comment that "It would be hard to better President Arthur's administration" since he never stayed in Washington long enough to do any damage. He also stated that I bore "an unsettling physical resemblance to another political livewire, G. Gordon Liddy," except that I had a sense of humor. The next few weeks would tell whether any of this would translate into votes or not.

The final and most successful stunt of all, in terms of free publicity, occurred about a week before Election Day. Among the ranks of FLP volunteers was a gorgeous young model and aspiring actress named Jane Mitchell. Fortunately for us, when Wonder Woman approached her about riding virtually unclothed on a horse we named *Taxpayer* in a vivid reenactment of Lady Godiva's romp through the streets of Coventry, Jane responded like a real trooper and agreed to do it.

Legend has it that Lady Godiva, the Earl of Mercia's wife, appealed to her husband to reduce the burden of taxes he imposed on his subjects. The earl replied that he would grant her request only if she agreed to ride naked on a horse through the town's crowded marketplace. This she supposedly did, her alluring private parts covered by her curtain of long, flowing hair. Her husband was as good as his word and abolished the most noxious of his taxes. If true, God only knows what kind of perversion motivated the good earl to send his wife out naked in public, but the taxpayers under his dominion benefited from his peculiar tastes.

We sent out a press release announcing that we would be conducting our special reenactment on Sunday morning, October 27, 1974, beginning at 11 A.M. To get around the issue of actual nudity and the peripheral problems that it would lead to (not the least of which was a photographic boycott of the event by the media), our latter-day Godiva donned a flesh-colored body stocking before climbing onto the lucky beast's back. Feeling a bit stupid in my British tweeds with leather patches on the elbows and an ascot around my neck (a totally inaccurate replication of a medieval earl's attire), I led Jane eastward along Central Park South from the Avenue of the Americas toward Fifth Avenue, pulling Taxpayer by his bridle. Jane sat perched on the horse's back, the body suit fitting her like a tight layer of skin and her long wig cocked a bit crookedly over her forehead. A comet trail of FLP volunteers walked behind her, stepping gingerly over the horse's excrement as we wound our way along the southern boundary of Central Park. By the time we reached Fifth Avenue, it had become apparent that the media response was the best we could have hoped for. Everyone was there, TV, radio, and print crews from every major organization in the city.

The cameras clicked away, recording Jane with her crooked wig, a beatific smile adorning her pretty face, as I read a statement protesting uncommonly high taxes combined with waste and corruption in the state and across the land. Aside from the daily newspapers and the networks, all of which gave ample coverage to the event, the stunt earned us a full page in *Newsweek* magazine, which called our campaign an extravaganza staged by Ayn Rand and Adam Smith, with elements of W.C. Fields and Groucho Marx added to the mix. Libertarian purists deplored the so-called trivialization of our philosophy, as they called it, but it was the only way to gain attention for a third party campaign backed with minimal capital compared with major party expenditures. In the euphoria of the moment we began to believe that the stunts of the past few weeks might actually put us over the top of the 50,000 vote total we had hoped to achieve. Two percent or three percent of the vote would amount to 100,000 to 150,000 votes. Surely that was not out of the question.

21

Down and Out in the Belly of the Beast

In the final week of the campaign we blitzed the airwaves with a slew of commercials and received the endorsement of four independent newspapers in the state. There was one more televised debate, the second and last one including the entire panoply of left-wing splinter groups that made the Communist Ristorucci look like a Rotary Club member. Essentially, they all accused one another of being "paid agents" of the Rockefeller family, "running dogs of capitalist imperialism," and "neo-Trotskyites in disguise." Amato of the Courage Party looked as though he would rather see his goon squad bust their heads open with baseball bats than listen to their twaddle. We closed out the campaign in high spirits, and on election night we gathered at our unofficial headquarters, the Kangaroo Pub on First Avenue and 81st Street, to celebrate what we fully expected to be a successful end to an exhausting, scintillating, and intoxicating (in more ways than one) gubernatorial campaign. I truly thought I would come out of it as the titular head of the most dynamic new minority party in New York. Employment be damned! For the moment at least, all such mundane concerns faded into the ether like the cigarette smoke in the bar.

As the night wore on, the pall of gloom hanging in the air of the Kangaroo Pub grew thick enough to hack apart with a meat cleaver. The media was slow to report the vote count of the minor party candidates, but the most telling news was that there was *nothing unusual* to report. The biggest news of the evening, outside of who won the election, would have been that a new minor party had achieved permanent status in New York by garnering one percent of the vote.

It was not to be. By 11 P.M. most of the FLP campaign staff had drifted soundlessly into the night, and by midnight it was painfully apparent that no minor party candidate had gotten the magic 50,000 votes. At 1 A.M. I was the only one of our group left in the pub, too numb with defeat to feel the effects of too many bourbons consumed through the long night's vigil. The letdown following the euphoric high of the campaign was one of the most painful I had experienced in my life. Gone were the lights, the reporters, the television and radio crews, the columnists, the well-wishers, and legions of volunteers. In their place was a black hole of failure with no glimmer of light visible anywhere. Shock. Numbness. As bad as it was, the full impact of the letdown had yet to fully sink in.

The man from CREEP had called it right. Six dollars a vote, he had said. When we tallied it all up later on we found we had raised a bit more than $70,000 and gotten about 12,000 votes. It was over before it was over, as far as he was concerned. He knew it was over as soon as he saw how much money we had to spend. Wonder Woman knew it was over as well. The rest of us believed it was possible to beat the odds and pay only one dollar a vote. But it didn't happen. All the free publicity we could possibly hope for didn't change the price of a vote.

Now it was time to go home and face the music. Time to go home and shop for a job. Time to decide what to do with the rest of my life. At the moment, I had to admit, I didn't have a clue.

PART V
The Woeful Interregnum

22

John Galt Rides Again

After the nightmare of the Nixon Years, two depressing years with dismal Gerry Ford, and four years of misery with Jimmy Carter, the political climate seemed hopeless. Gerry Ford had left everyone in a catatonic state. Ayn Rand had admired him in the beginning, particularly after he appointed her protégé Alan Greenspan as his economic advisor. She even had her picture taken at the White House with tall, ruggedly handsome President Ford in the middle, bespectacled Alan Greenspan with a face like a bloodhound on one side, and a radiant Rand on the other. Truth be told, I believe dear old Ayn had a crush on Ford. It was probably his chin, jutting forward like Goldwater's with a Galtian cleft in the middle.

The problem with Gerry Ford was that he never stopped acting like a congressman, even after he became president following Nixon's resignation. During a memorable debate during the 1976 campaign against Jimmy Carter, the power suddenly failed in the studio. Instead of taking charge like the President of the United States, the Leader of the Free World no less, Ford stood around like a dummy waiting for some lowly electrician making a union scale wage to fix it. He stood there fidgeting, rocking back and forth from foot to foot, staring frozenly into the camera.

Carter did much the same thing, but nobody expected him to do *anything*. He looked like a sheriff from Dogpatch, this pretender to the most powerful job on earth, and he sounded like a televangelist with four pounds of hairspray molding his hair. Ford, however, was our *leader*. Instead, he acted like a congressman waiting for a committee to study the problem and tell him what course of action to take.

Ford's most endearing accomplishment during his brief two years in the White House was his humiliation of liberal Republican Nelson Rockefeller. Rockefeller would die a few years later of a heart attack in his mid-seventies, while servicing his young mistress with his penile implant. At the time Rockefeller was Ford's vice president. Prior to that, Rockefeller money had helped fuel Gerry Ford's many congressional campaigns, and Rockefeller used to brag that he had Ford in his hip pocket. Once Ford became president, however, Rockefeller complained that he needed an appointment to get in to see him. It was Ford's way of exacting revenge on the manipulative former Governor of New York who used to pull Ford's puppet strings.

Carter went on to win the election that November, and he saddled the country with four more years of *malaise,* as he himself characterized the economic environment at the time. Inflation had soared to the mid-teens, the prime rate hit 21 percent, and a pervasive pall of stagflation clouded the atmosphere, seemingly for good. Into this depressing state of affairs strode a Republican presidential candidate who could have been created by Rand herself. It was as though the swinging doors of Galt's Gulch had opened wide and out stepped the tallest, proudest cowboy of all other than John Wayne on a mission to save the Western World. True, Ronald Reagan was less than perfect from a libertarian perspective, but his free market, pro-capitalist, individualist rhetoric was a stirring tonic in the miasma of collectivism that had prevailed for so many decades past.

This was not Reagan's first pass at the presidency. He made a half-hearted attempt to secure the Republican nomination in 1968 but backed off when it became clear that he would have a difficult time stopping Nixon. Then again, there was talk of Reagan joining the Ford ticket in 1976 as a type of "co-president," a term invented by the left wing media who were terrified that Reagan might succeed in beating the more moderate Ford in a convention floor fight. In 1980, however, the conditions favoring a successful Reagan campaign could not have been better.

The United States of America was a mess. Sky-high interest rates accompanied by a grinding recession had created an atmosphere of hopelessness and gloom. Reagan strode onto the national scene tall and erect, an indomitable smile set in place as he told his fellow citizens that he would dispel the storm clouds with a healthy dose of free market economics and a drastic cut in income taxes. Margaret Thatcher, the most lovable Iron Lady in modern history, had already conquered England where she was routing the socialists with an unrelenting campaign of privatization. Thatcher was a no-nonsense, take-no-prisoners heroine out of a novel by Rand, and Reagan was Howard Roark with a winning smile hell-bent on a mission to clear the collectivists out of Washington. Suddenly, for the first time since the Goldwater days, your blood started to flow with a sense of purpose.

Victory was in the air. Goldwater had disappointed, but Thatcher plus Reagan was more than 1964 redux; *real* heroes had stepped into the void spoiling for a fight, charged up to their eyeballs with the power of ideological conviction. For the first time in sixteen years, a politician had come along whom you could enthusiastically follow into combat.

As the 1980 campaign for president got under way, Reagan's victory over Carter was by no means assured. Reagan stumbled several times with a series of ill-advised statements, which the press was only too happy to take out of context and misinterpret. The left-wing media was in a panic over the idea that Reagan—not only a Republican, but a right wing Republican with uncompromising ethical principles—might occupy the White House for the next four years. They would do anything short of calling for Reagan's assassination to keep him out of office.

In an attempt to consolidate his forces, Reagan moved his campaign headquarters east to an estate in Middleburg, Virginia, about forty-five minutes west of Arlington in the verdant countryside not too far from the Appalachian Trail. In September, following a few mishaps with the media on the road, Reagan's campaign staff met at the estate to see how the problem could be fixed. In attendance were the candidate and his wife Nancy, Jim Baker, Bill Casey, Ed Meese, Pete Dailey, Mike

Deaver, Bill Timmons, and F. Clifton White, who had orchestrated the 1964 Goldwater campaign. They all sat around the cavernous living room in a circle, with Nancy hovering nervously in the background. The consensus was that Reagan's staff was making him nervous, critiquing everything he said on the campaign stump to a point where Reagan no longer trusted his own judgment and communication skills—his strongest suits. Finally, Cliff White exploded,

"If you leave him alone and let him do what he wants to do, what he feels comfortable with, we won't have any problems. The problem is you guys, not him. Let Reagan be Reagan."

White gave birth to a battle cry that would resonate in Republican ranks throughout Reagan's eight years in office: Let Reagan Be Reagan. Nancy Reagan was particularly delighted with White's assessment, and everyone in attendance murmured in agreement. How could any of them do otherwise? With Reagan sitting in their midst taking it all in, who was about to suggest that the candidate needed to have his lines spoon fed to him as though he were a retarded child?

James Baker bristled inwardly about being backed into a corner by White. Of all the people present at the meeting that afternoon, Baker was the one who wanted to rein Reagan toward the center the most. Jim Baker, a friend of George Bush, was a so-called moderate Republican who felt more comfortable with a Bush-Rockefeller-Romney liberal agenda than he did with Ronald Reagan's quasi-libertarian slash taxes, shrink the government rhetoric. Baker showed his true stripes during the car ride back to Washington D.C. after the meeting. Sharing the limo with Baker were White, Bill Timmons (a White acolyte), and Dean Burch (another Bush Republican brought into the Reagan campaign by Baker). Suddenly, Baker turned to Burch and said, referring to Reagan,

"He really isn't very smart, is he?"

"I disagree," Cliff White jumped to Reagan's defense immediately. White had idolized Barry Goldwater in 1964 and he had all but deified Reagan since 1968. "Reagan is probably the most underrated man intellectually who's ever sought the presidency."

White explained to Baker that he had gotten to know Reagan well during his unsuccessful presidential bid in 1968 and during his tenure as Governor of California. In White's view, Reagan had unerring political instincts and was bright and knowledgeable, although not overtly intellectual. Cliff White not only failed to convince Baker of Reagan's mental astuteness that evening, he also positioned himself as a leading candidate for removal from Reagan's inner circle after the election, when Baker purged the Reagan White House of its more right wing elements.

But that came later.

Reagan turned the campaign decisively in his favor during his debates with Jimmy Carter. Reagan was a natural performer, as relaxed in front of the camera as Carter was awkward, especially adept at using humor to make his point while his opponent bored the viewers with his ponderous intellectualizing. In the modern media age, style carries far more weight than substance in so-called political debates. How a candidate delivers his lines and who gets off the best one-line putdown scores heavily with viewers. In that department, Reagan clearly outclassed Carter. In addition, voters were more than ready to give capitalism a chance to keep inflation from totally destroying the value of their assets, and Reagan swept to victory in November.

From the beginning, Baker played the role of Machiavelli in the Reagan administration. Baker had his own political agenda, which was totally at variance with Reagan's. Baker was extremely bright and capable, but devoid of any political ideology except one: whatever further his own career was all that mattered. Some of those closest to Reagan viewed Baker as the ultimate pragmatist, others as a crass opportunist. He was smart enough to avoid antagonizing Nancy Reagan, who was the ultimate means of access to the president. Baker cozied up to Mike Deaver, Nancy Reagan's batboy and number-one amanuensis, and ran his ideas past Deaver first before presenting them to Reagan. It was only a question of time, however, before the tug-of-war for Reagan's soul between Baker and Bush on one hand, and Cliff White and the conservative/quasi-libertarian faction on the other, erupted into the open. In the end, the Wesley Mouch brigade would win.

Mike Deaver was the key to Baker's eventual victory. After Reagan's 1980 victory over Carter, Deaver established the White House Troika composed of himself, Jim Baker, and Ed Meese. Deaver had been a failure for most of his life. He started off playing piano in a bar. After that he tried his hand selling life insurance without success. Serendipitously as it were, he met Bill Clark, a friend of Reagan, who hired Deaver to work in Reagan's first gubernatorial campaign in California. Suddenly, Mike Deaver had a career: Ronald Reagan. Reagan became Deaver's ticket to respectability. When Reagan became governor in 1966, his chief of staff Ed Meese hired Deaver as his assistant. Survivor that he was, Deaver quickly realized that the primary line of access to the governor was Nancy Reagan. Mike Deaver positioned himself as her go-fer, main flunky, and all-around errand boy.

Nancy wanted Ronnie home by five o'clock every evening, so Deaver made sure he got the governor home by five. He picked up Nancy's groceries along the way, catered to her every need, and took care of Ronnie for her. He was an accomplished cocktail lounge piano player, which meant he was always fun for Nancy to have around at parties. Deaver became Nancy's key to the governor's office, and she was his to the governor. It's not clear whether people like Mike Deaver are born with a congenital talent for butt-wiping or if they have to cultivate it. Whatever the case, Deaver had an uncanny genius for subservience, and like most talented operatives who have to find a way to survive, he was shrewd enough not to let anyone else get as close as he to his bread and butter.

Deaver's biggest worry was Bill Clark, the guy who rescued him from obscurity and lifted him onto the Reagan bandwagon. Following Reagan's election as president, the common wisdom had it that either Ed Meese or Bill Clark would become Reagan's chief of staff. Nancy was the linchpin in the decision. Deaver turned her against Clark, whom he viewed as his major threat, and maneuvered Meese into a supposedly more elevated role as Counselor to the President. He positioned Baker as chief of staff, since he regarded him as a kindred spirit of sorts, and then set up the Troika with himself as the main barrier between Reagan and everyone else of whom Deaver disapproved for one reason or another.

Once the Troika was in place, Jim Baker had a free hand in staffing much of the government. Ronald Reagan's primary weakness was that, unlike Carter who micromanaged to a fault, he was never a hands-on manager in charge of what was going on around him. His casual indifference to the everyday affairs of his administration made him vulnerable to the manipulative designs of the Jim Bakers and Mike Deavers in his inner circle. Reagan's strength was his ability to articulate a grand vision centered in a relatively consistent ideology. He was a master helmsman who set a course, then stepped back and delegated the job of following it to those around him.

While Reagan gave lip service to the religious right, particularly on the abortion issue, his primary focus in the beginning at least was on the economy. To his credit, while Reagan did not believe in abortion himself, he also did not believe in imposing his personal moral convictions on the country through legislation, preferring to lead by example instead. The religious right lapped up his rhetoric on social issues, only to be disappointed when Reagan failed to follow through with political action. His early concentration on the economy made Reagan more acceptable to libertarians, while social conservatives had little choice but to support him since there was no viable alternative in sight. Only after Reagan left office did Ralph Reed and the Christian right wing say that they were tired of settling for rhetoric instead of substance.

With President Reagan officially sworn into office, there was a dramatic improvement in the spirits of both conservatives and libertarians. The left wing media, however, were in a royal snit, and they tried to cripple Reagan at the outset with attacks on his "Kitchen Cabinet," which the media claimed exercised too much influence over the president. William French Smith, Reagan's lawyer who later became attorney general, presided over this group. The money boys included Jack Hume, a San Francisco investment manager; Henry Salvatori, chairman of the Western Geophysical Company of America; Holmes Tuttle, who built a fortune after beginning as a Ford dealer in Oklahoma; Justin Dart of Dart Drugs fame; and A.C. Rubel, former CEO of Union Oil Company of California.

If the media were exercised over the influence this group of wealthy businessmen had over the president, they need not have worried. Jim Baker was also concerned about it since he had no leverage over this group himself. The Kitchen Cabinet raised money for Reagan, made public policy suggestions, and lobbied for key appointments, but Baker made sure they made no headway on White House staffing. Baker and Deaver working together succeeded in shutting the money boys out, leaving them high and dry on the California coast while the two of them pursued their own agenda, which only occasionally dovetailed with Reagan's.

Over time, their nefarious scheming would deflect the Reagan Revolution from its original course and slow much of its early momentum. In 1981, however, when Ronald Reagan first took command of the executive branch of the federal government, his presidency offered the greatest hope for a libertarian revolution since the Tuccille for Governor campaign of 1974.

23

The First 100 Days

In 1980, libertarians were charged up politically for the first time since 1970. For a decade they had been off on their own with mixed results. Now, suddenly, Margaret Thatcher and Ronald Reagan had entered the political arena—the Dynamic Duo, which was going to change the way the world did business and conducted its affairs. Hope was in the air and everything seemed possible once again. As then Congressman Jack Kemp wrote in his Foreword to my 1981 book, *The New Tax Law and You:*

"Ronald Reagan was elected President on November 4, 1980, primarily to deal with one issue: the economy. Tired of more than a decade of burdensome government, the American people approved Reagan's plans to establish a foundation for economic recovery. That foundation is based on four pillars—tax-reduction to revive economic growth, spending restraint to reduce the burden of government, regulatory revision to improve efficiency, and monetary reform to end inflation.

Within the first six months of Reagan's term, the first two of these pillars—tax cuts and spending restraint—were enacted by a bipartisan coalition in Congress. The centerpiece was the Economic Recovery Tax Act of 1981, a bill designed to restore incentives to work, save, and invest in creating new jobs and enterprises ... Jerome Tuccille's book is useful for everyone who wants to know how the new tax law can create a climate of renewed prosperity and opportunity in which all Americans may share."

That was the old Jack Kemp who still believed in limited government. After that, unfortunately, Kemp disassociated himself more and more from that view. As a Supply Sider and Laffer Curve convert, he believed that lower tax rates would generate more, not less, revenues for the federal gov6rnment. During the next decade-and-a-half, Kemp's interest in reducing taxes shifted from an interest in shrinking the state to raising more money for his own state-sponsored programs. In 1981, however, as his own words indicated, spending restraints on government were still one of his top priorities.

Reagan's first 100 days in office were a whirlwind of free market reforms, as he intended. He started off with a burst of energy worthy of a man 20 years younger than his 69 years. The single, overriding issues of the day were the twin problems of stubbornly high inflation and punishing taxes, particularly for middle class wage earners. With all the tax loopholes in effect at the time, those ostensibly in the highest marginal tax bracket of 70 percent were usually able to avoid taxes through shelters designed for the wealthy and marketed by financial advisors.

In quick order, Reagan established the framework of the revolution he had promised the American people during the presidential campaign. On Inauguration Day, January 20, 1981, Reagan imposed a moratorium on federal hiring. Two days later he announced a cutback on government travel, froze new business regulations that were soon to take effect, and appointed a task force to eliminate other regulations already in existence. On February 18, Reagan submitted to Congress the first step of his economic program, calling for a 30 percent reduction in income taxes over three years and nearly $50 billion worth of spending cuts. On March 26, Reagan created a council to identify specific areas of government waste and fraud as targets for future budget cuts. On April 6 he jettisoned 34 separate safety and environmental restrictions on the automobile industry. On April 8 the president set up an advisory group to implement a new federalism, restoring many decision-making powers to state and local governments. On April 11, after recuperating from a gunshot wound inflicted by some lunatic who was infatuated with actress Jodie Foster, Reagan returned to the White House and stepped up the campaign to get the entire economic package enacted by Congress.

It was an invigorating performance—tough, decisive, courageous, and thoroughly uplifting for advocates of free markets and limited government. Tax cuts, budget restraints, deregulation, decentralization. Reagan clearly planned to deliver even more than his most ardent supporters had hoped for. For the first time in decades, libertarians had more than mere rhetoric to bank on; Reagan was taking forceful action to trim the tentacles of the American Welfare State just as Margaret Thatcher had begun the wholesale dismantling of Socialism in Great Britain.

Even Reagan's political opponents were in awe of his early accomplishments. Democratic Congressman James R. Jones, chairman of the House Budget Committee, forecast that President Reagan was "well on the way to reshaping American government more radically than any occupant of the Oval Office since Franklin D. Roosevelt."

"The president is a very secure personality," commented Thomas E. Cronin, a presidential historian who taught at Colorado College. "He's bullish on the future, and that is a morale-building quality. Leadership is largely a matter of building morale."

Reagan was almost impossible to dislike, blessed as he was with the ability to charm those whose own political ideology was diametrically opposed to his. "He's a beautiful man," admitted the avuncular liberal Thomas P. "Tip" O'Neill, the Democratic speaker of the House. "Too bad he doesn't agree with my philosophy."

Dick Cheney, a more traditional Republican and vice president under George W. Bush, who wanted to wait for real spending cuts before lowering taxes, was moved to say, "[Reagan] doesn't raise the hackles on your neck even if you disagree with him."

Erwin C. Hargrove, the director of the Institute for Public Policy Studies, hardly a libertarian organization, commented, "I would give him an A, not necessarily in policy but certainly in political craftsmanship. Reagan has demonstrated, in a way that Jimmy Carter never did, that he understands how to be president. He knows that a president can deal only with a relatively small number of issues at a time. He also understands that his principal task is public leadership. Therefore, he has concentrated primarily upon economic policy and in particular on forming public opinion and developing working relationships with Congress."

In August 1981, following two masterful televised appeals to the American people by Reagan, and his whirlwind courtship of conservative Democrats, Congress gave the president just about everything he wanted in the way of tax and spending cuts. Reagan at age 70 was well on his way to reversing the leftward drift of the nation's political system, first set in motion 50 years earlier. For the first time since the beginning of the New Deal, there would be a real shrinkage in the federal government's role in economic affairs, a curtailment of the power of the regulatory agencies, an emasculation of the entrenched bureaucratic establishment, and the first substantial cuts in federal income taxes in 20 years.

Or so the common wisdom had it at the time.

Careful analysis, however, revealed that the tax cuts commencing in 1981 were the most revolutionary aspect of Reagan's economic package. As far as federal spending was concerned, Reagan did not so much propose to reduce the level of spending as to *reduce its rate of growth*. Under Carter, spending had increased 13.6 percent annually during the last three years of his administration. Reagan's so-called "draconian" cuts merely lowered the rate of growth to a projected 4.7 percent a year. Granted, with inflation thundering along at more than 13 percent a year when Reagan took office, a reduction of that magnitude in the rate of spending growth was significant, but it was hardly a complete castration of the federal Leviathan. Still, it was a good start, a deflection in the trend line if not a total reversal in direction. Reagan had grabbed the monster by the horns, a first step in the battle to wrestle him down onto his knees.

The 1981 bill reduced individual income taxes for everyone over three years. The new marginal rates under Reagan ranged from 11 percent to 50 percent, down from 14 percent to 70 percent under the old law. (Reagan's 1986 tax bill further reduced the top bracket rate to 28 percent, but it also increased the capital gains tax from 20 percent to 33 percent while tossing out all the tax shelters except for mortgage deductibility.

The ink was scarcely dry on the most wide-ranging tax reform package in decades, when the moderates in the White House conspired behind Reagan's back to water it down. Early in 1982, Baker and his cohorts managed to convince the Gipper that he had gone too far, and Reagan agreed to backtrack by repealing most of the tax cuts affecting business.

Norman B. Ture, who founded the Institute for Research on the Economics of Taxation and was the principal architect of the 1981 bill, was so disgusted by Reagan's early capitulation to the soft and squishy moderates that he resigned his post as Under Secretary of the Treasury for Tax and Economic Affairs and returned to his institute.

"[Norman] was one of the few people to join the Reagan administration on philosophical principle, and one of the first to leave for the same principle. He didn't compromise," said Stephen J. Entin, resident scholar at the institute when Ture died in 1997.

Ture may not have been willing to compromise, but Ronald Reagan apparently was. Fiscal conservatives and libertarians grew increasingly alarmed by the power exerted by the Troika in the White House. By the end of Reagan's first year in office, Baker, Deaver, and company succeeded in isolating the free market types and denying them access to Reagan. Ture had left, and Martin Anderson, an economist who subscribed to the philosophy of Ayn Rand (whom someone described as Friedrick Nietzsche in a bad mood) was gone shortly later. The situation deteriorated through 1982. Clif White, a political consultant whose memoir I co-authored, had enjoyed Reagan's friendship and confidence since the late 1960s. White made several attempts to speak directly to the president but was stymied each time. He called Nancy Reagan in exasperation, and managed to set up an appointment with Ronnie in the spring of 1983. To his surprise, when White arrived for what he thought was going to be a one-on-one with the

president, he was greeted in the lobby of the White House by Deaver and Assistant Political Director Lee Atwater.

"We'll go up to the residence now," Deaver told him.

Sizing up the situation quickly, White fell in with them as they rode up in the elevator together. Reagan was waiting in his office upstairs and stepped across to shake White's hand with his trademark grin stretched across his face. White made an initial attempt to get Deaver and Atwater out of the picture.

"Do you want to make this private, Mr. President?" he asked. "If so, we'll at least know who leaks it to the press."

Reagan laughed heartily at that but refused to take the bait. Deaver and Atwater sat stiffly in their chairs as Clif White launched into perhaps the gutsiest proposal of his political career. He presented a plan to Reagan that would essentially have kicked Baker upstairs out of harm's way and reassigned someone else who was totally committed to the Reagan agenda as chief of staff. In elaborate detail, Clif itemized a laundry list of recommended changes, including moving Baker over as Director of the CIA and getting rid of Deaver and Atwater altogether.

"You've got to turn Mike out, Mr. President," Clif said to Reagan with Mike Deaver sitting there by his side. "Mike's got to make some money. The poor guy hasn't made any money all his life, and if he goes out there now while he's still on top, he can make a fortune. Nobody deserves that more than he does."

Deaver squirmed visibly in his chair, and the diminutive Atwater slunk down further in his own chair in an attempt to make himself even more invisible than he already was. Reagan took it all in without changing the expression on his face in what had to be stunned silence as Clif White made his pitch. The meeting rambled on past its allotted half hour with no one saying a word except for White. Finally, someone knocked on the door and Reagan rose from behind his desk, a signal to everyone that the meeting was over. The president looked White straight in the eye as he extended his hand and said, "Clif, I really appreciate this very much."

That was it. Deaver, Atwater, and White left Reagan's office and rode down on the elevator together. When they reached the lobby, poor little

Lee Atwater was shaking so badly he couldn't speak. Deaver said to White, "Clif, I couldn't disagree more with what you said in there."

"Fine, Mike, that's your privilege clearly. We're all entitled to our opinions, and this is mine."

Deaver turned and continued on his own way while Atwater walked with White across the colonnade, visibly agitated. "I shouldn't have been there. I shouldn't have heard any of this. I don't want to know anything about it," Atwater yelled over and over.

"Don't worry, Lee," White said. "I won't say a word about it to anyone. It's strictly a private matter among those of us who were in the room with the president."

White left Atwater quaking in his shoes as he walked toward the garage to get his car. But that was not the end of the matter, as Clif suspected at the time. Mike Deaver went immediately to Baker's office and gave him a detailed rundown on what had just transpired. Baker decided on the spot that he "didn't want Clif White to set foot inside the White House ever again."

White rolled the dice that day and risked whatever dwindling influence he had over the direction the Reagan White House would take in the future—and lost. "Breaking up the Troika was, of course, my main objective," Clif said years later. "I laid it out straight on the line, figuring this would be my one and only opportunity to present my case to Reagan." As it turned out, it was. White stretched his neck way out on a limb as lie spoke his mind, Reagan listened intently, and Jim Baker and Mike Deaver continued to run matters pertaining to the Oval Office as they saw fit. Whatever hope there was of keeping Reagan on the fiscally conservative, quasi-libertarian track on which his administration started off was lost forever.

The big question that arises is: why was Ronald Reagan so susceptible to the wiles of Baker and Deaver, and later on to the more moderate economic policies of Don Regan? White's assessment was that Jim Baker was the worst culprit. "He and the others over-briefed the president for his press conferences and generally would not let him relax and be himself. They corrected his statements afterward to the point where he was almost afraid to say anything. Baker was convinced that Reagan was a dummy, and he felt a need to second-guess every statement he made.

"For example, when Ron said something to the effect that trees emitted more carbon monoxide than automobile exhaust did, Baker responded immediately with a press release saying that the president really didn't mean it. Yet I had read the environmental report that supported Reagan's conclusion, and I told Baker he should have backed him up on it. He should have told the media to study the report if they didn't believe it, and figure it out for themselves. Baker corrected the president so often that the media picked up on it and perpetuated the myth of Reagan's alleged stupidity."

Still. The question persists: why did Reagan permit Baker and Deaver to wield so much power in his White House? According to White and other Reagan apologists, Reagan did not have a lust for power himself in the same way that Kennedy, Johnson, and Nixon did. Reagan did not need to be president as Kennedy did; he had a comfortable and agreeable life apart from politics.

Yes, but if Reagan was guided primarily by the ideal of reversing the statist direction of the country, why did he allow those around him to thwart his principles? Many of the fiscal conservatives and libertarians who had joined the Reagan ranks during his 1980 campaign were leaving in droves. Surely Reagan was aware of their departures. White maintained that Reagan put too much "trust in the people around him, people he thought were guided by the same principles he was."

But how could Reagan have believed that when those who *shared* his principles were the ones who were leaving? Reagan apologists claimed that Baker and company managed to convince the president that it would be next to impossible to get many of his programs through Congress. Democrats soon realized that Reagan would not go to the mat for much of his legislation. His Congressional liaison staff advised him to be careful and avoid unnecessary battles. The careerists hi Reagan's own party constantly urged him to be cautious. "We really don't want to risk losing a big one," they told him. "Let's go along with the Democrats on this bill and keep our ammunition dry for when it really counts." Without the firebrands in the Republican Party there to say, "You'll never know if a battle is winnable or not unless you fight it," Reagan succumbed to Baker's middle-of-the-road, let's-not-rock-the-boat approach. "You can't pass it, you haven't got the votes, we'll never get it through, the press will beat up on us if we try it," was the battle cry of the Jim Baker contingent around Reagan.

Yes, but the firebrands had all left because they were not being listened to in the first place. Why would Reagan believe that he could not get his legislation passed by Congress when Congress gave him 100 percent of what he asked for eight months into his first term? The excuses for Reagan's capitulation came all too easily for Clif White and the other apologists. That was understandable, considering that Clif truly loved Reagan and all but deified the man. But the truth was, the only reason why Reagan allowed Baker, Deaver, and Regan to emasculate his programs was because, deep down inside, he was not totally committed to them himself.

That, plus the fact that Baker's assessment of Reagan was closer to the mark than Clif White's was: when you got right down to the bottom line, Ronald Reagan, with all his charisma, all his charm, all his communication skills, really was an intellectual flyweight engaged in intellectual combat with world-class heavyweight opportunists.

24

Where's the Rest of Him?

Reagan had written an autobiography (with Richard G. Hubler) entitled *Where's the Rest of Me?* I'm sure he didn't intend his title to be ironic, but those who supported Reagan in the beginning were also wondering where the rest of Ronnie was by 1983—or, at least, where the rest of his revolution was. Ronnie, himself, was as big as life all over television, all over the front pages of international newspapers, grinning from ear to ear as he "communicated" inimitably with his worldwide audience. We knew where you were, Ronnie, and we heard what you said. But, where was the rest of *you*? If Nancy knew, she wasn't talking.

The Supply Side/Laffer Curve tax cutters were right in one major regard: lower taxes did indeed result in greater tax revenues for the federal government, just as had been the case whenever taxes were reduced earlier in the century. The Revenue Acts of 1921, 1924, and 1926 lowered the top bracket rate in stages from 71 percent to 25 percent, which resulted in a rapidly expanding economy and a 61 percent increase in federal tax revenues with virtually no inflation. In 1963, John F. Kennedy proposed legislation reducing the top bracket rate from 91 percent (where it had soared under Herbert Hoover and Franklin Roosevelt), once again leading to the longest economic expansion in U.S. history to date and a 62 percent surge in government tax revenues. The top income tax rate under Reagan declined all the way back down to 28 percent, accompanied by a massive bull market in stocks, a growing economy over seven years, and a 54 percent jump in federal tax revenues through 1989.

So the Supply Siders were right, Laffer was right, and Jack Kemp was right. But Milton Friedman was right as well when he said that government expenditures inevitably rise to meet and eventually exceed incoming revenues. Reagan was supposed to put an end to that practice, not spend all the extra money. Even with Reagan's slowdown in the rate of spending growth, the federal deficit as a percentage of the gross domestic product increased from about 2 ½ percent when he took office in 1981 to more than 6 percent in 1983. True, it declined thereafter, but by the end of his second term in 1988, the deficit as a percentage of GDP was still above 3 percent, a bit higher than when he entered the White House.

Libertarians and fiscal conservatives didn't jump onto the Reagan bandwagon for a replay of the Kennedy years. We wanted real tax cuts, which we got, followed by *real* spending cuts, which we did not get, and a dramatic reduction of the federal government's role in human affairs. Not only did Reagan fail to cut the federal budget, he increased the deficit 69 percent in nominal dollars and 22 percent in real dollars, adjusted for inflation. The national debt (all those dollars borrowed to fund the deficit) doubled under Reagan, from about $1 trillion when he took office to more than $2 trillion eight years later.

(A trillion dollars is the number 1 followed by 42,000 zeros.)

As a percentage of GDP, the debt load rose from 27 percent to 42 percent. As far as the federal bureaucracy was concerned, after some initial attempts to dismember the beast, Reagan lost interest and let it survive with barely a nick.

We knew it was Bedtime for Bonzo, Ronnie, but we didn't expect you to retire quite so early.

To be fair about Ronnie and his putative revolution, his tax cuts did usher in one of the greatest financial parties since the Roaring twenties. The stock market exploded in August 1982, roaring from a low of 777 on the Dow Jones Industrial Average straight up into the stratosphere with hardly a glance earthward. Real estate prices also boomed, leaping ahead 25 percent to 35 percent a year in some prestigious communities for much of the decade. Many residents of Greenwich, Connecticut, for example, were able to subdivide their property and sell off tiny parcels containing only the family dog house for over a million dollars.

Later, during the George Bush Bust of the late eighties and early nineties, many property owners went bankrupt. A dentist I knew filed for Chapter 13 when he couldn't find any buyers for his four ski condos, two weekend beach houses, and his million-dollar bungalow in Greenwich.

"How traumatic for you," I commiserated.

"Yes, but God it was fun while it lasted," he said, just before borrowing a buck and quarter for subway fare so he could get to a job interview at a McDonald's in the Bronx.

But that came later, after Ronnie spent all the extra money from the tax cuts on more nuclear bombs and space-age weapons because we and the Russians had only about 30 times more than we needed to annihilate one another. During the first Reagan administration, however, it still paid off to pile up the debt, leverage yourself up to the rafters to buy as many condos and ski chalets as you could find, and charge off the interest to Uncle Sam. The federal government stopped subsidizing us taxpayers to run up our credit cards after 1986, but the real estate subsidy remained in effect.

Why?

Because going in debt to buy property is as American as apple pie, while going in debt to shop in Bloomingdale's is highly immoral, presumably because most of the sales help there were gay and, therefore, un-American. Lower taxes fueled the market, despite the arrival of Wall Street Wizard Don Regan from Merrill Lynch—or Bull, Banks, Forbes & Trotsky, I forget which. Regan left Wall Street for Washington at the behest of Jim Baker, who had the uncanny ability to recognize a man equally unprincipled as himself from three hundred miles away. Don Regan joined the Reagan administration with one major goal in mind: to promote the *Regan* agenda, which was not to be confused with the Reagan agenda. Jim Baker had no problem with Regan promoting the Regan agenda as long as it did not get in the way of the Baker agenda. President Reagan had already begun his long snooze after his 1981 tax bill was enacted, so he paid little or no attention to the *Reagan* agenda for the next six years, which made everyone associated with the Troika extremely happy.

And what was the Regan agenda? Thwarting the president at every turn, it appeared, which was not all that different from the Baker agenda. When status-quo moderates on both sides of the aisle started bleating about ensuing budget deficits if Reagan's tax cuts went through, Don Regan, Jim Baker, and Bob Dole convinced Ronnie to reduce his tax cut in the first year from 10 percent to 5 percent. This compromise lowered the overall reduction in taxes during Reagan's first term to about 25 percent instead of the 30 percent he originally wanted. Fortunately, Reagan was still sufficiently alert in the beginning to stand most of his ground against Baker, Regan, Dole, and the others, and the tax cut he delivered was substantial enough to trigger a major economic revival and a massive run-up in stock prices.

The negative influence exerted by Don Regan over the Reagan White House cannot be overstated. Regan was a status quo, country club conservative from way back. Don't rock the boat. Compromise. Leave well enough alone. If the system ain't broke, don't fix it. As long as Wall Street makes money, how bad can it be? The municipal bond market thrived on the complexity of the tax code, so where was the benefit in simplifying it? Tax shelters, bruited partnerships, municipal bonds, IRAs, and other tax-related schemes were a major source of revenue for Wall Street brokerage firms. The last thing Don Regan wanted to do was throw out the incomprehensible 10,000-page tax law and replace it with a flat tax. As for Baker, he had made his fortune in the oil patch of Texas, which had benefited during the 1970s from inflated oil prices. Oil and gas drilling limited partnerships were a favored dodge of Baker and his colleagues, and a simplified tax code with low marginal bracket rates, accompanied by moderate inflation, would put most of them out of business.

Yes, Don and Jim made quite a team. Unfortunately, they didn't belong on the Reagan team, but for one reason or another Ronnie failed to understand that. Or maybe he *chose* not to understand it. Maybe he was really one of them after all. The clue to understanding Reagan was discernible during his tenure as governor of California. Governor Reagan started off as an ardent tax-cutter way back in the 1960s, calling for legislation to limit the taxing power of the state while simultaneously increasing real spending at the fastest rate in California's history. In retrospect, he seemed to be an out-of-control spender begging for taxing restraints to help him kick his own habit, much like a heroin addict asking to be deprived of his drug supply.

Reagan's rhetoric was always good, although he moderated it to a great extent during the 1980 campaign, caving in to political expediency. Before the campaign, he had given any number of resounding speeches criticizing farm subsidies, Social Security, urban renewal, public works programs, government regulations, the progressive income tax, federal aid to education, energy regulation, deficit financing, and other controversial issues. In 1980, however, there was a perceptible softening in his views about deficit financing and dismantling Social Security.

We understood that you didn't want to repeat Goldwater's mistakes, Ronnie, but we didn't expect you to actually *relocate* to the middle of the road after the election.

Perhaps worst of all, under the tutelage of Secretary of Treasury Regan and Chief of Staff Baker, free trader Ronald Reagan erected more barriers against international trade than any president since Herbert Hoover. Reagan bashed Japanese automobile imports at a Chrysler plant in Detroit, he promised the National Maritime Union higher tariffs on imported goods as well as increased subsidies, he imposed higher tariffs on imported textiles at the behest of Strom Thurmond of South Carolina, and higher tariffs on imported tobacco to placate Jesse Helms of North Carolina. Reagan also cut private deals with the Teamsters and construction industry unions to protect their turf.

Of course Ronnie was lovable. He was all things to all people, left, right, and in-between. Of course he was popular. He went out of his way not to piss off anyone. Reagan knew what he was doing all the time; he didn't need Baker or anyone else to mislead him. Clif White was correct in his assessment that Reagan had uncanny political instincts. Unfortunately, his ideological principles became increasingly invisible through-out his administration, until they all but faded from view in the end.

Many of his apologists argued that Reagan had a broad political coa-lition to keep happy. Those who backed him included traditional Republicans, fiscal conservatives, libertarians, Supply Siders, neocon-servatives, social conservatives, conservative Democrats, blue collar workers, neo-fascists, and several unions, many of whom were totally at odds with one another about economic and social issues as well as for-eign policy. It was simply impossible to formulate a coherent program that would be acceptable to all of these disparate groups.

The problem was: that's *exactly* what Ronnie attempted to do. Reagan got elected on the basis of his stated ideology, which was sol-idly rooted in classical liberal-libertarian, limited government princi-ples. He had a clear mandate to deliver the package he promised: lower taxes, a *real* reduction in spending, deregulation of the economy, and the elimination of bureaucratic bungling, fraud, and waste. The first 100 days of Reagan's administration proved that he could get most of what he wanted through the Congress. He had no need to backslide, to dilute his own program and move toward the soggy center. The great tragedy of the Reagan presidency was that he allowed himself to be deflected from his original course without good reason. There was no need for him to suddenly change direction, and in allowing himself to be seduced by the spineless careerists in the Baker-Regan-Deaver wing of the party, Reagan blew a once-in-a-century opportunity to reverse the warfare/welfare statist path the nation had taken for more than 50 years.

Ronnie, you were already *70 years old* by the time you took office. It was *twilight* time. Didn't you want to put your own stamp on history before calling it a day? Apparently not.

Ronnie, did you really expect George Bush and Danny Boy Quayle to finish the job for you? What the hell were you thinking of?

The pattern was established early when Treasury Secretary Regan squared off in policy sessions against David Stockman, Director of the Office of Management and the Budget (OMB). To put it kindly, theirs was not a friendly rivalry from Day One. Stockman was an ex-congressman, a policy wonk, who sometimes referred to himself as a libertarian. He was definitely a fiscal conservative who knew the workings of the federal budget better than anyone in Washington, including Regan, Baker, and the president. Stockman was also brash, brilliant, opinionated, somewhat arrogant, and possessed of a mop of thick, untrainable hair that drove Regan wild. All Regan—former Marine Corps officer as well as former chairman of Bull, Banks, Forbes & Trotsky—wanted to do was lunge across the conference table, knock Stockman to the floor, and shave his head with hedge clippers. *Everything* about Stockman drove Regan wild, from his haughty intellectualism to his hair to his condescending style toward those who opposed him on the budget.

Don Regan had been used to presiding over one of the largest financial service institutions in the world. He had hundreds of David Stockmans working for him as analysts in his past life, reporting their findings to him, then following his orders promptly and efficiently once he made a decision. Here the shoe was on the other foot. Stockman ran the budget and insisted that budgetary restraints should drive public policy as he proposed to slash spending across the board.

"No, no," Regan said. "You've got it ass-backwards. Policy should drive the budget, not the other way around, and we don't want *real* spending cuts, just a reduction in the rate of growth." The two reached an impasse and neither would back off. Unfortunately, Regan had on his side Baker, Deaver, and Secretary of Defense Cap Weinberger, who was champing at the bit to launch a massive and obscenely expensive military buildup. All Stockman had in his camp was an army of young budget-cutting zealots like himself who had zero influence on the White House. At the end of the day, the spenders won the battle, which prompted Stockman to go public with the statement that, if the federal government refused to lower the level of spending, the result would be expanding deficits that would require tax hikes down the road.

The media ran a story reporting that Ronald Reagan personally took Stockman "to the woodshed" for daring to suggest that taxes might have to be raised. The public got the impression that Ronnie dragged Stockman out to the shed, kneed him in the balls, slapped him around for a while, then spanked him with a two-by-four. The truth was that the whole episode was manufactured by Baker and leaked to the press as a means of humiliating Stockman and keeping him in line with the Baker and Regan agenda, as distinct from the Reagan agenda. The upshot of the entire fiasco was that taxes were indeed hiked, as Stockman had predicted, by weakening the provisions of Reagan's tax cut bill, and government spending proceeded to spiral out of control.

Stockman may not have won any personality contests, but he was one of the few people in the administration who was seriously committed to the Reagan agenda. His mistake was in believing that Ronald Reagan was as committed as he was.

25

The Randian Altruist

While Regan and Stockman were sparring in the background, Ed Meese established a highly visible committee to review spending called the Private Sector Survey on Price Control, popularly known as the Grace Commission after its chairman J. Peter Grace. Members of the Troika considered Meese to be little more than a fifth wheel in the administration. He was only there because he had known the president for twenty years since their days in California and he was the closest thing to a buddy that Reagan had. Other than his staying power within the Reagan orbit, however, Meese had no discernible talents. Memos tended to get lost in his in-box for months at a time before he discovered them, and sometimes they were lost forever. As far as Baker and Regan were concerned, Meese was a tower of mediocrity whom they tolerated since he never posed a threat to anyone. In an effort to make himself useful, he set up the Grace Commission under the mistaken notion that Ronald Reagan was interested in reining in government spending.

Grace and a small army of volunteer businessmen met regularly to identify areas of "waste" in the federal government, and after many long months of analysis, they produced forty reports outlining some 2,500 separate recommendations for cuts in federal expenditures. Meese presented the Grace Commission findings to Reagan in the company of Baker, Regan, Deaver, and a few budget wonks, who had all they could do to keep from laughing out loud as Ronnie's eyes glazed over before he lapsed into a coma from which they thought he could never be revived.

More as a gesture to make Grace and his fellow executives feel that their many hours of volunteer labor were not spent in vain, a few of their recommendations were actually implemented. Mostly they had to do with eliminating some publications, monstrous tomes that no one read anyway, and firing a few employees who were more than made up for by increased hiring in the Department of Defense. In all, Reagan claimed to have put some $46 billion "to better use," mostly by shifting the money into the military budget. In any event, the alleged savings amounted to about 1.4% of total expenditures.

Libertarians did not expect any more than token spending cuts from Baker and the rest of the Wesley Mouch brigade, but they did hope for progress in this area from former Ayn Rand protege, Alan Greenspan. After all, hadn't Alan been one of Ayn's favorite boy-chicks from the Inner Circle days, when he lapped up Objectivist wisdom at the feet of the Grand Goddess herself? Prospects for real budget restraint brightened considerably in 1983, when Greenspan was tapped to head up a commission on reforming the Social Security system. Greenspan and his cohorts put on their green eyeshades and labored long and hard over a veritable sea of information, crunching numbers, analyzing data, and making projections. Finally, they were ready to release their findings.

Surely Greenspan, dedicated Objectivist that he was, had come up with a truly *Galtian* proposal for revamping this federal Ponzi scheme that had been set in motion by the Fascist dictator Roosevelt half a century earlier. We held our breath, leaned forward in our chairs, and focused our undivided attention on the nuggets of wisdom that were about to issue from Greenspan's mouth. "We have decided," Alan said, "that the key to addressing the Social Security issue is …"

Yes, Alan, tell us. Scrap it altogether? Privatize it? Farm it out to financial services firms? Let all Americans decide for themselves how to prepare for their own retirement?

"… is to …"

Yes, Alan, yes. Tell us, tell us.

"… is to raise taxes."

What? What did Ayn Rand's boy-chick say? What was this heroic individualist on leave from Galt's Gulch advocating? *Raise* taxes! Surely he was misquoted. Surely he didn't mean it? He must have said *phase* taxes out, not raise taxes, and been misunderstood by the press. Say it ain't so, Alan. You're giving me a nervous breakdown. You should be ashamed of yourself. It's a good thing Ayn was dead or she'd give you a spanking you'd never forget. Come back from the grave, Ayn, and give this man a slap!

Yes, that was Greenspan's recommendation after months of tortured deliberation. Raise taxes. Specifically, the Greenspan Commission on Social Security Reform advocated a program of dedicating general tax revenues to the Social Security fund for the first time ever. Coverage would be extended to employees of nonprofit organizations and to all new federal employees. Further, state and local government employees would be prohibited from dropping out of the system. Tax hikes scheduled for 1985 would be accelerated into 1984, then raised again in 1988. Worse yet, self-employed people would have to pay Social Security taxes on 100% of their income instead of 75%.

Even Ronnie was stunned. Reagan thought Greenspan was a tax-cutter like him and had committed himself to following the recommendations of the Greenspan commission. Alan backed him into a corner, and Reagan felt he had little choice but to go along with Greenspan's proposal. Congress enacted it into law with a few minor revisions designed to *soften* the proposal's overall impact. Even Tip O'Neill thought it a bit harsh.

God, protect me from my allies; my enemies I'll take care of myself!

Other efforts to save money through privatization, sales of federal land, and similar measures were ignored or discarded. The government had grotesquely mismanaged its loan portfolio, which amounted to about $250 billion in 1983, and Reagan had a sterling opportunity to turn it over to private management. The federal government owned 770 million acres of land, much of which was underutilized and costing taxpayers a fortune. The government's vast sea of naval petroleum reserves was likewise hugely unprofitable. Other activities such as the postal system, the air traffic control system, Conrail and Amtrak, and the power marketing administration were woefully administered by the government. Talk about privatizing these programs was just that—talk with no serious effort to follow through on it.

During Reagan's first term in office, the administration's efforts at privatization were limited and generally unsuccessful. Ed Meese terminated the land sales initiative for political reasons. If Meese saw any contradiction between this action and the Adam Smith tie he always wore, he never bothered to explain it. Congress put an end to an early attempt to sell Conrail when the unions, as well as management, made a fuss. Congress finally did agree to sell Conrail in 1986, but only after Reagan gave in to a public offering of Conrail stock rather than a sale of the railroad to a private company. Reagan did make an effort to advance various privatization measures during his otherwise disastrous second term, but Congress rejected most of them.

One of the most stunning developments as Reagan's first term came to a close was the tax plan drawn up by Treasury Secretary Don Regan in the interests of simplification. By his own admission, Regan was not a flat-taxer; he believed that higher income groups should pay a higher proportional share of taxes, but he did want to revamp the existing tax code and reduce the number of bracket rates. The best part of Regan's proposal, which came to be known as Treasury I, was the substitution of three new brackets—15%, 25%, and 35%—for the existing fourteen brackets ranging from 11% to 50%. So far so good.

To make up for the anticipated revenue loss, however, Regan further proposed to substantially raise taxes on corporations to a level that made even the Democrats gag. When Ronald Reagan first saw Treasury I, he asked free market economist William Niskanen what he thought of it.

"Walter Mondale would have been proud," Niskanen told Reagan.

Donald Regan, after having spent his entire working life on Wall Street at the helm of Bull, Banks, Forbes & Trotsky, had suddenly discovered a populist streak in his political makeup. He now believed that corporations were not paying their "fair share." Neither apparently were the wealthy, for Regan also proposed to toss out all existing tax shelters except for the mortgage write-off.

Regan seemed to take pride in the cast of left-wing dunderheads who came to the defense of his tax bill. Such free market stalwarts as Ralph Nader, George McGovern, Charles Rangel, and Joseph Pechman of the cloyingly liberal Brookings Institute rallied to Regan's defense. Conservatives and libertarians were outraged, as was the president himself who didn't know what to *do* with this thing that had been foisted on him by his Treasury Secretary. If Regan thought he would win some brownie points with the liberal media, which uniformly despised him, he was sadly mistaken. The media had long resented Regan's arrogant manner, his haughty and patronizing demeanor, and had been flaying him alive for the past four years. Chrysler chairman Lee Iacocca, not exactly Mr. Nice Guy himself, had one brief run-in with Regan a couple of years earlier and summed him up perfectly.

"You're a nasty son of a bitch," Iacocca had told Regan to his face.

"I'm not a son of a bitch," Regan had replied.

The media did not buy Regan's newly discovered populism. They recognized the hypocrisy in his tax bill for what it was and continued to hound him as unmercifully as ever. No matter *what* he did, Don Regan remained a nasty son of a bitch who could not get *anyone* to like him.

Regan's tax proposal was put on the back burner until after the 1984 election, which Reagan won in a crushing landslide. The economy was strong, inflation and unemployment were falling, and Reagan was at the crest of his popularity. Even if it were revealed that he had been arrested as a serial killer in the past, Ronald Reagan could still have trounced his Democratic opponent. Walter Mondale was a cross between Prairie Socialist Hubert Humphrey, with a vapid smile fixed permanently on his face, and bloodless robot Al Gore (before he reinvented himself after losing to Bush II in 2000) who had a windup key growing out of his back. Reagan sauntered amiably to a second term, then promptly fell asleep.

In one of the more bizarre dances of modern politics, Don Regan and Jim Baker announced that they wanted to swap jobs. Jim Baker, who claimed he was burned out as chief of staff, became Secretary of the Treasury, and Don Regan, who was dying to get a foothold inside the

White House where he could preside as "chief operating officer," according to his own job description, became the president's new chief of Staff. Rumor had it that Baker and Regan swapped mistresses as well. That neither man was suited for his new position never occurred to Ronald Reagan; neither was well suited to his old position either. So Reagan gave his blessing to the manipulative duo, who proceeded to destroy what was left of Reagan's credibility as a leader.

The first thing Don Regan did as Chief of Staff was pick a fight with Nancy Reagan, who was an almost fanatic custodian of her husband's time and affections. Nancy believed in astrology and used Deaver as an accomplice in manipulating Ronnie's schedule, so that the president sallied forth into the real world only on those days Nancy's guru considered propitious. Ronnie indulged his wife's eccentricities up to the point where it bordered on the affairs of the Republic, but no further, and Deaver, dutiful chamberlain that he was, protected their little secret. Regan, however, lost little time in ridiculing Nancy's superstitions to everyone in the administration, thereby earning the First Lady's eternal enmity.

Fortunately, as Reagan's second term got under way, even Jim Baker realized that Treasury I, Don Regan's proposed tax plan, was loaded with dynamite. As the new Treasury Secretary, he went to work with Richard Darman, his new Deputy Secretary, to give Treasury I a make-over. Neither Baker nor Darman were tax experts, but they fiddled and fine tuned and finessed Regan's monstrosity until they thought it would meet with Reagan's approval, if not his unqualified support. So was born Treasury II, an improvement over Treasury I in that it lowered the top income tax bracket to 28%, which represented a further 6% cut in income taxes. However, Treasury II contained some nasty provisions as well, including an increase in the capital gains tax and the elimination of essentially all tax shelters except for the interest on mortgage payments.

That might have been acceptable to most taxpayers if the top rate had been flattened down closer to 20 percent, with a Constitutional amendment in place prohibiting future administrations from raising the

206 It Usually Begins With Ayn Rand

bracket rates again. But that was too much to ask of politicians of both major parties. Later on, under both Bush and Clinton, the bracket rates retraced their inevitable spiral back upward, reaching 39.6% within a year after Clinton took office. Reagan delivered a simplified and more equitable tax code, then Bush and Clinton put the screws on U.S. taxpayers by lifting the tax rates closer to where they were in 1981. The problem was: with the loopholes closed, *there was no place left to hide anymore!*

The second Reagan tax bill cemented over all the loopholes that had made high bracket rates somewhat tolerable in the first place. Gone were full deductibility of IRA contributions; deductibility of credit card interest; tax-sheltered equipment leasing, oil and gas, movie, and real estate limited partnerships; unregistered bearer bonds; mortgage writeoffs on second homes above a certain limit; and all the other legal dodges used by taxpayers to reduce their tax burden in the past. One of the consequences of Treasury II was to flush a lot of underground money out into the open. Bearer bonds were to be discontinued after July 1, which meant that all the drug dealers in the country, mom and pop retail store owners, pizza parlor owners, restaurateurs and ginmill operators, plumbers, electricians, and other beneficiaries of cash businesses had to drive to the bank, open their safe deposit boxes, take out their bearer bonds, and bring them in to their stockbrokers—no questions asked if they did it before July. Cash hidden in those boxes was flushed out too, since rules requiring financial firms to report deposits in excess of $10,000 went into effect at the same time.

So there you were, a broker at Fishball & Evans—or maybe it was Gruntal & Company—sitting at your desk watching the ticker tape run by overhead, when suddenly half your clients showed up en masse demanding immediate attention. There was Jack O'Brien, owner of Shannon's Irish Pub across the street where you sometimes drank for free, standing in front of you with a shopping bag stuffed with bearer bonds and a pile of cash that reeked of beer and whiskey.

Jack, you see, had been putting himself on the books for $25,000 in annual income while he stuffed another thirty or forty grand a year in his safe deposit box. Most of that money went into Treasury bearer bonds, the income from which Jack treated as though it were exempt from taxes. Jack sat down sheepishly and upended the bag onto your desk, depositing a quarter million or so in Treasuries and a hundred grand in booze-soaked cash that the IRS never knew he had.

"Oh my God, Jack, I'm getting high just smelling that stuff."

"I got to get rid of it," he said.

"No kidding. I'll sell the bonds and get you a certified check in a week."

"Can I get cash for them instead?"

"I'm afraid not. Not even gambling casinos dispense cash these days. It's got to be a check."

"This doesn't get reported to IRS, does it?"

"Not yet. But in a few weeks, sales transactions for stocks, bonds, and real estate have to be reported.

"Good. I'm selling out in time then."

"I don't need to hear any more. Whether or not you report it is strictly up to you. What do you want me to do with the cash you brought in?"

"I'd better hang on to it. I'm buying a house in the Hamptons for $350,000, only the listed price will be a quarter mil. I'll pay for it with the bond proceeds and slip the buyer a hundred grand under the table. That way I get rid of the cash and the buyer pays a smaller capital gains tax."

"Jack, for Christ's sake, I don't want to *hear* any more!"

After Jack left, Mario Fantozi who owned a pizza parlor came in and dumped a similar stash on your desk, except that his smelled like olive oil and garlic.

"I gotta to get rid of this," he explained.

"I understand, Mario."

"I'ma gonna sella the bonds and buy a nice house inna Hamptons for …"

"Say no more, Mario. Whatever you do next is strictly up to you. Just don't *tell* me about it, okay."

For the next week and a half, business was phenomenal as dozens of your best clients paraded through the door and unloaded their bearer bonds. You sold millions upon millions of dollars worth of hearer bonds, taking a hefty commission each time, and even converted some of the cash into stocks for those who wanted to play the equities market instead of buying real estate. And then, abruptly, they were gone. Business took a nosedive.

All the money disappeared and your office became a morgue.

You see, Ronnie not only closed all the loopholes and flushed out all the underground cash, he also destroyed your tax shelter business, which accounted for about 50 percent of your commission stream. Your clients merely shifted their wealth into different assets and you were ready for food stamps.

Thanks a lot, Ron.

26

The Patriotic Subversives

The net effect of the 1981 and 1986 tax bills was a significant reduction in the overall tax burden, as well as a simplification of the code. We were a long way from genuine tax reform of the type libertarians could live with, but Reagan had made a giant stride forward toward that goal.

Reagan's record in other economic matters was far less satisfactory, as we've seen. During his eight years in office, the United States imposed more restrictions on foreign trade than it had eliminated. Ronnie failed to take the initiative, as the leader of the Western World, in promoting freer global trade, one of the primary tenets of his free market ideology.

In 1987, Paul Volcker announced that he wanted to step down as chairman of the Federal Reserve. Volcker's tenure at the helm of the Fed was admirable. In the absence of a gold standard to support a nation's currency, the role of a chief banker is critical. Tight controls over the money supply had led to the lowest inflation rate in twenty years, thereby restoring the integrity of the dollar and underpinning the growth of the economy under Reagan. Volcker's decision to leave was likely to unsettle world financial markets unless Reagan appointed a suitable successor, someone equally committed to monetary restraint. So Ronnie searched and searched and decided to give the job to …

… to *Randian muscle-mystic Alan Greenspan,* the same Objectivist hero who had done such a notable job of preserving Franklin D. Roosevelt's Social Security scam.

Well, this was Alan's opportunity to redeem himself by making atonement for his unforgivable act of treachery. Alan was sworn in as the new Fed chairman in July 1987 and went on to distinguish himself as a worthy successor to Volcker for the next nineteen years.

Alan, your epistemological mother would have been proud of the way you acquitted yourself, but she'll never let you return to Galt's Gulch even if you crawl back on your knees.

As far as foreign policy under Reagan was concerned, it was literally conducted *under* him during his second term—in the *basement* under the White House. Its two main architects were Marine Corps Lieutenant Colonel Oliver North and former Navy Admiral John Poindexter. If Ronald Reagan was somewhat, um, inattentive shall we say during his last few years in office—out to lunch, perhaps, or tucked in for a long nap—what can one say of his chief of staff Don Regan who fancied himself as the administration's chief operating officer? Did ever a chief of staff serve his boss so poorly as Regan did Reagan? Hardly. Regan would have done the country a bigger favor attending to the affairs of the nation instead of concerning himself with Nancy's astrology hobby.

On Regan's watch, while the president was snoozing, two zealots named North and Poindexter (with the blessing of Bud McFarlane who later tried to kill himself over the fiasco) used Israel as an intermediary to sell weapons illegally to Iran, without the approval of the president or the Congress. That was bad enough in itself except that they screwed the Iranians by overcharging them, and then channeled most of the money to the Contras in Nicaragua. For those who missed the episode, the Contras were a group of right wing thugs who were at war with a group of left wing thugs called the Sandanistas. In their fevered paranoid state, North, Poindexter, and McFarlane imagined that the right wing thugs were a bastion of freedom standing tall against a Godless Communist menace that was about to engulf the Western Hemisphere, citing as proof the left wing beachheads they had already established in Berkeley, California, and Cambridge, Massachusetts.

Everyone in the administration knew what was going on except the president. North, Poindexter, and McFarlane were the point men, but Vice President George Bush, CIA director Bill Casey, Attorney General Ed Meese (who had been kicked upstairs once again), State Department official Elliott Abrams, Secretary of Defense Casper Weinberger, Secretary of State George Shultz, CIA operatives Clair George and Alan Fiers—and possibly Nancy Reagan's astrologer—were privy to information about the Iran-Contra initiative. Everyone knew except Ronnie, who later claimed he didn't know, or didn't know if he knew, or couldn't remember if he knew or not or if and when he had ever been informed.

Lawrence Walsh was appointed independent counsel to investigate exactly what had transpired, and he proceeded to botch his case. He later accused Ed Meese of being the architect of an attempted cover-up—the same Ed Meese who had trouble locating his in-box, let alone anything in it. Walsh won convictions against both North and Poindexter, which were later overturned on grounds of weak evidence. He hounded Weinberger unsuccessfully while letting Shultz off the hook, for no other reason than he found Weinberger to be "arrogant" while Shultz was a "voice of courage and reason." Walsh detested George Bush—certainly one of the most detestable men in Washington—but Bush got even later by pardoning everyone connected with the sorry adventure. Aside from the problem of having unelected swine such as these running covert operations without anyone's permission, Iran-Contra occupied the spotlight during Reagan's last two years in office, diverting attention from the much-needed economic reforms.

By 1988 the revolution that had gotten off to a promising start during Reagan's first 100 days in the White House sputtered pathetically into oblivion. Reagan's most ardent defenders were forced to admit that his second term was a dramatic departure from his first. Ronnie was like the month of March, roaring in like a lion and leaving town like a whimpering lamb, waving and smiling valiantly as his most trusted lieutenants were being carted off in handcuffs. Through it all, however, his popularity was still high with the voting public. The American people refused to believe that the president who had lowered their taxes, given them six years of booming prosperity with moderating inflation, and who had brought the "Evil Empire" to its knees by outspending it could have been a part of the sordid operation that had taken place almost literally beneath his nose.

So Ronnie waved bye-bye to America and flew back to LaLa Land with Nancy on Air Force One. Bye-bye, Ronnie. It was bad enough that Reagan had let us down in the end, but did he have to compound his weak finale by leaving his vice president in charge? Dear God, say it isn't so. One of the great benefits of having King George I as vice president for eight years was that he was all but hidden from view. Georgie Boy lurked there in the background, biding his time, biting his tongue, trying not to fidget noticeably as he waited obediently in Reagan's shadow for his own chance, finally, to run the show.

Did King George believe in *anything* at all?

Let's see, he was a Rockefeller Republican when it suited him. Then George dashed into the phone booth to change his ideological attire in time for the 1988 presidential race. Zap, the man who had once denounced lower taxes as "Voodoo Economics" suddenly emerged as a born-again Reaganite, vowing that he would never raise taxes under any circumstances. More incredibly, this ideological chameleon also embraced Reagan's antiabortion rhetoric in an effort to convince the Christian Right he was really—really and truly—one of them. Reagan, at least, had never acted on any of his socially conservative rhetoric. Reagan sang the praises of family values, but in real life he rarely went to church and didn't get along with his own children. He and Nancy presided over a typically American dysfunctional family. But King George, in his shameful attempt to convince everyone that he was the true heir to the Reagan legacy, actually adopted the Christian Right's social agenda as his very own.

What did King George believe in? Nothing apparently.

"After years of observing him in his role of vice president," said economist William Niskanen, "I find his views still unclear." Unclear? Nonexistent would have been more accurate.

George Bush believed in one thing only: that he was born with a divine right to be president. His early mentor Nelson Rockefeller had believed the same thing about himself but, in the end, the prize was denied him. Unfortunately, George Bush succeeded. The warm glow of Reagan's popularity descended on Bush almost by default; there was no one else around to benefit from it. Bush was also assisted by the specter of Michael Dukakis, the sorriest candidate for high office since—since the beginning of time. What was one to make of this humorless little machine from Massachusetts who looked like a cross between Mr. Bean and Pee Wee Herman? The man was grim. He was totally devoid of a sense of irony or whimsy. He was diminutive, not necessarily evil in itself, but almost a lethal physical flaw in American politics. Dukakis was not merely a bleeding heart liberal, he was a bleeding heart robot who looked as though he slept in starched pajamas.

Of course George Bush was elected president in 1988. President Michael Dukakis was *unthinkable.* President of Bulgaria perhaps. President of Azerbaijan or some equally grim little slave state over there in Eastern—*far* Eastern—Europe perhaps. But President of These Here United States of America? Never! The little dork was only capable of winning a race in some ultra-left concentration camp like the Peoples Republic of Massachusetts or Vermont.

It was bad enough being saddled with President George Bush for four long years, but King George committed the unforgivable sin of foisting Danny Boy Quayle on the country as his hapless, hopeless, inept, semiliterate vice president. The choice of Dan Quayle as his running mate spoke volumes about Bush's low character and lack of self-esteem. After all the years of loitering in some greater man's shadow, Bush finally had a chance to run his own show, and he was *not* going to be overshadowed by someone with more, um, charisma than he had—that is to say, by someone with any substance at all. So he reached down into the grab hag of possible running mates, and reached lower and lower until he could not descend any further, and plucked Dan Quayle from the bottom of the pile.

Dan Quayle.

What was one to make of this simple-minded specimen of American mediocrity? It was a testimony to Ronald Reagan's lingering popularity that his vice president was able to capture the White House in 1988.

214 It Usually Begins With Ayn Rand

King George was unelectable on his own, let alone with a cretinous albatross like Dan Quayle slung around his neck. To put it kindly, Dan Quayle was an embarrassment. If the 1988 presidential race had been a contest between Quayle and Lloyd Bentsen, the Democratic vice presidential candidate, Bentsen would have won in a landslide. During the heat of the campaign, Danny Boy actually announced,

"Republicans understand the importance of bondage between a mother and a child."

Thanks for sharing that illuminating tidbit with us, Dan.

He also had a touching insight into the Holocaust. "The Holocaust was an obscene period in our nation's history. I mean in this century's history. But we all lived in this century. I didn't live in this century."

Dan, you didn't live on Planet Earth in *any* century.

The campaign was going downhill in a hurry when Dan announced that "It isn't pollution that's harming the environment. It's the impurities in our air and water that are doing it."

The man certainly had a gift for tautology. Fortunately, nobody was listening to this guy or the race would have been over in August when Danny Boy stated, "Let me just tell you how thrilling it really is, and how what a challenge it is, because in 1988 the question is whether we're going forward to tomorrow or whether we're going to go past to the—to the back."

It's inconceivable that anyone actually tuning in to what he was saying would consciously have voted him a heartbeat away from the presidency. This was George Bush's hand-picked running mate, the person who would be directing the affairs of the most powerful nation on earth in the event of Bush's early demise—a distinct possibility considering Bush's dietary habits.

Eat your broccoli, George. It's more important now than ever! Not that we wanted *you* to be president, but Quayle as president was even more absurd.

This was the dilemma libertarians were faced with in 1988, eight years after the Reagan Revolution had started off so promisingly. Dukakis? God help us all. For those libertarians who were inclined to vote, the decision was agonizing. Clench your teeth and vote for Bush or waste a vote on Libertarian Party candidate Ron Paul?

This is what you left us with, Ronnie.

As you stepped into the voting booth that chilly November, you could not justify pulling the lever down for Bush/Quayle under *any* circumstances. Not even if Jesse Jackson were the Democratic nominee. Not even if Fidel Castro were running against Bush. No way, no time, not ever. Reach for the muskets! It's time for a *real* revolution. So you shed a tear and voted for Ron Paul, knowing that you had cast your vote into a black hole. Not that you had anything against Ron Paul personally, but it was just an exercise in futility. Maybe there was a point in registering a protest vote—after all, you yourself had gone out looking for them in 1974. But you had grown far more cynical during the ensuing fourteen years. Everything seemed increasingly hopeless, particularly in the aftermath of the aborted Reagan Revolution that left you feeling, once again, that there was no way out of the mess we were in.

That Reagan had selected Bush to be his own running mate in 1980 had been a cause of great concern that Ronnie was a bit ambivalent about his professed ideology. You had been troubled by it at the time, but chalked it up to political expediency. Most mainstream political tickets are "balanced"—a westerner with an easterner, a southerner with a northerner, a Catholic with a Protestant. This was supposed to be the best way—the *only* way—to appeal to a broad cross section of the voting public.

But Reagan with Bush?

Why not balance Adam Smith with John Maynard Keynes or Ludwig von Mises with John Kenneth Galbraith? How about Ayn Rand with Jesse Jackson? Geographical balance is one thing. Sexual balance—a man with a woman—is fine. But how about some ethical compatibility, some agreement on principle? Shouldn't running mates at least be in the same ballpark, the same hemisphere, when it comes to fundamental values? The idea that George Bush had become a born-again Reaganite as he approached his dotage was laughable. Sadly, as it turned out, Reagan had been a closet Bushite all along, a tax-cutter, yes, but a big-spending moderate Republican beneath his soaring free market rhetoric.

So, in 1988, we had Bush and Quayle to look forward to for the next four years. A middle-of-the-road aristocrat who believed in nothing, and an inarticulate frat boy who believed that "the loss of life would be irreplaceable" after the 1989 San Francisco earthquake. Dan Quayle gave a bad name to the causes he espoused. Every time he said he believed in free enterprise, you wanted to throw up.

Why couldn't you have been a Marxist, Dan? You would have driven the final nail into the coffin of socialism forevermore. That capitalism still has any credibility whatsoever, after *you* got finished singing its praises, speaks volumes about its viability as the only ethical economic system imaginable. Thank God that free enterprise has managed to survive Dan Quayle and George Bush—everywhere except in the United States, of course.

So George and Dan took the oaths of their respective offices in January 1989, and you were suddenly plunged into the deepest depression since Johnson beat Goldwater in 1964. There was no hope for the future. All was gloom and doom. "Read my lips!" King George had snarled during the campaign, sounding for all the world like a born-again tough guy. "No new taxes!"

Hooray for George.

After he was elected, Georgie reverted to type and socked us with the biggest tax hike in decades. Just great! Four years of Bush and Quayle to look forward to. Worse yet, there was no one on the horizon who was capable of rescuing the Reagan Revolution from oblivion, who was able to rekindle the spark of Ronnie's first 100 days and ignite a fire that could not be smothered. Once in office, Bush worked hard to put his own stamp on the presidency and to distance himself as far as possible from the Reagan legacy.

"When Bush got in he wanted to distance himself a little from Reagan," Reagan loyalist Bill Rusher told me in 1993. "Unfortunately, he did it all too well ... His attempt to invoke family values was just plain laughable ... Reagan understood that the social issues, which are real issues, are not like the economic issues on which you can often pass a bill in this session. Social issues deal with great fundamental beliefs as to what America is about. American opinion moves slowly and the president's job is to be, in a sense, almost our spiritual leader—not to expect a bill to go sailing through Congress in this session, or even to demand that. Reagan pleaded for the great social issues. A lot of these ideas are going to take time to work their way through the system. Whoever understands that, and still stands for the social issues and for the economic issues and for the libertarian issues, is going to be the one who will pull us together again."

Cliff White's assessment of George Bush was equally critical. "[Bush] was on to something during Desert Storm when he talked about the new world order; it was the germination of a grand theme. The problem is that George didn't have the foggiest idea of what the new world order was. If he had possessed the vision (which he trivialized as 'the vision thing' in his reelection campaign), he could have used this theme to formulate a great concept of where the world was heading throughout the rest of the decade and beyond, and the role the United States would play in this evolving new world order. Instead he let the opportunity slip by. What could have been a spiritually and morally uplifting battle cry for his presidential campaign became nothing more than a public relations slogan penned by one of his speech writers. Incredibly, George Bush followed up a decisive victory in the Middle East with a thoroughly inept and disgraceful campaign for the presidency."

Neither Bill Rusher nor Cliff White (who died before his memoir was published: *Politics as a Noble Calling,* which he asked me to write for him) have been libertarians in the strict sense, but they are the type of conservatives most libertarians can work with. Both have been staunch fiscal conservatives, tilting toward low taxes and fiscal restraint. Both have also been fairly conservative on social issues, but neither has ever believed that his moral views ought to be legislated into law. Cliff White, whom I got to know better during the course of interviewing him for his book, was one of the most honest, spiritually attuned human beings I've ever met. If Cliff had one major failing it was his naive belief that something he called "good government"—limited government with responsive representatives who didn't abuse their power—was possible.

Sorry, Cliff. It ain't so.

Jefferson had it right when he said it would take a revolution every generation or so to preserve our individual liberties. Ben Franklin was right on target when he announced after the Constitutional Convention that the Founding Fathers had delivered a republic "if you can keep it."

So we were stuck with George Bush and Danny Boy for four long, painful, agonizing, and embarrassing years. George later admitted that he "blew it" when he tapped Quayle to be his vice president. Wrong, George. Hopeless as he was, Quayle didn't blow a second term in office for you. After frothing at the mouth all those years to finally become President of These Here United States of America, you blew your presidency yourself—and the tattered remnants of the Reagan revolution along with it.

It was your own dishonesty that did it, George. Your own lack of principles. Your own venality. Your own moral and philosophical impotence. And you blew it all in 1992 to a slick con artist from Arkansas who was born with the Mark of the Beast on his dick.

27

The Mark of the Beast

"Welcome to President Bush, Mrs. Bush, and my fellow astronauts," said Dan Quayle while addressing the twentieth anniversary celebration of the moon landing in 1989.

Lest anyone thought that Danny Boy had little grasp of extraterrestrial matters, the vice president announced the same year that "Mars is essentially in the same orbit ... Mars is somewhat the same distance from the sun, which is very important. We have seen pictures where there are canals, we believe, and water. If there is water, that means there is oxygen. If oxygen, that means we can breathe.'

Sadly, that was true. No one had yet thought of depriving Quayle of his oxygen supply, so he was still breathing.

On earthly matters, Danny was even more insightful. "Hawaii has always been a very pivotal role in the Pacific. It is *in* the Pacific. It is a part of the United States that is an island that is right here."

"What a waste it is to lose one's mind," Dan Quayle said during his 1992 campaign for reelection. "Or not to have a mind is very wasteful. How true that is."

Truer words were never spoken, Dan. And no one proved that point better than you.

Stop the world, I want to get off! Was there no end to this banality?

The Bush presidency was a disaster on every conceivable front from a libertarian perspective. First, King George committed the unforgivable crime of raising our taxes—and not just a little, but rather he socked us with one of the heftiest tax hikes in U.S. history. Second, he spent our money like a drunken blue blood and sent the federal budget deficit spiraling out of control. Third, he mismanaged his relationship with former CIA ally Saddam Hussein and turned him into an Iraqi version of Libyan lunatic Khadafi.

The subsequent war in the Middle East, stage-managed for public relations purposes under the jingoistic title of "Desert Storm," was a direct outcome of misguided U.S. foreign policy. Throughout the 1980s, the CIA (with Bush's approval) had subsidized Hussein because of his opposition to the Islamic dictators in Iran. Why the U.S. government finds it necessary to take sides in quarrels between totalitarian butchers is a subject worthy of book-length treatment in itself. The simplest argument seems to be that, in a world in which the Soviet Union backed one combatant, the only way to maintain the so-called balance of power was for the U.S. to support the other party.

Sorry, I don't see the logic there. If the communists wanted to spend billions of rubles they couldn't afford propping up a bankrupt regime, it didn't make financial sense for the U.S. to pursue the same policy. From an ethical standpoint, it was (and is) immoral to support a regime that brutalizes its own citizens. Militarily, it would have been more cost-effective to maintain a strong defense force rather than a military-industrial complex capable of embarking on worldwide adventures. And as far as American "international interests" are concerned, they are best left for the marketplace to sort out. It is not the government's business to tell private corporations where they can drill for oil or with whom they can trade. Private profit-making enterprises are capable of evaluating risks and making their own decisions about economic matters.

So, given the sorry history of American foreign policy as well as the role he played in it throughout his life, Bush had pretty much backed himself into a corner when Hussein decided to push his way south into Kuwait. George's own past had left him with few options. He had little choice personally except to stop his former pal dead in his tracks before Hussein made a mess in the desert, close to Saudi Arabia, close to Israel, close to Jordan and a few unlikely U.S. allies in the region, most of whom were hostile toward one another. So King George cajoled, he twisted arms, he promised all sorts of future payola to get our European allies and Japan to back him in Desert Storm.

Hey, guys! Your oil supply is at risk.

Well, it wouldn't have been if the marketplace, rather than career politicians and bureaucrats, ruled. So Bush launched Desert Storm with all the pomp and technological wizardry that the modern age could muster, and he turned it into the greatest worldwide miniseries that had ever been staged on Planet Earth.

And what a show it was—except for the poor sons (and daughters) of bitches who were forced to don uniforms and expose themselves to Hussein's scud missiles and chemical warheads. Bush staged an extravaganza that had the entire world tuned in for a blow-by-blow replay of the action. Manic-depressive comedian Jonathan Winters came out of retirement, changed his name to Norman Schwartzkopf, and launched a second career as a war hero. Joint defense chief Colin Powell became an instant celebrity with his daily briefings—from the safety of Washington. Book publishers stood in line with buckets and buckets of advance money for key participants in the interest of advancing the cause of literature.

Then, suddenly, barely 100 days or so into the action, King George declared victory and brought the curtain down on the final act. Why? Because "our objectives have been achieved," he said. What objectives? Saddam Hussein was still alive. Worse yet, so was Dan Quayle, as far as anyone could tell. How did Danny Boy feel about Desert Storm? "Bobby Knight told me this," Dan said. 'There is nothing that a good defense cannot beat a better offense.' In other words, a good offense wins." In other words, shut the hell up, Dan!

George's approval rating was up around 95%, so "why not quit while I'm ahead?" he figured. Wrong strategy, George. If the war was working for you, then the correct reelection strategy was to *prolong* the war, not end it. Why put a stop to the only thing you had going for you? You couldn't very well take any credit for lowering taxes after raising them. You couldn't benefit from the economy, which was plummeting into a recession. You couldn't boast about narrowing the budget deficit, which was exploding and likely to widen further thanks to a very expensive war effort. You had *zip* going for you, George, except for a highly successful war that had your fellow Americans cheering themselves hoarse as they marveled at U.S. military superiority from command centers—that is to say, from their neighborhood taverns—all over the country. And you wanted to end all that and allow voters to start focusing on the troubles brewing in their daily lives?

How silly of you, George. It was further proof of your own thundering incompetence.

No sooner did the curtain come down on the final act of Desert Storm, when Hussein came out of his bunker, returned to his palace in Baghdad, and picked up pretty much where he left off before Bush so rudely interrupted him. A few American soldiers lost their lives, a few thousand more suffered the long-lasting effects of Saddam's chemical weapons, and Jonathan Winters and Colin Powell inked lucrative book deals for their memoirs. Patriotic Americans all over the country climbed down off their barstools only to discover their jobs were gone as a nasty recession took hold. As a result, Bush's popularity ratings plummeted while a hale and hearty Saddam Hussein used the opportunity to rebuild his army and return to butchering the Khurds up north.

Great Victory, George.

So the stage was set for a bumbling George Bush and his tragic-comic vice president, who were forced to defend their incumbency in the midst of a brutish recession against a slick con artist from Arkansas with a "distinguishing characteristic"—the Mark of the Beast—tattooed prominently on his pecker. If you don't believe me, ask any female under the age of eighty in Arkansas. There is only one word that adequately describes the quality of the campaign staged by the Republican ticket in 1992.

Disgraceful!

Well perhaps *incompetent, boorish, vapid, insipid, banal, immoral, hollow,* and *utterly without substance* all come close to the mark as well.

Not even a tape recording of Bill Clinton engaged in verbal foreplay with Gennifer Flowers and making bigoted remarks about Mario Cuomo's Italian-American-Mafioso connections could save Bush and

Quayle from their well-earned defeat. The best thing anyone could say about Democratic candidate Bill Clinton was that he was *likable*.

Well, sure he was likable. He was fat, he played golf, and he cheated on his wife. In other words, he was a quintessential American male, circa 1992. How could anyone dislike Bill Clinton, unless her name was Hillary Clinton?

And so this smooth, slick, corrupt, amoral, technocratic, small-town politician ascended to the White House. This so-called New Democrat, packaged to perfection with a glittering surface concealing the vacuum underneath, assumed the role of the most powerful man on earth. Clinton was at least likable—a "sweet, undisciplined rogue," as Maureen Dowd referred to him in her *New York Times* column—but now we were stuck with Al Gore as well, "the most evil man on earth," according to radio talk show host Don Imus.

Gore, at least, had an agenda he believed in, even if he expressed it robotically at the time. But Clinton was nothing so much as a salesman willing to bend whichever way the wind was blowing. Clinton's guiding philosophy was to promote the cause of Bill Clinton, to do whatever was required to sustain his popularity and remain in office. If that meant tilting to the left by allowing Hillary to nationalize the health care industry—14 percent of the U.S. economy—that was okay. If it meant borrowing some free market rhetoric from the Reagan years, that was perfectly fine too. The only benefit of Clinton's waffling and constant changing of direction on the issues was that he ended up stealing Newt Gingrich's so-called "Contract With America" and promoting a semblance of free trade via NAFTA, reforming welfare, and balancing the budget. He had to do that to keep his presidency from becoming toothless following the Republican sweep of Congress in 1994. Of course, he also burdened the American people with the largest single tax hike in U.S. history earlier in his administration. He added two new, higher tax brackets on top of Bush's tax increase: 36% and 39.6%. Reagan had thrown out all the loopholes in the 1980s but at least lowered the top bracket rate to below 30%. Then Bush and Clinton drove the rates back up close to 40%, but with no place to hide any longer. The net result was that, by the end of 1993 the American people were saddled with the greatest overall tax burden in the nation's history. In this environment, Clinton had the audacity to declare, "the age of big government is over."

Really?

Financial wizards crunched the numbers and figured out that if the entire income tax were *eliminated* and the federal budget sliced by *one-third,* it would only bring us back to the situation that existed as recently as 1988. In 1988 the federal bureaucracy was far bigger and fatter than it was in 1971, the year *It Usually Begins With Ayn Rand* was first published, a year when even New Leftists referred to Washington D.C. as *Leviathan.* If the government was too big and intrusive *then,* what could one possibly say about the size it had grown to by 1994?

Anyone running for office in 1994, calling for the complete elimination of the federal income tax and a one-third reduction in the budget, would have been branded a *Radical Libertarian.* Yet, even that seemingly draconian political platform would only have whittled the state down to its bloated size of six years earlier. Those who believed that the "age of big government is over" had little or no dealings with the FBI, the BATF, or the IRS in Clinton's administration. Bill Clinton, as presidents before him had done, was fond of using all three Gestapo-like organizations to spy on and terrorize his political opponents.

The country was numb during Clinton's first two years in office. His whopping tax hike had taken hold and the economy was still struggling to emerge from the quagmire of the recession. In the aftermath of the off-year elections of 1994, the Republicans were elated over their so-called "revolution" at the polls when they found themselves in control of both the House of Representatives and the Senate for the first time in decades. Then, spearheaded by the leader of this latest Republican revolution, Field Marshal Newt Gingrich, the Republicans proceeded to snatch defeat from the jaws of victory. The "Contract With America" was not exactly a Galtian document to begin with. Where were the grand plans for dismantling the bureaucracy, for overhauling the ten-thousand-page tax code and eliminating the IRS, for privatizing Social Security and Medicare and getting rid of entitlement programs? They were nowhere to be found. The contract was a pale shadow of Milton Friedman's ideas for *truly* whittling down the size of government, but Clinton called the Republicans' bluff and embraced it as his own. The Republicans blew it and allowed Clinton to regain his footing well before the silly season began for the 1996 presidential campaign.

Indeed, the level of political discussion in the U.S. had sunk so low that you found yourself rooting for Al Gore in his much-publicized debate about NAFTA with that whining little demagogue from Texas, Ross Perot. This is what it had come down to: robotic Al Gore defending free markets and open trade from attack by one of the country's richest businessmen-turned-protectionist. It was Al Gore who conjured the specter of the anti-trade Smoot-Hawley bill as the cause of the Great Depression in 1929. What had the world come to when Gore, who had advocated an industrial policy to promote his favorite industries and whose wife was calling for censorship of song lyrics, had to defend free trade against assault by a billionaire businessman—and later, by Pat Buchanan and a coterie of fellow travelers on the conservative far right?

How depressing could things get?

Ayn Rand! Were you listening to all this? Send Ragnar, send John, send Dagney along to knock some heads together. I know we've had our differences in the past, but we needed a voice of reason, as well as some *real* free market revolutionaries, to straighten these guys out. Where were you when we needed you more than ever?

It looked as though we had hit rock bottom, but little was I to know that we had farther yet to fall. Little did I know that just a few years later, Bill Clinton would look like a better Republican than his successor in the Oval Office.

28

Rock Bottom With Bush II

The most amusing thing about the Clinton years was the Republicans' attempt to impeach him because he lied about his sexual peccadilloes, most famously, his dalliance with a chubby intern named Monica. Americans had always had a soft spot for stylish rogues and were willing to put up with them as long as they were amusing. Clinton amused us with his special talent for telling outrageous lies with a good ol' boy smile on his face. He knew he was lying and we knew he was lying, and somehow none of that mattered because the economy was strong again, times were good again, the stock market was booming, and everybody was making money. So what if Clinton was corrupt?

The negative side of the Clinton years was that the good times masked much of the political treachery that took place during his administration. Most dangerous among the abuses were the president's use of government enforcement agencies to attack his enemies. Through the FBI, he maintained a list of 900 secret files on former White House staffers and built a political database on hundreds of thousands of political opponents. Through the BATF he waged war on the Branch Davidians and Randy Weaver, to mention just two instances. Through the IRS, Clinton audited conservative and libertarian organizations, sent SWAT teams out to destroy innumerable small businesses, and arbitrarily terrorized ordinary taxpayers. Clinton routinely waged war against the U.S. Constitution and trampled all over the First, Second, Fourth, and Fifth Amendments in the Bill of Rights.

Our fat, golfing, adulterous president found a new way to conduct the business of government: extortion. He demonized the tobacco, health care, and technology industries (Bill Gates and Microsoft in particular) in a brazen attempt to seize hundreds of millions of dollars in fines and penalties for the federal piggy bank. You knew things had *really* hit rock bottom when former conservative and libertarian icon, Barry Goldwater, fell in love with Hillary Clinton and told his allies to "let Clinton get on with the business of governing."

Barry, what were you thinking? We didn't want this guy to govern any more than he was already governing! If he governed any more, we'd have federal SWAT teams kicking in our doors *every night.*

Perhaps most depressing of all about the schizophrenic state of affairs that characterized the country in the 1990s was the lack of viable political opposition. Libertarians who bothered to vote usually did so for either the Libertarian Party candidate or the Republican, as the lesser of major party evils. In 1996, we were stuck with cynical old political hack Bob Dole, who wore black socks on the beach, as the Republican opposition to Clinton. In 2000 we were forced to choose between wind-up doll Al Gore and Compassionate Conservative (read Big Government Conservative) George W. Bush as our leader for the next four years. So you held your nose, voted for Bush, and within two years realized that it was the biggest mistake you had made inside a voting booth in your entire life.

Now we had *really* hit rock bottom. Bush had actually lost the election to Al Gore, who ran one of the most unimaginative campaigns in modern political history. Gore, who was five times smarter than Bush Junior, managed to sound like the dummy in his debates with the inarticulate, tongue-tied scion of the Bush dynasty. Thanks to Boy George's father, however, Bush family apparatchik, hatchet man, and *consigliere* Jim Baker succeeded in stealing the election from Gore in the famous dust-up in Florida. Gore graciously stepped aside and let Junior ascend to the throne of the American power structure in Washington. And then Junior proceeded to saddle the American people with the worst administration since Lyndon Baines Johnson.

Bush started off by imposing tariffs on the steel industry and outspending LBJ on domestic discretionary programs by a ratio of two-to-one. In no time flat the budgetary surplus Clinton had presented to the

American people had vanished into the ether, and once again we were drowning in a sea of red ink. Then, in the aftermath of 9/11, Bush launched us into the most disastrous, unnecessary war since Vietnam. He invaded Iraq with about one-third of the troops he needed to accomplish the job. Against the advice of some of the country's leading generals, including his secretary of state Colin Powell, Bush sent in 150,000 troops to accomplish a mission that called for half a million. Julius Caesar had figured it out more than 2,000 years ago: to estimate how many troops it takes to occupy and shut down a country, multiply the population by two percent. In Iraq, with a population of around twenty-eight million, that would have meant 560,000 soldiers. But even that number begs the question of whether we should have gone into Iraq in the first place—particularly since we had yet to accomplish our primary mission of wiping out those responsible for 9/11 in the mountains of Afghanistan.

How bad had things gotten by 2004? So bad that you actually voted for vapid, wooden, empty-suit flip-flopper John F. Kerry, a man with no discernible convictions, just to punish Bush. Kerry was so inept that he, a man with combat experience, allowed himself to be put on the defensive against Bush who had used his father's clout to keep him out of harm's way in Vietnam. How dismal could things get? The Bush II presidency proved beyond a doubt that one-party rule in Washington—or any of the states for that matter—is the most dangerous type of government. The Republicans, with no restraints whatsoever since they controlled the executive and legislative branches of government, demonstrated that they could outspend the Democrats when given the opportunity. The only difference was in how they chose to paper over the budget deficits. The Democrats taxed and spent while the Republicans borrowed and spent. The former style pinches now, while the latter is a Keynesian formula for passing along the debt burden to our children and grandchildren.

It will take this country a generation or longer to undo the extravagances and outright bad decisions made by Bush II, Dick Cheney, and Donald Rumsfeld. And that's assuming that whoever wins the presidential election in 2008 is interested in pushing this country in a new direction entirely—a more libertarian direction.

In July 2007 I attended FreedomFest in Las Vegas, a free market extravaganza put on by economist Mark Skousen. At the event, I delivered a speech pretty much summing up my thoughts on the political environment and also, believe it or not, sat side-by-side with Nathaniel Branden on a panel discussing Ayn Rand. I am summarizing my speech below, since it reflected my thinking on the state of libertarianism in the country at the time:

In the aftermath of the 2004 presidential election, thanks to Bush's disastrous ineptitude, libertarians talked seriously for the first time in more than three decades of forging a new political alliance with the political Left. Many threw off their ideological blinders and developed a more pragmatic approach to achieving libertarian reforms in society. Instead of regarding libertarianism as an end in itself, they began to understand that achieving liberty is an ongoing process. If libertarians could wave a magic wand and usher in Galt's Gulch, popularized in Ayn Rand's novel *Atlas Shrugged,* or Murray Rothbard's anarcho-capitalist utopia, or Milton Friedman's strictly limited government—or any other model libertarians favored—within fifty years that society wouldn't look anything like it did when they started out. Jefferson understood this when he said it would take a revolution every generation or so to keep our freedoms. So did Benjamin Franklin when he said we've given you a republic, if you can keep it.

More realistic libertarians understood the lesson dramatized in William Golding's novel *Lord of the Flies*: put any three people together on a desert island and two of them will gang up on the third and take his toys away, then turn on each other until one of them is dominant. What a lot of libertarians acknowledged now that they didn't understand thirty years ago is that libertarianism is not an end, not a final solution in itself. It's a continuing process of constantly undoing the excesses of previous generations. How are libertarians, or any other group for that matter, going to *maintain* their political and societal model once they have achieved it?

Libertarianism had grown into a big-tent movement over the decades. Of course, some said they had a big tent back in 1970 as well; the only problem was: there was nobody in it. There were about 175 Objectivists in the country; 125 Rothbardians; fifty middle-of-the-road anarchists; and a few dozen even more exotic libertarian strains, including a few who wanted to colonize an unclaimed island in the South Pacific and build their libertarian utopia from scratch. Libertarians *needed* a big tent because none of them would sit within 100 yards of one another.

By 2004 libertarianism had come to resemble a free market rainbow coalition. It had become fractured into pro-war and anti-war libertarians; pro-life and pro-choice libertarians; pro-death penalty and anti-death penalty libertarians; pro-global warming and anti-global warming libertarians; pro-immigration and anti-immigration libertarians—in other words, libertarians who disagreed with one another on every key issue of the day. The only people missing from the coalition were Jesse Jackson and Al Sharpton, who had yet to declare themselves libertarians. In Maryland during the 2006 off-year election, a candidate ran for the U.S. senate with the backing of the Libertarian, Green, and Populist parties. So libertarians were a far more diverse group in the lame-duck years of the Bush II administration than they were during the Reagan years.

Yet, the spirit of libertarianism hadn't changed over the years. Cicero got it right when he said about his own government: "a fish rots from the head down." He went on to say that "the head is swollen with the poison of corruption and bloated with pride and arrogance." He was talking about the Roman Senate, but the same statement could easily be applied to the government in Washington, and most of the states in this country. The problem here has existed for the most part since the early 19th century. Mark twain got it right when he observed that "no man's life, liberty, or property is safe as long as Congress is in session." He also admired the administration of Chester A. Arthur, which he said was hard to beat since he spent more time fishing than he did trying to govern the country.

Then there was the great French philosopher and enlightenment figure, Denis Diderot, who also got it right when he stated: "man will not be free until the last king is strangled with the entrails of the last priest." Substitute the world *politician* for king, and the same principle applies. Ayn Rand got it right when she talked about "Attila and the witch doctor." Attila is of course the power of government, and the witch doctor is the stranglehold the church has had throughout history over the freedom of the people.

Today, the priests in our society come in many forms; they don't all necessarily wear a Roman collar. They include anyone who tries to impose his moral agenda on the rest of us. The priests today come in the forms of various safety Nazis and neo-prohibitionists. They want to use the power of the government to protect us from ourselves—from the harmful effects of overeating, from smoking, from transfats, from just about anything that other people want to do for personal enjoyment, whether it's good for them or not. They are neo-prohibitionists and neo-utopians hell-bent on creating their own vision of paradise here on earth.

Libertarianism was more clearly defined thirty-five years ago, while those calling themselves libertarians today come in a wide variety of political types. Still, there is a common thread running throughout the libertarian mindset. It starts with a distrust of government and centralized power and the knowledge that power always corrupts, and absolute power corrupts absolutely. These used to be left-wing concepts, and it is time for libertarianism to return to its left-wing roots. There is nothing *conservative* about libertarianism; it is radical at its roots.

It is worth taking a look at three basic libertarian models to see just how realistic they are: Ayn Rand's Objectivist model; Murray Rothbard's anarchist model; and Milton Friedman's limited government model. First Ayn Rand. On close analysis, does anybody really think that life in Galt's Gulch would be fun? It couldn't have been much fun for all those closet homosexuals sitting around in her living room, pretending they were all interested in screwing Dagny Taggart, her primary heroine in *Atlas Shrugged*. Rand preached individualism but was an unyielding authoritarian within her own circle. She also denounced people with facial hair, anybody who believed in the supernatural, and she thought people should get down on their hands and knees and worship environmental polluters since they created jobs for the masses. Her views on literature were totally absurd; anyone who puts Mickey Spillane ahead of Hemingway in the pantheon of American writers, or tap dancing ahead of ballet, is talking unadulterated drivel. There was no element of the divine in Rand's philosophy, dogmatic atheist that she was.

In Murray Rothbard's anarchist utopia, the only people who would get rich are the lawyers. According to him, just about everything should be litigated since he allowed for no government to regulate anything. He defined pollution as an act of aggression, but then he said that aggrieved parties had to prove their rights were violated in a court of law. That's all well and good if you're Donald Trump and can sue everybody else into bankruptcy, but what about Joe Sixpack who has trouble paying his rent let alone hiring a high-priced lawyer? According to one diehard Rothbardian with whom I corresponded, people who couldn't afford to pay their bills in Rothbard's world would be *enslaved!!!* That's his word, not mine. Imagine that: libertarian slavery. There's a message that's bound to resonate with mainstream society. If pollution is an act of aggression, why not just outlaw it the same way we outlaw breaking and entering and rape?

Milton Friedman's model is the closest we have to the real world since it is *based on* the world we live in. He proposed a scaled-back version of the American republic that exists today—lower taxes, less government spending, broader civil liberties, no war on drugs, educational alternatives to public schools, an overhaul of Social Security and Medicare. I have no illusions that we'll see anything close to even that much classical liberalism in my lifetime—and my grandchildren's lifetimes for that matter. But Friedman was the only one of the three who presented a practical plan for the real world, modeled on the principles established by our founding fathers and delineated in the U.S. Constitution and, most important, in the Bill of Rights.

Clearly, it is long past time for libertarians to sever their bonds with the political Right and make common cause with forces on the progressive Left.

Essentially, there are only two ways to approach politics in any society: the utopians among us on both ends of the political spectrum choose to remain holier than thou, above the fray, true to their own principles without compromise, apart from the political debate, outside the mainstream—in other words, irrelevant. The other course is to pick and choose your battles, get involved, hook up with other activists and parties you feel *relatively* comfortable with, and try to influence policy as much as possible, particularly on a local level.

In retrospect, Bill Clinton with all his faults turned out to be a better Republican than George W. Bush because he had a Republican Congress to deal with. They held his feet to the fire, kept him off balance. He governed by stealing Newt Gingrich's "Contract with America" and leaving the Republicans without any issues of their own. Thanks to pressure from the other side of the aisle, Clinton promoted free trade, welfare reform, and a balanced budget. Divided government seems to be the best those interested in reducing the size and scope of government can hope for.

In November 2006 we got rid of one-party rule in Washington, and with any luck we will maintain that kind of balance in the years ahead.

Today libertarians have no natural allies, as far as I'm concerned. The rift with conservatives is greater now than it was thirty-five years ago, thanks to Iraq, thanks to the bloated, corrupt, out-of-control federal government that George W. Bush has foisted on us. It seems to me that libertarians today are once again at a crossroads. Brink Lindsey has written recently of *liberal-tarianism* as a means of finding common cause with the Left. Markos Moulitsas (the daily kos) has been blogging about the new *libertarian democrats* and asking traditional libertarians to throw their lot in with them.

The risk is that we end up with liberalism lite—or libertarianism lite, if you will—but then the question is: are we better off with libertarianism or liberalism lite or with big government conservatism?

Each of us has to make his or her own decision: remain irrelevant and refuse to compromise, continue to work with the Right if you feel more comfortable with conservatives, or open a dialogue with the Left if you feel more culturally attuned to liberals.

So we're bigger now, more mainstream, more a part of the public debate than we ever hoped to be thirty years ago. I think everyone interested in seeing a libertarian transition to a more tolerable society has a major choice to make as we look to 2008 and beyond. The beauty of libertarianism today as opposed to way back then is that we will all go off in twenty different directions, off on our own, making an impact where we can, and not nearly as much in lockstep as we were in the early years of our movement. And that, it seems to me, is a damned good thing.

PART VI
As Things Look Now

29

A Grizzled Old Iconoclast Looks Back

Toward the end of 2006, a delightful young libertarian named Sunni Maravillosa asked me to bring her up to date on what had been going on in my life during the past thirty years and more. Following is the interview, which was originally published online at Sunni's Salon (http://www.endervidualism.com/salon/intvw/tuccille.htm). Sunni is a prolific and energetic pro-freedom writer.

S: Hi, Jerry, and thanks for taking some time out of your schedule to talk with me. How've you been?

J: I'm doing better than I have any right to be. At my age most writers are washed up or past their prime. They seem to have used up everything they have to say and start repeating themselves or else become caricatures of themselves. Hemingway and Fitzgerald were classic examples. They did more drinking than writing later in life. But I consider myself fortunate that I have enough ideas left to last the rest of my life. I've always defined happiness by how well the writing is going, so at the moment I'm doing swimmingly well.

S: That's great to hear. I imagine most folks reading this will know you primarily as the author of *It Usually Begins with Ayn Rand* and its follow-up, *It Still Begins with Ayn Rand*. But you've written a slew of other books and had a very interesting life so far. What else would you like people to know about you, by way of background?

J: By way of background, I come from a working class neighborhood in the Bronx where street fighting was the major contact sport. Combine that with a stultifying Catholic Church upbringing, and you've got someone who couldn't wait to get away from the old neighborhood as quickly as possible. Somewhere along the way, in a life filled with a quest for alternative spiritual fulfillment along with sexual adventure, I became a lean, mean writing machine, trying to work out the old devils by putting words down on paper. It was a form of therapy, although it had unforeseen consequences in that it was a compulsion. You might call it creative neurosis since I was driven to write and get published at all costs. That kind of obsession makes you a bit ruthless and totally self-absorbed, which is tough on those who choose to share their lives with you. Despite it all, I've managed to stay married to the same woman for 41 years with many bumps along the way. At this stage of life I have two grown children and three grandsons, who have the effect of mellowing me somewhat.

S: Does that therapy work for you? How effectively does it banish those old devils?

J: As a writer I'm reluctant to banish all my devils. I believe some of those devils are what drive writers to keep on writing. You never want to lose the passion that motivated you to write in the first place. I guess I have a fear of losing my edge and becoming too comfortable with the status quo.

S: It is impressive to me that you've stayed married through some tough times, which were hinted at in your latest book, *Heretic*. How have you accomplished that?

J: Love and friendship and a lot of hard work are what keep a marriage or any relationship going. I don't think most of us are comfortable with monogamy, but you're got to make that sacrifice and commitment to keep it going.

S: You're currently working in financial services, right? Isn't that something of a wild ride these days?

J: The world of personal finance and investments is always a wild ride. Things are pretty tame now compared with twenty-five years ago when the Dow Jones Industrial Average bottomed out at 777, mortgage rates were in the high-teens, and the Hunts were trying to corner the silver market. Before that we had stagflation—a sluggish economy combined with high inflation. For more than a decade the Dow traded in a rut, back and forth between 750 and 1000. Things are pretty rosy now compared with then.

S: What's your take on how things are looking in this country, economically speaking? It seems to me that Fed chairmen mostly make soothing sounds, and most of the mainstream media accept what they're saying, but others, most notably Bill Bonner and Richard Daughty, think things are going down the tubes.

J: Pessimism sells while optimism doesn't. Back in the 1970s, Harry Browne and Doug Casey were predicting the end of the world as we know it, their books became best-sellers and they made a lot of money terrifying the investing public. After them we had Ravi Batra and others saying essentially the same thing. Guess what? They were all wrong. I wrote a book in 1978 entitled *The Optimist's Guide to Making Money in the 1980s* and my book probably sold one-tenth as well as those by the end-of-the-world brigade. In my forecast I said the Dow would start rising around 1982 and never look back, and that's exactly what happened. Now, incredibly, the stock market—at least the Dow—is soaring to new heights despite a disastrous war in Iraq and ongoing mayhem in the Middle East and elsewhere. Bush is the very antithesis of libertarianism, yet the economy keeps humming along and stocks keep going up.

The lesson here is that the economy continues to expand despite the best efforts of politicians to regulate it to death and spoil the party. The reason why the economy keeps expanding is the spread of capitalism and free enterprise globally. The emerging world, China, India, and other areas that were formerly socialistic and communistic are freeing up their markets. This has unleashed a torrent of wealth creation and buying power around the world. Looking back to 1927, the S&P 500 has grown at an annual rate of about 11% and small-cap stocks have done better. This has happened in an environment of world wars, Korea, Vietnam, and now Iraq—not to mention earthquakes, tsunamis, hurricanes, and other natural disasters. It's happened despite FDR, Jimmy Carter, LBJ, Richard Nixon, and Doofus W. Bush, the circus clown in Chief. Obviously, the market fluctuates from time to time. We are bound to pull back sooner or later. But I see nothing on the horizon, short of a meteor hitting planet earth and wiping us all out, to deflect the historical trajectory.

S: I guess I've somewhat unwittingly fallen in with the pessimists, then. It seems to me that the falling dollar, the large trade deficit, and an increasingly rapacious federal government make some kind of unpleasant correction inevitable, and soon.

J: No question that a policy that fosters a weak dollar combined with the trade deficit poses problems down the road. The question right now is, how well are people doing? The average person is doing relatively well in terms of standard of living. Those who want to travel to Italy, however, have a problem with the expensive euro relative to the dollar. But what's going on is not all that new. We've been running trade and budget deficits for decades, except for a brief spell during the Clinton years. So far our economy has been able to absorb it. You need to hedge yourself against disaster at all times, which means you need to be holding gold, foreign stocks and bonds, and other securities besides U.S. stocks and bonds. Unless there is a global collapse, a diversified strategy should see you through most eventualities.

S: I know that the federal government cooks its data to some degree; they have to keep up the pretense of being in control of markets. Discontinuing M3 is a good example of trying to hide important information from foreign investors as well as the American public. However, does it necessarily follow from that that shadow government statistics are necessary?

J: Discontinuing M3 was largely a result of not being able to measure money supply that accurately anymore. Government data are always suspect. The government lies mostly about its budget deficits. It has always engaged in a game of smoke and mirrors where the public purse is concerned. Obviously, the more information and data that the public has, the better off it is. But most of the information is already out there. Certainly, Wall Street and the financial institutions are privy to their own data, which is more accurate than the government's. I'm always amused that libertarians think the private sector can do anything better than the government can, and rightly so, but they make an exception when it comes to compiling data. Sophisticated investors view government figures with skepticism, if not outright scorn. The market is always discounting the data because the information is already out there in the marketplace. The stock market doesn't lie. Prices reflect the reality under the surface. If you want to know what's going on in the economy, how healthy or unhealthy it is, just look at the stock and bond markets.

S: One thing I'm finding particularly interesting is that many who probably cheered when Alan Greenspan was appointed Fed chairman have been jeering his work of late. You wrote a biography of him some years back. Is our current economic situation the mess that Greenspan made? Or is that too harsh a judgment?

J: The economy's not a mess at all. It's growing at 3% to 4% a year, and we're fully employed with 4.5% unemployment. I remember when 6%

unemployment was considered full employment. You can argue about the quality of jobs, but anyone who wants to work can find employment. During Greenspan's tenure as Fed chairman, the economy grew at better than 3.5% annually and inflation was held under 3%. His record is outstanding. I know that gold bugs would detest the man even if he managed to walk on water, but they live in a utopian universe. The fact is, we don't have a gold standard, we do have a central bank, and Greenspan did a superb job of fine-tuning monetary policy even though he never renounced his preference for a gold standard. Ask yourself if you would rather have the Federal Reserve run by a man with Greenspan's philosophy or by someone like Robert Reich or J. Kenneth Galbraith in his heyday. Given the environment we live in, I don't know anyone who could have done a better job of balancing economic growth against the threat of inflation. Of course the revisionists are out in droves now, inevitably so, in an effort to humanize the image of a man who seemed holier than God when he was in power. The pendulum always swings too far. But on balance, Greenspan's record speaks for itself.

S: Robert Reich? Absolutely no way! So Jerry, I take it you aren't a gold bug. What do you think of returning the dollar to a gold standard—would you be in favor of that?

J: Any currency needs to be backed by something with intrinsic value. For many that something should be gold. Our currency is backed by the stability of our political and economic system and the power of our economy. Greenspan proposed floating two kinds of money in the form of Treasury certificates, one the present dollar and the other a security backed by gold. He maintained that the marketplace would decide which one it wanted to own. The market would decide which one would survive over time—the gold-backed currency or the current one. I think that approach might be a good way to sort it out. Competition would resolve the issue.

S: A very interesting idea; too bad it didn't get implemented. How did it happen that you started writing biographies? You've done several: Greenspan, Trump, Rupert Murdoch, F. Clifton White, the Hunt family … is that writing easier than other kinds of nonfiction, or than fiction?

J: I started writing biographies by accident in a way. A publisher contacted my agent to find out if I was interested in writing a book about the silver crash in the early 1980s. When I researched that book, I discovered that the story of the Hunts of Texas was truly larger than life. H.L. Hunt, the patriarch of the clan, started life as a degenerate gambler, a womanizer, a bigamist, and worse, when he finally struck black gold in Texas and made his fortune. He had so much money rolling in from oilfield royalties that he couldn't possibly gamble it all away fast enough. Then his sons Bunker and Herbert came along and almost managed to blow the family fortune on their silver futures. So my book on the silver crash turned into a three-generation family saga going back to the time right after the Civil War. The book sold well, so a publisher asked me to write a book about Donald Trump, who was not yet a superstar. I got lucky there since he emerged as the golden boy of real estate just as my book came out. That led to Murdoch, the Cliff White memoir, and finally to Greenspan. As far as which type of writing is easier, *none of it* is easy. But fiction is most difficult because you're essentially making up a story as you go along, biographies are next because you're using the techniques of a novelist but the story is laid out for you, memoir is difficult but more fun because you get a chance to write about yourself. For me, essays and political writing are least difficult since you get a chance to spew your brilliant insights from the pulpit with no restraints.

S: I didn't realize when I reviewed *Heretic* that *It Usually Begins with Ayn Rand* is also something of an autobiography. Dare I confess that I've not read that yet? [laughs] Has its enduring popularity surprised you?

J: Shame on you for not reading that book, Sunni. [laughs]

S: [laughing] I know, Jerry!

J: I think it would be right up your alley if you like political fun and games. The book is considered a somewhat fictional political memoir, although I left out the sex that I put into *Heretic*. No, I never thought it would become a perennial seller when it was published, particularly since sales were underwhelming in the beginning. But as the years wore on I kept getting letters and later emails from new generations of libertarians who claimed it turned them on. It became something of a Gonzo phenomenon, compared with Hunter Thompson's books, and took on a life of its own. My son J.D. Tuccille alerted me to that about ten years ago, when he told me it was still being read and discussed in chat rooms, etc. It's always a great feeling for a writer to discover that one of his books has become a cult classic. Who knows what I'll be remembered for fifty years from now, but for the moment I'm enjoying it. The book is a favorite of mine since I was a young writer at the time, still unsure of what I was doing, and I decided to let it all hang out and go crazy having fun with that book. And it worked. To some extent, *Heretic* is similar except that I was a grizzled old writer when I wrote it and, presumably, had learned a few things about writing over the years. I think those two books are the funniest ones I've written.

S: I haven't read it because I misapprehended it, based solely on the title. I'm sure I would enjoy it—I've enjoyed each book of yours that I've read. From what I've read about the book, you came upon the freedom philosophy at an opportune time—having personal contact with people like Ayn Rand, Karl Hess, and Murray Rothbard, just to name a few. Who among those luminaries made the deepest positive impression on you?

J: I was a libertine, not a libertarian, when I discovered Ayn Rand. I dismissed her early on when I learned she was totally inflexible in her beliefs, intolerant of homosexuality and even facial hair, if you can believe it, and realized that life in an Objectivist society would be akin to a science fiction nightmare devoid of humor. Then I met Murray Rothbard and Karl Hess and joined up with them. Karl was a very decent guy, whose heart was in the right place, but he didn't have an ounce of economic sense. He became something of a syndicalist socialist, if it's possible to quantify what he believed in economically. Murray and I enjoyed a good ride together, but we eventually broke when I challenged him on Israel and on foreign policy in general. I was never totally isolationist, as Murray was, and thought the U.S. should have strategic military alliances with various nations, including Israel. Murray's anti-Zionism bordered on anti-Semitism in my view, and we parted over that. I'm told that he later took issue with some of the lampooning I did of him and others in *It Usually Begins with Ayn Rand*, although at first he had no problem with it. So my political luminaries turned out to have feet of clay, which is probably the way it should be. Even Jefferson had his flaws.

S: We're veering into territory I've been thinking about a lot lately, and will probably write on at some point—the delicate balancing act that seems to be required when dealing with egos. So many libertarians become personally invested in their ideas that a challenge to an idea gets taken as a personal attack, which often has the effect of shutting down what could be a productive exchange of ideas. And even more libertarians—maybe; I'm not sure of the relative proportions—become so invested in their heroes that to offer a valid criticism of one is tantamount to accusing the hero of feeding an infant crack cocaine. I suppose that's inevitable, since freedom-loving individuals are human too, but it's damned frustrating to see that dynamic at work in people who are ostensibly individualists.

J: It's similar to the infighting on the left among right- and left-wing Trotskyites, communists and syndicalists, social labor crazies and welfare statists, ad nauseam. None of them want to give an inch in their ideologies. That renders them irrelevant in the grand scheme of things. Put 10 libertarians in the same room and they will come up with at least seven or eight different ways of organizing society. They are all so convinced that their own model is correct that they refuse to see the value in someone else's ideas. I prefer to believe that my political opponents are as intelligent as I am, give or take a few IQ points, and have ideas worth listening to. Hard-core ideologues just want to preach. They are lousy listeners.

S: Ah yes, left and right .. . All these years out from those days when you first hoped to create a left-right coalition, and freedom-lovers still haven't been able to create one—do you still think it's possible? Is it even worthwhile any more?

J: Actually, I think the chances are better now than ever. A candidate for the U.S. Senate in Maryland in 2006 had the backing of the Libertarian, Green, and Populist parties. He pulled off a political trifecta. Someone from the Cato Institute recently published an article saying libertarians are better off joining with Democrats on social issues since the Republicans have abandoned any pretense of promoting small government. And the election of more individualistic western Democrats who believe in gun rights and free markets provides libertarians with another opening to the left. Unfortunately, we live in a two-party state in which third-party candidacies have no chance of going anywhere unless they're backed by someone with star power. H. Ross Perot was the last example of that. Ralph Nader to a lesser extent. So, we're left with working within the two-party system if we want to have any impact. The best we can hope for is divided government, which we've just achieved on the federal level. In retrospect, the Clinton administration worked as well as it did because he stole Newt Gingrich's Contract with America and pushed for free trade, welfare reform, and a balanced budget. He left the Gingrich Republicans without any issues of their own. Doofus Bush has made me nostalgic for Clinton and his White House blowjobs. The problem with many libertarians is that they are "purists"; they insist on

100% of what they want, or else they think they're "selling out." Yet, there are appealing candidates out there with libertarian-ish or liberal-tarian tendencies in both parties. Jesse Ventura and Kinky Friedman come to mind, although they were both independents. I want politicians to amuse me, to make me laugh. It's the least they can do in return for the power we give them, particularly power over the purse. We don't live in a vacuum, and we don't elect dictators who can impose libertari-anism by waving a magic wand. The system works through give-and-take, through horse-trading in an attempt to achieve our goals. Everyone who gets into office will eventually sell out to special interest groups, with precious few exceptions.

S: Very interesting observations, Jerry, but your last two sentences neatly summed up why I'm an anarchist who doesn't vote. I want to do my own horse-trading, thank you, because I can control who I'll be get-ting into bed with, and I can't do that with elected officials.

J: You can be an anarchist and still vote. I'm not saying you should. Whether one votes or not is a personal choice. But in a tight election, voting is a form of self-defense. It depends on the circumstances. I don't think it's a moral issue.

S: The word *libertarian* has been stretched a lot of late: I've lost count of the number of Republican-types who claim to be libertarian but cheer Bush's Islamic jihad; and I've seen some left-socialists apply the term to their value structures too. Recently I wondered aloud if genuine liber-tarians—by that I mean those who understand and try to live by the non-aggression principle—should abandon the term for something else. Others have too; I'm far from the first. Is this the same old argument in a slightly different suit, or something qualitatively different, do you think, Jerry?

J: Over the past few years, Sunni, I've corresponded with anti-war and pro-war "libertarians," pro-choice and pro-life "libertarians," pro-death penalty and anti-death penalty "libertarians," pro-gay marriage and anti-gay marriage "libertarians," no-tax-at-all and flat-tax "libertarians"—in short, people calling themselves libertarians who disagree on some of the most critical issues of our time. So, you're right, what the hell does the word mean anymore? We seem to be living in the age of Big-Tent Libertarianism, if you will. Perhaps that's a condition of the word catching on and going mainstream to a great extent. That said, I don't think we should abandon the word *libertarianism* itself. It derived from liberal, which we now call classical liberal to distinguish it from FDR liberalism, but it still stands for a distinct philosophy of liberty and government. To the extent that someone believes that individual liberty is paramount, that government is to be distrusted under all circumstances, that the Bill of Rights is the most important part of the constitution, that government has to be kept small, that the private sector should largely be left untrammeled, that trade should be free, the tax burden low, and that war should be *defensive*, that person fits within libertarian parameters. I'm afraid that I have a hard time characterizing someone who believes the preemptive strike in Iraq was justified as a libertarian. Yet I have several good friends, one calling himself a Randian anarchist, who was in favor of going in. We've reached a point, Sunni, where we have agreed to disagree and still call ourselves libertarians. We've worked so hard to get the word *libertarian* recognized, it would be a shame now to replace it with something else. If the term *dedicated public servant* makes you cringe, I suppose you're off to a good start down the libertarian path.

S: True enough, Jerry, but you didn't mention the one thing that ties all those perspectives together: the Non Aggression Principle. To me, any tax—not user fees; those are a different creature entirely—is aggression; so I'd have a very hard time calling someone who advocates for the so-called Fair Tax a libertarian, for example. So yes, label me a purist, but I think of myself as a pragmatic purist who realizes that to get where I want to be, incremental steps are necessary. I'm just not willing to be content with any middle points along the way.

J: Yes, but a lot of libertarians don't want to be bothered with even considering the middle points along the way. The Non Aggression Principle poses an interesting dilemma. Philosophically it is probably the cornerstone of libertarianism to many. Yet I can think of any number of circumstances where preventive aggression is justified. For example, if someone threatens to harm me or my family, I have no problem kicking the shit out of that individual before he can act. Is that self-defense, or is it an act of unjustified aggression? Israel today is faced with a hostile neighbor, Iran, which is on the verge of acquiring nuclear weapons. Iran's head of state has stated explicitly that he won't rest until Israel is wiped off the map. Does Israel have the right to preemptively attack Iran before it can act? Is that self-defense, or is it a violation of the Non Aggression Principle? I am essentially a social Darwinist, Sunni. I believe in the survival of the fittest. If I have to split someone's head open before he can injure me, I have no problem acting in advance. So that's where I stand. The Non Aggression Principle sounds fine in theory, but in the end we all want to survive and protect our interests. There are a lot of evil bastards and outright scumbags out there. So fuck them! If I have to aggress against them beforehand, then so be it.

S: Well, without getting bogged down in this topic too much, because we could dance on the head of this pin all afternoon, I agree with you. I don't think aggression is limited to physical force; a serious threat of imminent physical aggression is itself a sort of initiation of force, and should be met with what you called preventive aggression. In doing some research for this interview, I was surprised to see that you'd written a few columns for Lew Rockwell—you aren't listed on the contributors page for some reason. In your last column there, you wrote: "The LP has displayed a genius for assigning itself a role in American politics akin to irrelevance, and I am sad to say that this record of genius is likely to remain unbroken as campaign 2004 unfolds …" I assume that you're aware of the "takeover" of the LP by a reformist faction that gutted the party of principle. Would you characterize that as continuing irrelevance, or something worse?

J: Any party that has succeeded in getting a decreasing number of votes for president over the past thirty-four years is irrelevant by definition. Perhaps if Barbra Streisand or Leonardo DiCaprio or someone else with major star power announced tomorrow that he or she was a libertarian and wanted to run in 2008 as the LP candidate, that would elevate the party to relevancy, and possibly to the status of the trendiest party of the moment. But, failing that, the LP is doomed to get plus or minus 1% of the vote at each quadrennial bloodletting, which means it will continue to be irrelevant. The best political strategy for libertarians is to work with liberal-tarian Democrats, or libertarian-ish Republicans, if they want to engage in politics. The Greens have a higher profile than the LP, so why not join with them if you want to influence environmental policy?

S: I believe some people have, but I've not been keeping up on environmental issues much these days. A friend of mine has launched an ambitious project to create a free America, without relying on bullets or ballots. While I admire what he's trying to accomplish and wish him success, deep down I can't help but wonder if it isn't too late for this country. Between the economy being in poor shape and government at all levels feasting on our freedoms, leaving the country has become a tantalizing option. Or am I being too pessimistic?

J: Sunni, put three people on a desert island, and two of them will gang up on the third and steal his loincloth. Read *Lord of the Flies* for a great view of what would happen if kids started their own society from scratch. I've heard about another group in New Hampshire called the Free State Project. That sounds good on the surface as well, but New Hampshire is not exactly a libertarian paradise either. It has no income tax or sales tax but it does have hideous property taxes, plus the state owns all the liquor stores. I don't understand why high property taxes are more libertarian than an income or sales tax, yet libertarians froth at the mouth about the latter two taxes. As soon as you allow government to do anything at all, it has to raise revenue from somewhere. Does it matter how it balances its budget? Our main concern is that public expenditures and the overall tax burden remain low. For years Connecticut had no income tax, yet it was one of the most heavily taxed states in the country on a per capita basis. So it's fun to look at all these utopian solutions to getting rid of the status quo, but I prefer to operate in the real world.

There are essentially three viable libertarian models—although I'm sure many libertarians would also include some archaic alternatives: the Randian model, which is harsh and humorless limited government; the Rothbardian model of utopian anarcho-capitalism; and Milton Friedman's model calling for classical liberal reforms to our modern Republic. I would submit that the Friedman model is closest to reality and has the best chance, although slim, of ever coming to pass. Like it or not, all U.S. citizens have been forcibly co-opted into the system through Social Security, Medicare, ad nauseam, and we need to find a way to see that they get their money back. Friedman's ideas on the subject were the only ones that made any sense and have any chance of being implemented.

S: I haven't read *Lord of the Flies* but I did see a movie version, which made me wonder to what degree some libertarian enclave might follow that course. It continues to astonish me that Ayn Rand so beautifully portrayed the value of a positive sense of life, and yet most Objectivists—to this day!—largely ignore that and live what seems to me a very grim, narrow life.

J: They are grim, narrow-minded cultists. They are religionists and Rand is their goddess. Most of the ones I've met are borderline psychopaths. To me that is reflective of an essential flaw in the Rand model.

S: While we're back on heroes, Jerry, it makes sense to touch on the recently deceased Milton Friedman. While many essays focused on his many contributions to liberty, L. Neil Smith wrote a thought-provoking article reminding readers that it was Friedman who devised the withholding system of collecting income tax. That's a *huge* foot of clay.

J: Yes, sometimes the best of intentions have rotten consequences. Friedman gave the state the ability to act more efficiently. But that's because people thought he was important enough to listen to. Rand and Rothbard didn't have the opportunity to fail so publicly because no one tried to adopt their ideas in the real world.

S: Is there any specific reason why you stopped writing for LRC? Or are you not interested in politics any more?

J: Sunni, I was, am, and always will be a political animal. My book projects have been taking up so much time lately, that I have little or no time to write elsewhere. At the moment I am trying to finish up a new book, update some of my earlier biographies, and get started on the next book.

S: Have you given any thought to starting a blog? It's an easy way to get your thoughts out, and some folks have even found ways to make some money with it—even if all they do is dash off quick "Look at this" or "Here's my take on this" posts. And speaking of writing, where do you find the time to write? It's amazing that you've been able to write all the books you have, while working full-time.

J: I've recently cut back to a schedule that gives me almost three months off a year. But as I mentioned, I'm compulsive about writing, still driven to write while also finding time for kayaking, hiking, golf, skiing, and, of course, spending time with my grandsons and family. Writers don't realize, you have to break a project down into small components. If you write one page a day, you will have a 365-page book written in a year. But if you start off saying, "Oh my God, I've got to write a 90,000-word book," the thought can paralyze you.

S: Oh yeah, absolutely. The thought of writing my doctoral dissertation paralyzed my work on it for over a year. Once I created an outline with specific sections for each chapter, and items to do to complete each section, the writing came very easily and flowed fast. Too bad I don't always remember that when I start new projects [laughs ruefully].

J: [laughs] Too bad I didn't learn that lesson myself when I started out.

S: What kind of writing do you enjoy most—fiction, biographical, financial advice?

J: Fiction and memoir. After writing about the rich and powerful over the years, it's fun to write about someone else—me. Memoir is close to fiction in that you adhere as close as possible to the truth you remember, but you also have to recreate dialogue that took place, in my case, several decades ago. The financial books I wrote mainly to make some money and I had a steady market for them twenty-five or more years ago. I gave the best advice I could, but over the years those books get dated. I'm more concerned about writing about what I enjoy most at this stage of life.

S: Your biographies sold well, and I imagine *It Usually Begins with Ayn Rand* and *It Still Begins with Ayn Rand* have also. Yet your autobiographical book, *Heretic*, was published through a self-publishing company, iUniverse. Was that your preference, or was it the only way to get it out?

J: At the time I was between agents, and these days it is virtually impossible to approach publishers directly unless your books are selling like John Grisham's or Steven King's. Many of my books sold well, but *Trump* was my most successful with 500,000 copies sold, and it was already fifteen years past its prime when I wrote *Heretic*. I had lined up another agent for *Heretic*, but she flamed out after she left a big agency to strike out on her own. I got impatient and decided to bring the book out through iUniverse instead of screwing around with it for another six months or so. Agents and publishers live in some sort of nineteenth-century time warp where it takes six months just to open their mail. It's terribly frustrating for anyone who wants results now. It's still largely a paper-driven industry, just getting up-to-speed on electronic submissions. When I started publishing back in 1970, there were 50,000 books a year published in this country. Today there are close to 200,000, which slows things down by a factor of four. Now I've lined up a new agent, so with any luck the next project will come out with a mainstream house.

S: I encountered a lot of this stuff when I was peddling a manuscript several years back. It is absolutely maddening how slowly this system works! Yet electronic publication, and e-books in particular, seem to be catching on very slowly. Why do you think that is?

J: Actually, the industry is expanding. Barnes & Noble bought a good piece of iUniverse because it sees potential profits there, and Random House owns most of exlibris. More and more books are coming out that way, and mainstream publishers are being forced to examine ways of exploring new distribution channels as a result.

S: It seems to me that you took a lot of risks with *Heretic*, Jerry. It's intensely personal, seems to pull no punches, deals with challenging subjects—and is written in perhaps the most challenging voice to do well, second person narrative. Was it hard for you to write it?

J: The second person is very risky, as you pointed out, Sunni. People either love it or hate it. I've run into people who put the book down because of it, and others who found it a page-turner. The problem is, the writing style shouldn't get in the way of the story, so I've decided to use first-person point of view for the next one, which will also be a memoir. I liked writing *Heretic* the way I did and decided to abandon the second person narrative reluctantly. I hate to give up something that seems to be working, in my view. It was an attempt to draw the reader into the story by creating an Everyman character. But the next story is compelling unto itself and I don't want the writing to put people off. So, back to the tried and true. Call me chicken, if you want.

S: [laughing] I'm not going to call you chicken! The second-person voice worked very well for me and I'll miss it in the next memoir. How's that project coming?

J: The book is moving along smoothly. I hope to finish it in 2007. My new agent is concentrating on movie rights first, since that's where the big money is. A book deal will be a no-brainer if that comes to pass. So we'll wait and see what happens on that end. But I hope to see it in print by the end of 2007. After that, as I mentioned, Barnes & Noble wants to reissue some of my biographies, so I have to update them. And then I have another story dealing with illegal betting in baseball that I want to write. I originally wrote the book for a major New York publisher, but it was killed by the legal department because of potential libel suits. *Penthouse* published it as an article boiled down to 3,500 words in 1991, but I want to go back now and rewrite it as a book. So I've got enough on my plate to keep busy for the next ten years I think.

S: Movie rights? To which book or books? And how much of your baseball book will cover Pete Rose? Growing up near Cincinnati and being a Reds fan from a young age, that whole episode was very sad for me.

J: Movie rights to *Gallery of Fools*, the true crime story. No guarantees, but we'll see what happens. Pete Rose is part of the baseball story. There's evidence that he not only bet on baseball but on the Reds, and even against them. That's why there's so much resistance to putting him in the Hall of Fame.

S: I've resigned myself to the fact that he'll never get in. Back on *Heretic* now for a bit, Jerry. Why did you want to share such an intimate look not only into your life, but also your parents' and other family members' lives?

J: My wife and daughter are not very happy with parts of the book, but one of the risks of being related to a writer—or just knowing a writer—is that sooner or later a lot of intimate details get out. The next memoir will be even spicier, not sexually, but with the revelation of a true crime involving some members of my family. It's set against the background of my political campaign in 1974. It's an incredible story, one I've been sitting on for more than thirty years, and I can only tell it now because most of those involved are either dead or in jail. Why reveal such things? Well, because I'm a writer and my life has been wild enough to serve up some interesting material. The option is to fictionalize it all as a novel or write it as memoir. James Frey chose to write fiction and present it as nonfiction in *A Million Little Pieces*. In my case, fictionalizing the real events would diminish them. It's one of those stories you can't make up. So I'll let it all hang out. Maybe I'm just an exhibitionist at heart, Sunni.

S: Perhaps more so than many writers care to admit, but as you intimated, writing is itself an exhibitionist activity. Even when one isn't writing directly, explicitly about oneself, a lot of hints as to how the author thinks and feels about particular subjects or issues suffuse his work. The element in *Heretic* that most intrigued me in it was your spiritual journey. If I understand rightly, most of your "supernatural" dabblings came before
you discovered Rand. Is that accurate?

J: Yes, and they continued during and after the Rand period as well. I was not only reading my astrological charts, but actually doing them while I was learning about Objectivism. How's that for schizophrenia?

S: [laughs] I thought of that as a good and proper discordian path. Did your interpretation of any of your dabblings change after the Rand period?

J: I just kept searching. I went from astrology to psychic phenomena to faith healing to, you name it, I was there. I kept reading, studying, analyzing my own experiences, learning about comparative religions, finding out what each had to offer, trying to reconcile my belief in reason and logical thought with things I saw happening that could not be explained by the tightest logic.

S: How do you [pauses] *justify* isn't the right word, but I'm not coming up with anything better; how do you maintain a value of reason and rationalism alongside some of the experiences you've had? The story you told about Pauline comes to mind …

J: Pauline Messina is a perfect example, Sunni. How do you explain logically a woman who meets two people whom she has no way of knowing are involved, and accurately forecasts that they will be married, have children, etc? Over the years I've met other such people, people who had foreknowledge of events that would shortly take place. I've also had dreams myself with visions of a city I would soon be relocating to before I had actually seen what the city looked like. There are any number of instances like this that cannot be explained logically. This tells me that there is a reality, another sphere of existence, that we do not know about yet and, therefore, can't be explained rationally. Rand claimed to be the most rational person on earth, but I pity her and her followers because they have their minds closed in advance to areas of knowledge that they haven't discovered yet. They refuse to entertain the possibility that things they can't explain rationally may actually exist.

S: It reminds me of the leap in understanding we gained from the invention of the microscope—all of these things that were previously attributed to ill humors or capricious gods became fairly comprehensible and predictable. And with all the technological advances since then, I think many have the view that if something's out there, we should be able to observe and measure it by now. I have problems with that, though; there's a lot we still don't know about the human body, for example. What do you think generally gives rise to supernatural phenomena? Poorly understood workings of human energy flow? Spirits? Some kind of higher being? All of the above?

J: I hesitate to use the word God, because then you have to define what you mean by God. Are you referring to the God who ordered Abraham to stab his son on a rock to prove his faith? The God who terrorized Job because of a bet with Satan that Job's faith would not weaken? The New Testament God who sent his only son down to earth to be tortured and crucified? All of these Gods sound like despicable creatures to me and I want no part of them. Then there is the deistic view, shared by Jefferson and other of our forefathers, who believed in a Higher Intelligence that we are all capable of tapping into. That is easier to defend. What gives rise to this type of speculation on supernatural phenomena is the kind of mystery I mentioned earlier. How do you account for prophetic dreams, people who are healed after visiting certain healers, the presence of spiritual beings in our midst—including spirits that have been known to haunt houses, etc.—except by entertaining the possibility of a spirit world? The point is, no one knows what happens to us after we die. We would all like to believe that the grave is not the end of it all, that life continues on a different plane. Some anecdotal evidence suggests that a different plane of existence may be real. So why not search for answers instead of dismissing it all as nonsense?

S: Exactly. I came across a very interesting article recently, published in the *Los Angeles Times*, in which the author—I think it was the science editor or something like that—made that same point. It appeared to cause quite a stir. You really didn't delve much into your paranormal research in *Heretic*. Would you care to share some of the resources that you found most valuable or thought-provoking?

J: You might want to read Jess Stearn's book, *Edgar Cayce: The Sleeping Prophet*, about psychic and faith healer Edgar Cayce. Stearn was a skeptic, a prize-winning journalist, who went to Virginia to debunk Cayce and instead came away a believer. Cayce had the ability to put himself in a trance, transport himself telepathically, diagnose illnesses from thousands of miles away, and prescribe cures. He also predicted the discovery of the Dead Sea Scrolls and claimed to have recollections of past lives. As far as I know, no one has come up with an explanation for Cayce's psychic and spiritual healing gifts. There are many other books out there on the subject, not only dealing with Cayce, but others with similar gifts. I personally have seen a Catholic priest, a Father D'Orio I think his name was, hold hundreds of people in thrall for ten solid hours while curing them of various ailments through the power of the Holy Spirit, as he claimed. Perhaps mind over matter is at work here, but I believe we are doing ourselves a disservice by dismissing such phenomena too readily.

S: Howard Gardener was one of the first psychologists to hypothesize about multiple intelligences, and in his framework he included "intrapersonal intelligence"—the ability to introspect, analyze, and understand oneself. Speaking very broadly, because individuals' introspective abilities vary enormously, it seems to me that that is an important part of spiritualism for many people—being able and willing to look deeper than the rudiments of daily survival. Would you agree?

J: Yes. It almost sounds like Buddhism. Buddhists are essentially atheists, but they delve within to find a greater understanding not only of themselves, but the mystery of existence itself. This also borders on the Jeffersonian concept of a Superior Intelligence. Perhaps we are all part of that Intelligence and have the capability of tapping into it through meditation, prayer, and similar reflective exercises. The Christian contemplative or centering movement is close to Buddhism, and its primary proponent, Father Thomas Keating, has held meditation seminars jointly with the Dali Llama. They use centering or meditation techniques designed to help people achieve a degree of inner knowledge not available through conscious thought. It's a very enlightening path for people looking for spiritual fulfillment outside organized religion.

S: I've just recently begun exploring meditation—it's hard to create a niche of quiet time when one has two energetic children around all day, though. Although I'm an atheist—by which I mean that I don't believe that Jesus Christ was the literal son of God who died for our sins, and like you I have deep problems with the God of Abraham, nor have I seen any reason to believe that other entities some call gods exist—I too am very interested in
spiritualism, in terms of understanding myself and life better, and attaining some peace and perspective about it all. But I've noticed, in talking with many people about the subject over the years, that some—and not all of these were hard-core rationalists—some people don't seem capable of thinking in that way. Attempts to explore those ideas were met with blank stares or other signs of noncomprehension. Some people might take the existence of such individuals as evidence that spirituality is, to put it rather crudely, a side effect of human consciousness and self-awareness. What do you say in response to those who try to attribute paranormal experiences to biological—especially brain-based—processes?

J: Brain-based processes seem to explain the phenomena of near death experiences—people declared dead who recall hovering above their bodies and seeing themselves from a distance until they were rejoined with their bodies and returned to life. This phenomenon has apparently been duplicated in the laboratory. But many of the other phenomena we discussed defy this explanation.

I don't believe that Jesus was the son of God who died for our sins either, Sunni, but I do think he was tapped into the intelligent force Jefferson talked about and was, therefore, a gifted prophet with lessons to teach. Perhaps Cayce is a latter-day example. Thomas Aquinas said that we are all co-creators with God and have a hand in shaping existence. This is a concept that even Ayn Rand explored, which explains her tolerance for him among religious philosophers. Someone once said that the fact you are searching for God means you have already found him. We're not going to find the answers to these questions in our lifetimes. But searching for answers is a spiritual quest, and you don't have to subscribe to traditional notions about heaven and hell to be spiritual. In my view, the Catholic Church and organized religion in general are evil. Any organization that countenances the sexual abuse of children and then tries to cover it up is evil by definition. The churches have always existed to suppress human inquiry and turn people into spiritual slaves. In that regard Rand was right. Her notions of Attila and the Witch Doctor are right on target. That's why I've abandoned organized religion and pursued this search on my own. I'll let you know when I'm finished, Sunni, but I don't think it will be anytime soon.

S: I didn't put it quite as forcefully as you just did, Jerry, but in my introductory psychology classes I invariably created a stir by pointing out how hugely destructive organized religion has been to humankind throughout its existence—and it still is. Some people advance the view that Jesus was the first libertarian; between that and his emphasis on peace and love, I understand why many admire him. But you've reminded me of another, much more personal reason I have for being skeptical of an afterlife. My mother was also very interested in these subjects, and did a lot of reading. She told me—and numerous other friends—that if she died before us and it was in any way possible, she'd come back and get in touch. To the best of my ability to tell, that hasn't happened. Maybe she couldn't because a frontal lobe brain tumor destroyed much of her brain before it killed her, but you'd think that a spirit wouldn't be hampered by damage to physical structures.

J: Some people claim they've been contacted by children who died, but who knows if this is wishful thinking or self-delusion. The truth is, none of us knows for sure what happens after death. The best-case scenario would be a paradise where life is perfect, and the next best case would be total oblivion. I just don't want to fry in some hellish netherworld.

S: Yeah. Mostly I don't think about it a lot, though; I'd rather enjoy living today than worrying about tomorrow—especially things that may or may not come to pass, and that I have no control over. Your thoughts regarding the importance of your writing struck a very deep chord in me, Jerry, because I feel the same way about cooking. And I think I've been resisting that grokking for years, because I'd thought that any "cornerstone of existence," as you put it, would necessarily be more crucial to physical success. [pauses] Maybe it would have been in my life, if I'd ever been willing to jump through all the regulatory hoops necessary to open a restaurant or bakery. Do you think we—and I mean individuals, not just state-based interference—make deep personal fulfillment harder than it has to be? Is that a necessary result of our increasingly complex and technologically-dependent society?

J: Well, we have that in common too, Sunni. We both like to write and we both like to cook. [laughs] Cajun dishes are my specialty.

S: Ooooh! A wonderful cuisine I haven't explored nearly enough!

J: Unfortunately, we live in a world governed by rules and regulations that make no sense. But our society is not unique. The Romans had a kind of free enterprise going, but it was corrupt as hell with licenses to trade and set up shop going to the highest bidder. Bribery was rampant. This has been the human condition since time immemorial, and it's not going to change as long as we have government. A republic or a democracy is only a system of government, and ours is an improvement on the Greeks and the Romans. But it is inherently corrupt. The power to dispense licenses and other favors is a recipe for corruption. So the question is, how badly do you want to open your restaurant or bakery? If it's something you lust after, then you have no alternative but to jump through the hoops and do what you have to do to get what you want. Fortunately we don't need a license to write, not yet anyway, but if you need a cook who makes a world-class jambalaya for your restaurant, I'm your man.

S: I think I do have an alternative—it won't make me as much money as an aboveboard business could, but as another interview victim and I discussed, I'd much prefer to set up an underground restaurant or bakery. I know that course is much riskier, but at least I wouldn't be adding to the corruption I so loathe.

J: If you have a dream, go for it, Sunni. We don't get many opportunities to do what we really want to do in life.

S: Actually, I am working on it now, Jerry; thanks for the encouragement. [pause] Yikes, Jerry, I've just realized that we've been going on and on! And I could continue—there's lots we could delve into still—but perhaps we'd better save it for another day. Before we go, are there any other words of wisdom or forthcoming projects you want to mention?

J: Only that I've always been amused by attempts to pigeonhole me politically. First I was an anarchist—"everyone's favorite right-wing anarchist," as one reviewer called me. Then, when I attacked libertarian isolationism in the pages of *National Review*—an indirect jab at Rothbard—some libertarians said that I had become a conservative. Never mind that I was also writing for *The Nation* at the time. No one maintained that I had become a liberal because of that connection. The truth is, my ideas haven't changed much over the years. I am a libertarian with a bit of a leftist bent. I am essentially, philosophically anarchistic, but I am also a realist. I am happy that libertarianism has evolved to a point where Camille Paglia can call herself a libertarian Democrat and Bob Barr has deserted the Republican Party and joined the LP. How much do Paglia and Barr really have in common? Probably more than is immediately apparent on the surface. Murray Rothbard and I used to joke about being middle-of-the-road anarchists. I think that's still a good thing to be.

S: I hope you're right about Paglia and Barr—and I'll have to think about that middle-of-the-road anarchist descriptor. Maybe I'm a radical middle of the roader. [laughs] Again, Jerry, thank you so much for the stimulating exchange! Happy holidays to you and yours, and best wishes for much more authorial success.

J: Thank you, Sunni. Spending time with you is delightful and stimulating as well.

Part VII
Afterword

Many of the early libertarian leaders are dead now. Ayn Rand. Murray Rothbard. Karl Hess. Roger MacBride. Joe Peden. Roy Childs. Milton Friedman. We'll miss them. I'm sure they are all in libertarian heaven, even though some of them didn't believe in an afterlife. How is it up there, Ayn? Is Howard Roark sitting at the right hand of John Galt? How about Ragnar? Or else … don't tell me Dagney Taggart is the dominatrix of the spirit world. Anyway, I hope it's more fun up there than life in Galt's Gulch would be.

In some ways, those heady days of the 1960s and 1970s seem to have happened a century ago; in other ways, it seems as though they are still with us. Did we learn nothing from Vietnam? Apparently George W. Bush didn't; he's given us a replay, with potentially worse consequences thanks to the proliferation of nuclear weapons. The battle to sustain the Bill of Rights is more challenging now than ever, the fight for freedom is far from over. In many ways things have gotten worse over the decades. Government is grotesquely big, taxes are too high, civil liberties are getting crimped a bit tighter every day. Yes, capitalism has spread around the globe and third-world countries are getting richer, but the U.S. system of government has become more militaristic and imperialistic. George W. Bush has driven the country in the wrong direction at breakneck speed, and the Democrats have been virtually impotent in their opposition. Bush should have been impeached long ago, but so far no one on the Democratic side of the aisle has had the guts to launch proceedings against him.

Our old heroes are gone, but most of them turned out to have feet of clay. In his dotage, Barry Goldwater fell in love with Hillary Clinton and put lust ahead of reason and common sense. Ronald Reagan never lived up to his potential as a libertarian savior. His rhetoric was okay on economic issues at least, but his policies were sorely lacking. Reagan's 1981 tax bill lowered the marginal tax brackets and reduced the general burden of taxes, but the law he put in place in 1986 reversed much of the good he did. Reagan also left out an important part of the equation: he forgot to cut spending by a commensurate amount.

Oh well, nobody's perfect. Still, we expected better than that. Disappointed once again. So what else is new? The First and Second Amendments to the U.S. Constitution are under constant attack, as they were in the early 1970s, and the Fourth and Fifth Amendments get trampled on every day.

The major problem now is that there is no one on the political horizon libertarians can look to with any degree of enthusiasm. Who is there out there with a libertarian message we can't ignore? Show your face, show us your jaw, show us your muscle tone and bone structure. We're surrounded by an army of Wesley Mouch clones.

The comparison has been made many times before, and it's getting to be a bit overdone. Still, it's hard to ignore the similarities between the U.S. today and ancient Rome in the first century B.C. Cato has impaled himself on his own sword rather than submit to the tyranny of Caesar, and Cicero is trying to hold on to what's left of the constitution of the falling republic as Caesar assumes the role of supreme dictator. Today we have our Decider in Chief. At least the Roman conspirators cut their own dictator down with a few dozen dagger thrusts inside their Senate. What's missing today are the drawn daggers in our own Senate.

We have to make do with mere character assassination.

It's getting late. The republic is falling. Our liberties are evaporating with it. Things look bleak as we look forward to the presidential election of 2008. All the declared candidates are latter-day Caesars.

Where are you, Ragnar? Don't you dare let me down again.

That's it for me now. Anyone who wants to contact me can email me at jtuccille@verzizon.net. Please also check out my Website at www.jerometuccille.com.

978-0-595-47757-9
0-595-47757-7

7685658R0

Made in the USA
Lexington, KY
09 December 2010